Leadership & Management in Healthcare

2nd Edition

Neil Gopee & Jo Galloway

Los Angeles | London | New Delhi
Singapore | Washington DC

Los Angeles | London | New Delhi
Singapore | Washington DC

SAGE Publications Ltd
1 Oliver's Yard
55 City Road
London EC1Y 1SP

SAGE Publications Inc.
2455 Teller Road
Thousand Oaks, California 91320

SAGE Publications India Pvt Ltd
B 1/I 1 Mohan Cooperative Industrial Area
Mathura Road
New Delhi 110 044

SAGE Publications Asia-Pacific Pte Ltd
3 Church Street
#10-04 Samsung Hub
Singapore 049483

© Neil Gopee and Jo Galloway 2014

First edition published 2008
Reprinted in 2009, 2011 and 2012
This edition first published 2014

Editor: Alex Clabburn
Assistant editor: Emma Milman
Production editor: Katie Forsythe
Copyeditor: Solveig Gardner Servian
Proofreader: Audra O'Brien
Marketing manager: Tamara Navaratnam
Cover design: Wendy Scott
Typeset by: C&M Digitals (P) Ltd, Chennai, India
Printed in Great Britain by Henry Ling Limited, at
the Dorset Press, Dorchester, DT1 1HD

Library of Congress Control Number: 2013933559

British Library Cataloguing in Publication data

A catalogue record for this book is available from
the British Library

MIX
Paper from
responsible sources
FSC
www.fsc.org
FSC® C013985

ISBN 978-1-4462-4881-2
ISBN 978-1-4462-4882-9 (pbk)

CONTENTS

ABOUT THE AUTHORS

Neil Gopee is currently employed as lecturer in Health and Life Sciences at Coventry University, having also previously worked as Associate Lecturer for the Open University. He has been an external examiner at various Higher Education Institutions which has given Neil wide-ranging insights into the two subject areas that he teaches on and researches in: (1) learning, teaching and assessment (under- and post-graduate), and (2) management and leadership in care settings.

Having qualified in Adult Nursing, as well as in Mental Health Nursing, Neil's nursing career has included a combination of clinical experiences in acute care and primary healthcare. Studying for his doctorate provided Neil with further in-depth insights into these subject areas. His publications include various peer-reviewed articles, and two other textbooks *Mentoring and Supervision in Healthcare* and *Practice Teaching in Healthcare*.

Jo Galloway is Executive Nurse, Quality and Patient Safety, at NHS Redditch and Bromsgrove Clinical Commissioning Group and NHS Wyre Forest Clinical Commissioning Group. With more than 20 years experience in health care, Jo's career has spanned acute care, community care, practice development, education, and commissioning. She has held a number of senior management positions both in the NHS and Higher Education. Jo has previously worked as a Nurse Consultant for Older People, and Lecturer Practitioner in Rehabilitation Nursing. Her areas of clinical expertise and publications include rehabilitation, care of older people and leadership. In 2012, Jo was awarded a Leadership Scholarship by The Florence Nightingale Foundation and Burdette Trust for Nursing. Jo is also an Honorary Research Fellow at the Faculty of Health and Research Centre, Health and Lifestyle Interventions, Coventry University.

LIST OF ILLUSTRATIONS

Boxes

Figures

Tables

ACKNOWLEDGEMENTS

With special thanks to Roberto, Robyn, Sacha and Eileen for their ongoing support and encouragement
– Jo Galloway

Thank you to my daughters Hema, Sheila and Neeta for always being proud of my scholarly avhievements
– Neil Gopee

LIST OF ABBREVIATIONS

ACL	Action-Centred Leadership
AHP	Allied Health Profession
AQP	Any Qualified Provider
BEICHMM	Buildings, Equipment, Information Technology, Consumables, Human Resources, Methods and Money.
CAF	Common Assessment Framework
CCG	Clinical Commissioning Group
CHC	Continuing Healthcare
CHRE	Council for Healthcare Regulatory Excellence
CLP	Clinical Leadership Programme
CNO	Chief Nursing Officer
COPD	Chronic Obstructive Pulmonary Disease
CPA	Care Programme Approach
CPD	Continuing Professional Development
CPR	Cardio-Pulmonary Resuscitation
CQC	Care Quality Commission
CQUIN	Commissioning For Quality and Innovation
CSW	Clinical Support Worker
DCM	Duty Care Manager
DH	Department of Health
E4E	Energise for Excellence in Care
EBHC	Evidence-Based Healthcare
EBM	Evidence-Based Medicine
EBP	Evidence-Based Practice
EPP	Expert Patient Programme
EWS	Early Warning Score
FT	Foundation Trust
GMC	General Medical Council
GP	General Practitioner
HCPC	Health and Care Professions Council
HEE	Health Education England
HRM	Human Resource Management
ICP	Integrated Care Pathways
ICU	Intensive Care Unit
IDPR	Individual Development and Performance Review (also known as Appraisal)
IHI	Institute for Healthcare Improvement

IIP	Investors in People
IWL	Improving Working Lives
JSNA	Joint Strategic Needs Assessment
LA	Local Authority
LEA	Leadership Effectiveness Analysis
LETB	Local Education and Training Board
LETC	Local Education and Training Council
MBO	Management by Objectives
MDT	Multi-Disciplinary Team
MEWS	Modified Early Warning Score
MRSA	Methicillin-resistant Staphylococcus aureus
NAO	National Audit Office
NHS	National Health Service
NHS III	NHS Institute for Innovation and Improvement
NHS KSF	The NHS Knowledge and Skills Framework
NHS TDA	NHS Trust Development Authority
NHSLA	National Health Service Litigation Authority
NICE	National Institute for Health and Clinical Excellence
NMC	Nursing & Midwifery Council
NPfIT	National Programme for Information Technology
NPSA	National Patient Safety Agency
ONS	Office for National Statistics
PALS	Patient Advice and Liaison Service
PCT	Primary Care Trust
PHE	Public Health England
PREP	Post-Registration Education and Practice
PROMS	Patient-Reported Outcome Measures
PSA	Professional Standards Authority for Health and Social Care
QIPP	Quality, Innovation, Productivity and Prevention
RCN	Royal College of Nursing
RCT	Randomised Controlled Trial
RN	Registered Nurse
SAP	Single Assessment Process
SHA	Strategic Health Authority
SIGN	Scottish Intercollegiate Guidelines Network
SOP	Standards of Proficiency
SWOT	Strengths, Weaknesses, Opportunities and Threats
TQM	Total Quality Management
TTO	Tablets to Take Out
WBL	Work-Based Learning
WTE	Whole Time Equivalent

INTRODUCTION

The months leading up to and after the point of registration with the relevant professional regulatory body can be both an exciting and a challenging time for health and social care practitioners. Completing final assignments and practice competencies, applying for and securing your first post as a qualified care professional, coping with the accountability and responsibility of your new role as a registered practitioner, ensuring that you get the right support and fit into your new team are to name but a few of these challenges. This textbook has been designed to support you on your journey from an emerging registered care professional through to becoming a care manager.

Leadership and management are essential skills for all qualified care professionals, regardless of the position that they hold. These skills have relevance for everyday practice in delivering care today, and also in leading and managing change and new ways of working for the care that is delivered tomorrow. It is well recognised that if you do what you always do then the results will be the same, and therefore to effect change we need to work differently. This book has been developed as a composite resource on leadership and management to support the everyday practice of care professionals working at Bands 5 and 6, or their equivalent levels. It is also intended as an essential resource for emerging practitioners, namely care profession students who are in the final year of their pre-registration course.

From our experience of teaching leadership and management within higher education, we are aware that the majority of books on this subject area within health and social care are either aimed at Ward Manager/Band 7 level or are based around the healthcare systems of other countries. We recognised the need to have a core text that is set in the context of health and social care that is delivered in the United Kingdom and which also focuses on supporting leadership and management development for new and emerging care professionals. This book is therefore firmly rooted within management and leadership in care delivery and professional practice within the United Kingdom, albeit the majority of policies examined are those that have been issued, and apply predominantly to England.

Because management and leadership theories are generic and can be applied across disciplines and geographical boundaries, this book will also be of interest to care professionals from other countries, in order to facilitate comparative analysis with the care systems and care delivery within their respective countries.

We recognise that a gap can sometimes exist between what is taught at university and the care that is actually delivered in the practice setting. As authors, we have a strong background of working within clinical practice, managing care and also teaching in higher education institutions. The book has been written with the intention of bridging this theory–practice gap, through drawing upon relevant theories and supporting the reader through Action points to apply them to their individual practice settings.

Our shared philosophy is that learning should be enjoyable and that we can all learn something from our everyday experiences and interactions. The book uses reflection within the Action points as a way of supporting you to turn your experiences into learning opportunities. We hope that you find the book to be an invaluable resource to support you in your everyday practice to deliver high quality, person-centred care and to achieve your aspirations.

Organisation of the Book

Chapter 1

How does government policy relate to the care that is delivered within my practice setting?

Chapter 1 sets the scene for socio-economic and political contexts of care provision and care delivery. It examines the current demographic changes that impinge on care delivery as well as government policy that directly affect the care that you deliver daily in your practice setting as a care manager. This chapter will help you to translate some of these policies to your practice setting and your role.

Chapter 2

There are so many management theories, how do they relate to me and how can I use them to develop my management skills?

Chapter 2 begins by identifying the everyday management activities of the Duty Care Manager (DCM), and will enable you to explore the management theories, roles and styles to best advantage. It also explores the qualities and personal skills of effective managers and will also support you to organise care delivery, as well as ensure effective communication with your patients and colleagues.

Chapter 3

What is the difference between leadership and management and how can I be a good leader?

Effective care leadership is essential for the development of health and social care practice and the delivery of care services. This chapter distinguishes management from leadership and provides you with the opportunity to reflect on the various theories and styles of leadership, and to support personal leadership development.

Chapter 4

Problem-solving, decision-making and managing conflict, what tools can I draw upon to support my practice?

Health and social care professionals are faced with a range of decisions that they have to make on a day-to-day basis. This chapter analyses the nature of problems, decisions and conflict, and presents you with frameworks for decision-making, problem-solving and conflict resolution within the context of professional practice.

Chapter 5

How can I ensure my patients receive high quality care?

Quality improvement is everybody's business and the DCM has a key role in supporting ongoing quality improvement, monitoring and assurance. This chapter examines quality frameworks and tools that you can use to maximise use of time and improve the quality of care that is delivered within your practice setting.

Chapter 6

Change, change and more change – how can I inspire change and facilitate the change management process at my level in the practice setting?

Change is omnipresent in health and social care and is essential to the modernisation of care services, together with the quest for ongoing improvements to quality and patient outcomes. This chapter critically examines change management theories and provides a framework for you to plan and implement change effectively in your practice setting, together with ways of sustaining the change.

Chapter 7

How can I deliver high quality care whilst ensuring best value for money and working within a set budget?

Health and social care resources need to be effectively and efficiently managed in order to maximise outcomes for patients or service users and ensure best value for money. This chapter addresses both the management of human and consumable resources and supports you to develop budget management skills and a command of financial terminology.

Chapter 8

So many competing priorities, targets to meet and demands on my time – what can I do to ensure that myself and my team members feel supported?

Care professionals have a number of challenges, competing priorities and demands to manage throughout the course of their day-to-day practice. This chapter will support you to identify self-management strategies, support and coping mechanisms to ensure your survival.

Chapter 9

How can I involve patients in their care, and work with my team to deliver care that is person-centred?

Current national policy priorities include the provision of personalised care and patient and public involvement in the delivery of care services. This chapter explores the power base of both care professionals and patients, and provides you with opportunities to explore mechanisms to promote patient involvement in their care.

Chapter 10

Healthcare is delivered in the context of teams with a shared purpose, how can I be both a good team player and an effective team leader?

Achieving seamless services and ensuring timely transfers of patient care are reliant upon effective teamwork between primary, secondary, community and social care. This chapter explores team roles and supports you to identify and apply mechanisms to maximise and evaluate team performance.

Chapter 11

How can I teach and support colleagues and health and social care students and also develop my role as an effective leader and manager?

Education, training and personal and professional development are essential to support service development, and ongoing improvements to the quality of care and patient outcomes. The DCM has responsibility for their own development, and also to support the development of their colleagues and students. This chapter will support you to identify development needs and to capitalise on the opportunities that are available.

How to Use the Book

The book includes a number of features that have been integrated to support your learning and development. These features will support you to use the book as a resource that you can come back to again and again to further expand and reinforce your learning.

Action points: Action points are included throughout all of the chapters to support you to reflect on current practice and to learn from your experiences. Action points enable you to apply your learning to practice situations and to look at suggested supporting materials in more depth to enhance the scope of your knowledge in the identified area.

Chapter summaries: Summaries are provided at the end of each chapter as an aide memoir and to support you to relocate and revisit pertinent points as required.

Good practice guidelines: Good practice guidelines are provided at the end of each chapter to highlight the key messages that have been constituted, to inform your practice and for you to apply within your practice setting.

Glossary: A glossary of terms has been incorporated at the end of the book to help you understand the meaning of a number of key concepts that are inherent within leadership and management.

Terminology

The following terminology is used throughout the book.

The term **'patient'** is used as a generic term to refer to 'users' of health and social care in the widest sense and therefore also represents service users and clients.

The terms **'practice setting'** and **'care setting'** are used interchangeably to signify the locations where health and social care practitioners carry out their roles, that is to address patients' or service users' health or social care needs, and include hospital wards, clinics, GP surgeries, nursing homes, and the patient's own home.

'Care' is used as a generic term that includes nursing care, but also represents therapy and treatment.

The terms **'healthcare professional'**, **'care professional'** and **'registrant'** are used interchangeably to refer to qualified nurses, and allied health and social care professionals, who are registered with their respective professional regulatory bodies. **'Healthcare practitioner'** refers to all members of staff who are employed to deliver care directly to patients or service users, even if they are not registered with a professional regulatory body such as the Nursing & Midwifery Council.

'Duty Care Manager' (DCM) is the term used throughout the book to refer to a healthcare professional who has management responsibility for a group of patients, a team of staff, or a practice setting. This responsibility may be for the duration of a span of duty (e.g. managing the practice setting), or may be more permanent in nature (e.g. managing a team of staff or a group of patients). The term is used as a way of differentiating between the role and responsibilities of the identified figurehead or appointed manager of the practice setting. Please see the Glossary for definitions of other terminologies used in this textbook.

The authors would also like to thank Sheila Gopee who is a specialist social worker, for her contribution in providing social care perspectives in this textbook, especially Box 4.4.

1

LEADERSHIP AND MANAGEMENT IN HEALTH AND SOCIAL CARE

The duties and roles that healthcare professionals fulfil on a day-to-day basis can be grouped under six key categories, namely:

- care interventions (i.e. direct patient care activities)
- the organisation and management of care
- training and educating colleagues and students
- teaching and promoting health and wellbeing
- using research and evidence based practice
- leadership.

These are illustrated in Figure 1.1. The six categories also apply to social care professionals, although the focus of 'care interventions' is more related to assessment of service user needs and commissioning appropriate care to meet their needs rather than direct care delivery as applied to healthcare. This book focuses on the leadership and management components of care professionals' roles with the aim of providing the Duty Care Manager (DCM) with knowledge and evidence to inform and support the delivery of well-organised, safe and effective care and treatment for patients and service users.

This first chapter of this book starts by examining the work activities of the DCM in relation to the six categories mentioned above, which DCMs have to engage in with full consideration of the prevailing context and ethos of the dynamics of contemporary health and social care provision and delivery. It thereby contextualises the DCM's role by outlining government strategy and policy as

Figure 1.1   Roles of duty care managers

detailed in, for example, the NHS White Paper *Equity and Excellence: Liberating the NHS* (Department of Health [abbreviated to DH throughout], 2010a) in which the Government's vision for care provision and delivery under the NHS is set out, whilst retaining and building on the core values and principles of the NHS, these being 'a comprehensive service, available to all, free at the point of use, based on need, not ability to pay' (p. 1). The principal aim of the White Paper and subsequent *Health and Social Care Act* (DH, 2012a) is to establish the medium for delivering continuously improving healthcare, whilst building upon reforms that have already been made over preceding years. This chapter therefore explores the prevailing strategies, policies and ethos in which health and social care are delivered, providing the context within which healthcare professionals and DCMs carry out their daily duties; reference is also made to the roles of social care professionals in recognition of the important interface between health and social care in the United Kingdom.

The chapter therefore begins by highlighting the significance of leadership and management in today's care provision, and then examines the roles, responsibilities and duties of DCMs as well as the collaborative work that is fundamental to being part of a multi-disciplinary team (MDT) made up of both health and social care professionals. This leads to determining the contemporary social and economic context of care, healthcare legislation, strategies and policies, including the aims of the National Health Service (NHS) and the current structure of the NHS, together with the roles that each component fulfils to achieve these aims.

Consideration is given in this chapter to current issues and challenges, along with the respective directions in policy; for example, current financial pressures within the

NHS and the objectives of Quality, Innovation, Productivity and Prevention (QIPP) (DH, 2011a). The chapter then explores workforce issues in respect of health and social care delivery, the educational preparation of care professionals for the delivery of competent, safe and effective care, and finally it considers the codes of practice that healthcare professionals must abide by, and the regulation of care professions. All components are discussed with reference to the DCM's role within them. The chapter objectives are therefore as follows.

Chapter objectives

On completion of this chapter you will be able to:

- identify the roles and responsibilities of DCMs in relation to their leadership and managerial duties in practice settings;
- enunciate the prevailing social, demographic, economic and political contexts in which care is provided;
- review the current legislation, strategies and policies that underpin care delivery and their relevance to DCMs in their leadership and management roles;
- analyse workforce issues for health and social care delivery; and
- explore the educational preparation of care professionals for the delivery of competent, safe and effective care, as well as the codes of practice that care professionals must abide by, and the regulation of care professions.

Leadership and Management in Contemporary Care Provision

Leading and managing current health and social care provision

Outcomes of effectiveness, safety and patient satisfaction with health and social care services are generally good. There are, however, numerous high-profile examples of systemic failures in both health and social care services that have had adverse impact on patient and service user outcomes. An early example is that of children's cardiac surgery at the Bristol Royal Infirmary, with more recent examples including the case of Baby Peter's care in Haringay, the Mid Staffordshire Hospital scandal, and Winterbourne View. When such failures occur, effective management and leadership entails learning from such incidents so that appropriate safety measures are instituted to prevent recurrence. This section explores the fundamentals of leadership and management, focusing on the role of individual health and social care professionals and DCMs. Examples of good and poor leadership are discussed together with opportunities for DCMs to reflect on this and consider how they can apply good practice within their day-to-day practice.

From another viewpoint, as published in care profession regulator fitness for practice reports, the Nursing & Midwifery Council (NMC) and Health and Care Professions Council (HCPC), for example, summarise instances of registered care professionals being found guilty of neglect or other aspects of professional malpractice. The Care Quality Commission (CQC), whose role is that of a 'watchdog' which monitors standards of care in all health and social care settings, also publish details of instances where they identify poor practice that has put patients or service users at risk. Responsibility and accountability for care delivery is of prime importance, and the DCM must have a clear understanding of their role within this in terms of their own practice and that of their subordinates.

Furthermore, every care professional is accountable for their own standards of professional practice, and as implementer and disseminator of the highest standards of care. From a more positive stance, health and social care journals, professional trade union organisations, as well as the CQC and other professional organisations frequently publish information publicising and promoting innovation and examples of best practice in health and social care delivery. Thus nursing and health and social care profession journals comprise a rich source of examples of good practice and projects where vision and focus by individuals and teams in health and social care have had positive results in terms of care outcomes.

Areas of good practice are also highlighted by Royal Colleges, DH publications, bulletins from Chief Officers, and publications from other organisations such as the NHS Institute and the National Institute for Health and Clinical Excellence (NICE). National clinical guidelines and protocols published by NICE, and similar organisations such as the Scottish Intercollegiate Guidelines Network (SIGN) also support the delivery of high standards of care.

Where and how leadership has made a difference

The reduction in infections such as Methicillin-resistant Staphylococcus aureus (MRSA) bacteraemias and Clostridium difficile (C. diff) rates provide a positive and relatively recent example of how leadership in healthcare can make a difference. The approaches used include identifying a figurehead to lead and champion the approach, to promote a vision of how this will have a positive impact on patients, through surveillance, identifying outcomes, development and agreement of ambitions, benchmarking, incentives and penalties, and publishing and sharing best practice.

Action point 1.1   Learning from failure

Select a recent high-profile care or treatment failure (e.g. the case of Mid Staffordshire referred to above) on which to focus. Search for the investigation report on the Internet, and read the executive summary and recommendations. Consider the issues and findings in respect of leadership and management and how this relates to the DCM role. You may find it helpful to discuss this with a peer, mentor or manager. Consider what you can learn from this and how you can apply the learning to your practice as a DCM to safeguard quality and patient safety, and ensure that you are working within the code of practice for your profession.

Learning from failure is imperative for health and social care managers. In *An Organisation with Memory*, the DH (2000a) indicated that failure is almost always unintentional, and there is usually no single explanation for the type of major failures noted above, and that organisations should put in place measures to overcome such failures when they do occur, and also to learn from them so that they do not recur.

More recently, deducing from research conducted on the factors that lead to service failures, the researcher Andrews-Evans (2012) identifies a 'senior nurses' framework' that he asserts should prevent such failures. The framework incorporates the 'right skill-mix' and an appropriate culture and ethos amongst the factors for success in preventing failure. Chapter 5 provides greater detail regarding quality assurance frameworks and ensuring high quality care in health and social care services.

Leadership at all levels

Leadership can and should be demonstrated by staff at all levels in health and social care and should not be considered exclusively the domain of those in supervisory and management roles. Focusing on the needs and preferences of patients and taking personal responsibility for meeting those needs is central to good leadership and the achievement of high quality care and patient outcomes.

So what are the qualities of a good leader? Qualities of good leaders in health and social care transcend grades, bandings and status in the hierarchy of management, and include:

- *Being visionary*: forward thinking and having foresight in considering how things could work differently and be improved in the future.
- *Leading by example*: a role model who does the right things.
- *A patient/service user focus*: involving patients wherever possible and respecting their wishes.
- *Taking personal responsibility*: a proactive approach to problems and challenges.
- *Challenging poor standards*: escalating issues where appropriate and taking steps to improve standards of care; adhering to their professional code.
- *Having a positive outlook and 'can do' attitude*: recognising that every practitioner has the ability to make a difference and putting this in to practice.
- *Being proactive*: problem-solving and being resourceful.

- *Good communication*: with patients and all members of the health and social care team to ensure continuity of care.
- *Empowering others*: valuing the contributions of other team members, and supporting people to take initiative; demonstrate personal leadership.
- *Recognising and rewarding good care*: saying 'thank you' when it is deserved and giving positive feedback for a job well done.

Effective and poor leadership will be discussed in detail in Chapter 3.

What is management?

Management incorporates planning, organisation, directing or guiding, and supervising/ monitoring activities (see Figure 1.2 and Table 1.1) which are aimed at achieving goals and objectives. In health and social care, DCMs use management expertise to achieve patient and service user outcomes; for example, managing the commissioning of individualised packages of care or ensuring the delivery of high quality care for a group of patients during a span of duty.

Table 1.1 identifies brief details of the management process, which will be discussed in detail in Chapter 2. Having ascertained the nature of leadership and management, the next section examines DCMs' overall roles as health and social care professionals.

Table 1.1   Brief details of the management process

Planning	Organising	Directing/Guiding	Supervising/Monitoring
Identifying what needs to be achieved during the span of duty, e.g. any admissions, assessments, discharges, theatre list, ward rounds, MDT meetings, sorting out staffing issues/problems	How this will be achieved, such as skill mix, resources, scheduling and allocating care activities	Allocating resources and responsibilities, having discussions with staff, and identifying team leaders	Monitoring activities and achievement of outcomes, making sure care interventions are performed to the appropriate standard; taking action as required

Figure 1.2   The management process

Roles of Duty Care Managers (DCMs)

The range of daily professional activities and roles of the DCM

This section begins by exploring the roles, responsibilities and activities of care professionals as DCMs by focusing on the range and diversity of activities that DCMs engage in on a day-to-day basis. The answers to this question will enable us to identify components of DCMs' roles in care settings, which we will discuss in the context of nationally identified knowledge and competencies that are required for professionals in different health and social care professions to perform their duties to the expected standard.

In the light of the context of care delivery already discussed, the leadership, organisation and management of care of patients are crucial components of the DCM's responsibilities. It is important, however, to determine the specific activities that the DCM is accountable for in relation to the six key roles of care professionals outlined at the beginning of the chapter.

Action point 1.2   Roles of the DCM

Drawing on your own professional experience, make a list of professional activities that DCMs engage in over a number of spans of duty. Make your list against the six roles identified in Figure 1.1.

From the point in time when DCMs start their span of duty, they engage in multiple care activities. You should have been able to identify several such activities that health or social care professionals engage in. These may have included some or all of those listed in Box 1.1.

Box 1.1   Roles of DCMs

- Ensuring the health and safety of staff/patients/visitors
- Receiving/giving reports on patient/service users care needs, and progress
- Assessment of patients/service users health and social care needs
- Managing resources – human and material
- Participation in risk assessment and management initiatives
- *Hands-on care

(Continued)

(Continued)

- Care planning and documentation
- Care co-ordination
- Working with multi-disciplinary team (MDT) members
- *Drug administration
- Training and education
- Preceptoring and mentoring
- Ensuring evidence-based care
- Organising transfers of patient care
- Delegation of duties
- Supervising care delivery
- Complaint handling
- Patient advocate
- Monitoring and evaluating care delivery
- Conducting individual development and performance review (IDPR)
- Safeguarding

* specific to healthcare

Your answers to Action point 1.1 and the activities noted in Box 1.1 remind us of the wide range of roles that DCMs engage in, which naturally indicates that the DCM is both a care practitioner and a care manager-leader. Specific *management* roles will be examined in detail in Chapter 2.

The Contemporary Social and Policy Context of Care Provision

Having identified the significance of leadership and management in care provision, and the daily duties of DCMs, this section of the chapter delves into the contemporary social context of health and social care provision, including the nature of the population (demography) and the incidence of health problems (epidemiology) that health and social care provision needs to gauge, and to determine the amount and nature of care, prevention and treatment required for the population. The social context of care provision is followed by the current and recent relevant legislation and policies that directly influence care provision.

First, we focus on the demography of the population and the inherent challenges for the delivery of contemporary health and social care. The British NHS provides care and treatment for every British citizen, of which there were approximately 62.3 million in 2010, and projected to be 67.2 million by 2020 (Office for National Statistics [ONS], 2011). A variety of demographic statistics are available from ONS publications, which provide a helpful resource for information and analysis. The ONS highlights, for example, that there were 3.5 million people in the United Kingdom in the 75–84 age group in 2010, which is projected to increase to 4.2 million by 2020; and 1.4 million people in the United Kingdom aged 85 in 2010, which is projected to increase to 1.9 million by 2020.

As for the challenges for contemporary health and social care, the increase in an ageing population is also associated with an increasing number of people with long-term conditions or chronic diseases; for example, type 2 diabetes, chronic obstructive pulmonary diseases (COPD) and so on. These changes are further complicated by the prevalence of an increasingly ethnically diverse population, advances in technology that facilitate treatment for conditions which were deemed untreatable in the past, as well as rising consumer expectations and litigation, and the limits of finance that can be allocated for health and social care.

The NHS therefore has to provide and support high quality care in rapidly changing environments, and provide more care outside acute hospitals, in community and primary care settings. In addition to demographic challenges, there are also considerable financial challenges, in that the NHS delivers care and treatment with a budget of approximately £120 billion a year (National Audit Office [NAO], 2012). This budget represents approximately one-sixth of the government's total spending each year, which is a considerable proportion of the United Kingdom's total spend, and is one of the factors that has triggered the government's QIPP programme which involves achieving up to £20 billion of efficiency savings by 2015. The financing of health and social care and associated financial management and budgeting and so on will be explored in detail in Chapter 7.

Healthcare Strategies, Policy and Legislation

Health and social care policies and legislation that affect daily care

The day-to-day activities that DCMs perform are influenced and guided by various government strategies, policies and legislation, by codes of practice, guidelines, and also surveys and research. The DCM needs to have a working knowledge of relevant legislation and its application to their role in order to fulfil their role effectively. The more influential policies and areas of legislation are now briefly discussed. A strategy can be defined as a broader concept that comprises a set of firm long-term directions and a blueprint for the organisation's activities for three to five forthcoming years.

Usually, health and social care policy in the United Kingdom tends to emanate from the governing political party's values and goals linked to care provision. Policy-making is the process of changing an idea into an action, the idea being that of a political party or others such as the government, civil servants, society, voluntary organisations or community groups for instance, or that of a collective of many or all of them.

Although the NHS constitutes a service that is provided in all four UK countries (England, Scotland, Wales and Northern Ireland), funding for and provision of health services vary to some extent across the four nations. This is because since 1999, the responsibility for health services have been devolved to Scotland, Wales and Northern Ireland, together with the power to decide on policy priorities, and how services are to be delivered (NAO, 2012).

Government devolution and the creation of national assemblies for Wales and Northern Ireland, together with the Scottish Parliament have had an impact on widening differences in health and social care policy between the four nations. Although policy aims demonstrate similarities across the United Kingdom, each nation has developed its own policy direction to meet the needs of the population it serves according to local needs. The NAO (2012), for example, compares healthcare needs and healthcare provision in the four countries, and observes for instance that:

- There are substantial differences in average health need per person between the nations, and average life expectancy at birth varies for men from 75.9 in Scotland to 78.6 in England, and for women from 80.4 in Scotland to 82.6 in England.
- Prescriptions charges apply to patients only in England, although prescriptions are free for hospital inpatients, people under 16 or over 59, and others who meet certain other eligibility criteria.
- Scotland has more GPs per head of population than any of the other three countries.
- England spends less on health services per person than the other three countries.
- Health priorities vary across the NHS, although in the last decade priority has been given throughout the United Kingdom mostly to public health, waiting times, cancer services and mental health services.

The DCM needs to be knowledgeable about current national priorities for health and social care and how they relate to their area of practice, the organisation that they work for, and the resultant impact on their patients. Within England, this includes influential government policy publications in particular that have a major impact on the management of care. *Equity and Excellence: Liberating the NHS* (DH, 2010a), for instance, is a White Paper detailing the then newly elected government's strategy for the NHS, which reaffirmed the requirement to assure quality of care and treatment. The more outstanding components of the *Health and Social Care Act* will be examined shortly.

The 2010 White Paper *Equity and Excellence* focused on outcomes as experienced by patients or service users, which it outlined as being achievable by devolving power to patients and service users as well as to frontline health and social care professionals. The White Paper was developed into a 'Bill', but during the consultation process there was extensive opposition from a number of Royal Colleges, which resulted in a number of changes to the Bill (e.g. change from 'GP' commissioning to 'clinical' commissioning) before it eventually materialised into an Act of Parliament. However, the majority of White Papers are preceded by a Green Paper or other form of consultation publication.

Prior to any words being put to paper, usually a period of consultation occurs, which is followed by publication of either a 'Green Paper' or a 'White Paper', and members of the public are invited to comment on future 'Bills' using these papers as a basis for discussion, and they can take the opportunity to contribute to a response collated by a professional organisation, make a personal response or discuss the Paper with their MP should they want to.

The White Paper *Equity and Excellence* (DH, 2010a) set out the vision for healthcare for change that is premised on the need for greater patient involvement and clinical involvement in commissioning and decision-making, with statements such as 'no decision about me, without me'. The clinical involvement further builds upon the foundations set in *High Quality Care for All* (DH, 2008a), and another previous White Paper, *The NHS Plan* (DH, 2000b), that set out the then plan to reform healthcare, and introduced a number of targets, as well as investment in healthcare that led to significant reductions in waiting lists, waiting times and improved access to care.

Thus influential government strategy and policy publications in particular have a major impact on the management of care in the United Kingdom. Government legislation indicates that the safety of patients, for example, is paramount. Patient safety is discussed further later in this chapter and in detail in Chapter 9.

The DCM needs to be able to identify the impact of government health and social care policy for their respective professional disciplines and to translate this within their practice setting. The government benefits from a number of professional officers who are leaders in their professions and act in an advisory capacity to DH ministers, other government departments and the Prime Minister with expert knowledge about health and social care disciplines. The professional officers within NHS England include the Medical Director and Chief Nursing Officer. The Director of Nursing is the professional lead for nurses and midwives working in public health and social care, and is therefore also the principal adviser to the Government on public health nursing and midwifery.

The DCM must also be able to identify the objectives and subsequent impact of government health and social care policies, and how they will affect their profession and patients. Health and social care organisations need to translate this and assess the impact on their business/services. This can include organisational strategies, policies and guidance for employees which the DCM needs to be knowledgeable of, and work within, as both a manager and employee of the organisation.

In addition to national strategy and central policies issued by the DH, England's Chief Nursing Officer (CNO) provides additional key guidance for nurses and midwives on the delivery of high quality care. Some of the publications also include collaborative work of the four UK Chief Nursing Officers, such as those addressing the careers of registered nurses (RNs). The CNO for England at NHS England, in collaboration with the Director of Nursing at the DH and Lead Nurse for Public Health England, for instance, published *Compassion in Practice – Nursing, Midwifery and Care Staff Our Vision and Strategy* (DH, 2012b) soon after their appointment in 2012, which as the name of the publication implies is a strategy for incorporating a culture of compassionate care, in care and treatment across the NHS. The strategy sets out the components of compassionate care as: care, compassion, competence, communication, courage and commitment (the '6Cs') (see Box 1.2).

Box 1.2   Components of compassionate care (DH, 2012b)

Care is the NHS's and healthcare trusts' core business, and the care delivered helps the individual person and improves the health of the whole community. Caring defines the health and social care professional's work, and people receiving care expect it to be right for them, consistently, throughout every stage of their life.

Compassion is how care is given through relationships based on empathy, respect and dignity – it can also be described as intelligent kindness, and is central to how people perceive their care.

Competence means all those in caring roles must have the ability to understand an individual's health and social needs, and the expertise, and clinical and technical knowledge to deliver effective care and treatment based on research and evidence.

Communication is central to successful caring relationships and to effective team working. Listening is as important as what individuals say and do, and is essential for "no decision about me without me". Communication is the key to a good workplace with benefits for those in healthcare professionals' care and staff alike.

Courage enables health and social care professionals to do the right thing for the people they care for, to speak up when they have concerns and to have the personal strength and vision to innovate and to embrace new ways of working.

Commitment to patients and populations is the cornerstone of what health and social care professionals do. They can build on the commitment to improve the care and experience of patients, take action to make this vision and strategy a reality for all and meet health, care and support challenges.

The Director of Nursing for Public Health England has responsibility for operationalising public health with renewed impetus, in the light of public health being a key component of the NHS structure as noted in Figure 1.3.

The previous CNO for England also published a number of key documents pertaining to the four branches of nursing and for midwifery, the most recent being *Energise for Excellence in Care* (E4E) (DH, 2012c). This publication, for instance, 'is a quality framework for nurses, midwives and health visitors which aims to support the delivery of safe and effective care, and for creating positive patient and staff experiences' (p. 1). It also aims to enable frontline nursing and midwifery staff to share ideas with their peers, as well as to provide information on work developed in a local context. E4E has now been incorporated within the Chief Nursing Officer of England's Compassion in Practice strategy and will be explored in more detail in Chapter 5.

Policies and visions aimed at influencing health and social care UK-wide are published jointly by the CNOs of all four countries of the United Kingdom (i.e. England, Northern Ireland, Wales and Scotland). *Midwifery 2020: Delivering Expectations* (DH, 2010b), for instance, is one such publication that sets out the vision for midwifery care.

The NHS Constitution

The NHS was established more than sixty years ago, and as noted in *The NHS Constitution* (DH, 2012d: 1) it 'is founded on a common set of principles and values that bind together the communities and people it serves – patients and public – and the staff who work for it'. The constitution is legally binding and has been reviewed regularly over the years, with recommitment to the principles or values of the NHS, and the rights, pledges, duties and responsibilities set out in the Constitution.

Two examples of the principles and values of the NHS are:

- The NHS provides a comprehensive service, available to all irrespective of gender, race, disability, age, sexual orientation, religion or belief. It has a duty to each and every individual whom it serves and must respect their human rights.
- Access to NHS services is based on clinical need, not an individual's ability to pay.

The reviewed constitution provides a basis for provision of health services that current governments cannot renege on, and have to operationalise services with full compliance of its principles and values.

The Health and Social Care Act 2012

AS noted above, changes to healthcare were announced by the coalition government in *Equity and Excellence* (DH, 2010a). This document was followed by the publication of the *Health and Social Care Bill* (DH, 2011b), which in turn was approved in March 2012 as the *Health and Social Care Act*, which came into effect from April 2013. The Act takes forward the proposals in *Equity and Excellence*, and the subsequent Government response *Liberating the NHS: Legislative Framework and Next Steps* (DH, 2010c). See Figure 1.3 for a diagrammatic illustration of the NHS structure in England.

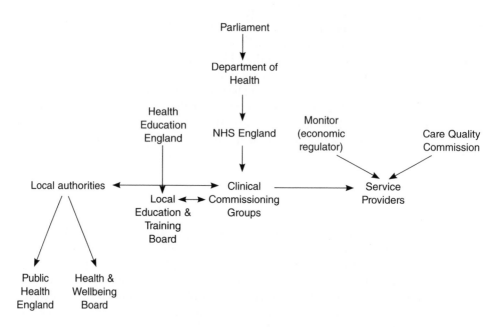

Figure 1.3   Structure of the NHS in England

In fact, the organisational structure of the NHS has changed quite a few times over the six decades of the NHS so far. More specifically, however, the healthcare system comprises the mechanisms identified in Table 1.2.

Key mechanisms that came into being with effect from April 2013 include establishment of NHS England following the dissolution of Strategic Health Authorities, and establishment of Clinical Commissioning Groups following the dissolution of Primary Care Trusts. Another key mechanism comprised transferring public health to local authorities. Briefly, the functions of the key mechanisms of the Act are as follows.

- *NHS England*: an independent body, which in 2012 was given statutory responsibilities principally for the authorisation of clinical commissioning groups (CCG). NHS England co-ordinates and commissions health services in England, and its role is to oversee the

Table 1.2   Mechanisms of care provision under the Health and Social Care Act 2012

Mechanism	Examples of provision
Providers of care	Include hospitals, health centres, GP surgeries, care homes, pharmacists etc.
Commissioners of care	Comprises mainly the NHS England and Clinical Commissioning Groups (CCG)
Public health	To be implemented through Public Health England
Safeguarding patients' interests	Though Care Quality Council (CQC), Monitor and Professional Regulators
Supporting the health and care system	Through National Institute for Health and Care Excellence (NICE), National Institute for Health Research (NIHR)
Empowering people and local communities	Include Health Watch England, and Local Health Watch
Education and training	Through Health Education England (HEE), and Local Education and Training Boards (LETB)

work of the 211 CCGs, and work with health and social care professional bodies and Royal Colleges. NHS England is responsible for ensuring that CCGs meet and maintain standards – as set out in the Health and Social Care Act 2012 and the NHS Constitution – and despite being one single organisation, it operates through 27 local area teams.

- *Clinical Commissioning Groups (CCG)*: initially referred to as 'GP consortia', and made up of groups of general practitioners (GP) and other health professionals; the 211 CCGs replaced their predecessors, the 152 primary care trusts, and together with NHS England took on responsibility for the majority of the NHS budget. CCGs commission care and treatment that is delivered by service providers (i.e. NHS Foundation Trusts, other NHS Trusts, and the independent sector). Each of the 8,000-plus GP practices in England is a member of a CCG, and the population which each CCG commissions care for does not normally cross local geographical boundaries of Local Authorities.
- *NHS Constitution* (DH, 2012d): CCGs and NHS England have a duty to comply with and promote the NHS Constitution (discussed above).
- *Public Health England* and *Health and Wellbeing Boards* (DH, 2012e): as public health is an important component of the Health and Social Care Act, it features in the structure of the NHS as Public Health England (PHE) and Health and Wellbeing Boards, which were also established in April 2013. They replaced various public health agencies (including the Health Protection Agency), as public health responsibilities for local public health were transferred to local authorities, accompanied by ring-fenced public health budgets.

Enhancing the health of the public in general has been on consecutive governments' agendas for several decades. The *PHE* (DH, 2012e) system is structured to provide comprehensive public health that builds on preceding public health activities, and is supported by the government's White Paper *Healthy Lives, Healthy People: Update and the Way Forward* (DH, 2011c), which also provides details of funding on public health.

Health and Wellbeing Boards are constituted as forums for public health and social care representatives to determine how to work collaboratively to improve the health and wellbeing outcomes of the people in their area, through discussion and involvement of local people, and therefore also to commission across health and social care services. Thus their aim is for patients and the public to experience a more joined-up service from the NHS and local councils, and more cohesive care. They also have other broader responsibilities (e.g. in reducing inequalities in access to health and social care).

- *Care Quality Commission (CQC)*: The quality of care and treatment are scrutinised by the CQC (2011a), whose role is to inspect the standard and effectiveness of healthcare and adult social care services. CQC is intended to be the safety and quality regulator (or watchdog) of these services in hospitals, care homes, care delivered at home and for GP and dental practices.

- *Monitor*: Both healthcare and social care professionals' care activities are inspected by CQC in the public sector, as well as those in the independent sector. Details of expenditure on care and treatment is scrutinised by the economic regulator 'Monitor', which is a component of the NHS structure, and whose role includes regulation of NHS Foundation Trusts against their own pre-determined set of criteria. As the independent regulator, Monitor works to make sure patients receive the high quality care they expect, which is done by monitoring how well Foundation Trusts deliver against their annual plans, so that trusts remain well-led and financially viable (Chief Nursing Officer Bulletin, 2012). From April 2014, together with NHS England, Monitor will take over responsibility for pricing NHS services through the national tariff.

  The activities of CQC and Monitor comprise components of a bigger picture of the way in which the whole health service is managed, as illustrated in Figure 1.2, and in particular are components of the *Health and Social Care Act* (DH, 2012a).

- *Health Education England* and *Local Education and Training Boards*: an essential component of the NHS structure identified in Figure 1.3 is Health Education England (HEE), which is the overarching national leadership special health authority responsible for ensuring that education, training and workforce development drive high quality health and social care, and positively influence patient outcomes as incorporated in the NHS Constitution. HEE is operationalised through a number of Local Education and Training Boards (LETB), whose role is explored in detail in Chapter 11 in relation to management of learning for healthcare professionals.

- *Foundation Trusts*: All NHS Trusts are expected to become Foundation Trusts (FT) by 2014, either on their own, or as part of an existing FT, or in another organisational form, as a small minority of NHS trusts will continue beyond 2014, with a specifically agreed later date to move to FT status. The NHS Trust Development Authority (NHS TDA) is responsible for overseeing the performance management, governance and clinical quality of non-Foundation NHS Trusts, and managing their progress towards foundation trust status.

A number of sub-structures of the NHS, and infrastructures, are established to ensure co-ordinated and smooth delivery of health and social care. Current national priorities for healthcare include 'care closer to home' (DH, 2008b) for an effective and sustainable shift of care that is more convenient for patients as they are provided nearer to the patient's home; and 'making every contact count' (DH, 2012a), whereby health and social care professionals use every contact with the public to help them improve their health, as a core responsibility in the NHS Constitution. Both concepts comprise a paradigm shift from the curative focus towards promoting wellness and preventing ill-health. Current national priorities for social care include personalisation and promoting independence.

Thus, health and social care professions are influenced by major paradigm shifts that currently see care being influenced by DH White Papers, new government policies, NICE guidelines, consumer surveys and research. Demographic changes such as an ageing population, the increasing number of people with long-term conditions and rising consumer expectations and demands, all need to be addressed in the current context of reduced levels of investment and maximising resources through efficiency (e.g. the work of QIPP [DH, 2011a]).

A key aim the QIPP programme is to achieve value for money, whilst also ensuring maximum benefit and quality care to patients and service users. These aims are to be achieved through developing integrated QIPP plans through a number of national work streams designed to support the NHS to achieve high quality and productivity, covering such areas as long-term conditions, and ensuring patients get the right care at the right time. QIPP is also referred to in Chapter 7, where funding and financial management for health and social care provision is explored in more detail.

Former policies and their impact on healthcare

An abundance of policies have been published over the years that have affected the workings and direction of the NHS, and the provision of health and social care, and no doubt new policies will emerge as the nature of the population that health and social care provide for evolves. Relevant recent policies that have influenced health and social care provision to a greater extent include the following.

The NHS Plan – A Plan for Investment, a Plan for Reform (DH, 2000b) constituted the then longer-term strategy for the NHS based on 'modernisation', which included targets to be achieved by specific dates; for example, increased number of staff undertaking a wider range of clinical tasks such as running clinics and prescribing drugs.

Standards for Better Health (DH, 2006a), which provided one of the updates on *The NHS Plan*, also shifted the emphasis with less focus on targets and more on standards and meeting local healthcare needs. *The NHS Plan* had resulted in improvements in key areas in tackling health problems such as cancer and coronary heart disease, and also a reduction in mortality rates.

High Quality Care for all – NHS Next Stage Review Final Report (DH, 2008a), which was published on the 60th Birthday of the NHS, recommended building upon the NHS reforms that had been achieved over the previous decade, and focused on the achievement of high quality care that is fairer, personalised, safe, effective and promote choice within health services. However, with a new secretary of state of another political party taking over government of the United Kingdom in the same year, more radical changes were afoot. Furthermore, as mentioned earlier, the responsibility for monitoring quality of care was by then firmly established as the main remit of the CQC (discussed further in Chapter 5).

The Equality Act 2010 (Home Office, 2010) is also an important piece of legislation, which replaced the then prevailing anti-discrimination laws with a single Act, the aim being to simplify, consolidate, streamline and extend existing equality legislation. It gives protection from discrimination for nine 'protected characteristics', namely: age, disability, gender, gender reassignment, marriage and civil partnership, pregnancy and maternity, race, religion or belief, and sexual orientation.

From Policy to Practice

With such a range of legislation, policies and benchmarks influencing the ways in which health and social care professionals commission and deliver care and treatment, we now consider the processes that healthcare organisations (i.e. NHS Trusts, independent sector, voluntary sector, social care) need to have in place to implement them. To a large extent the Director of Nursing at the healthcare organisation, or equivalent, plays a highly significant role in this. The Director of Nursing has a number of nurse leaders in post, some based within the clinical specialism in the organisation, while others have more generic roles. Post-holders such as practice facilitators tend to be specialism based (e.g. to design and implement care pathways), while modern Matrons' activities might cut across specialism (e.g. infection control, tissue viability, cognitive behaviour therapy). Usually, one such leader, or a very small group, is designated to lead on the implementation of the new policy or guidelines.

Commissioning

Commissioning relates to the way in which the NHS and local authorities use the financial resources available to them to improve the health and wellbeing of their populations. Additionally, commissioning is fundamental to the achievement of high quality services that represent value for money. At a practice level, DCM's need to have an understanding of commissioning, and the differences between commissioning and providing services. For social workers and staff working within Continuing Healthcare (CHC) however, commissioning is a central component of their roles as they commission packages of care to meet the assessed needs of patients and service users. Commissioning is an ongoing process that can loosely be divided into a cycle of four key stages as shown in Figure 1.4.

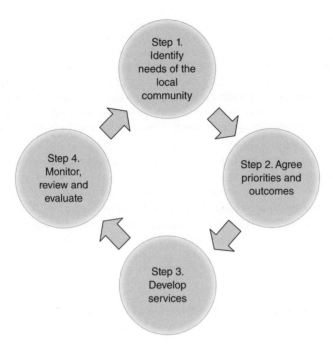

Figure 1.4   The commissioning cycle

Action point 1.3   Commissioning

Think about the demography of your local community and ask yourself the following questions:

- What are the population trends e.g. changes in the age profile?
- What are levels of general health like?
- What is the average life expectancy?

Access the Joint Strategic Needs Assessment (JSNA) for your community (these are generally widely available on the Internet). Consider the findings of the report together with the recommendations made.

Locate your local Health and Wellbeing Board's 'Health and Wellbeing Strategy' for your community and assess how well the strategy reflects and addresses the findings of the JSNA.

(Continued)

(Continued)

Now consider that you are commissioning a package of care for a patient with complex needs. Identify a patient to use as a case study and study the four interrelated steps in the commissioning cycle outlined in Figure 1.4 and focus on the following:

- Consider the care needs and preferences of your patient and what assessment tools and specialist input you can access to support you with this.
- What are the options available to meet the assessed needs and preferences in the community?
- How would you select a provider that delivers high quality care and represents good value for money? How will you involve the patient in the decision-making process?
- Once you have commissioned the package, how will the individual needs of the patient be monitored together with the quality of care that is delivered by the provider?

How policies are implemented into practice are examined in detail in Chapter 6 under the management of change, and also discussed in Chapter 5 in relation to ensuring quality of care.

The Healthcare Workforce

The healthcare workforce in the twenty-first century

The healthcare workforce is central to the delivery of high quality care for patients, and numerous examples of redesign and the creation of new and innovative roles are evident. Furthermore, the NHS workforce itself has been changing for some time in the broader context of employment and changes in society and expectations such as healthcare providing value for money. Changes include:

- Increasing specialisation and advanced practice.
- An increase in the number of clinical support workers (CSW) as part of workforce redesign.
- Changes in shift patterns such as twilight and 12-hour shifts and annualised contracts.
- New roles such as nurse/therapy consultants, community matrons, physician's assistants and others.
- Changes in educational preparation leading towards all graduate professions.
- Roles that transcend disciplines and/or organisational boundaries, e.g. rehabilitation assistants and teams that provide both health and social care.

The impact of these changes can include, for example, more cost effective care delivery and better use of resources, enhanced quality of patient care, improved professional career structures and delivery of care closer to home.

The DCM needs to be aware of the dynamics of employment, whilst ensuring that there are appropriate numbers and a skill mix of staff with appropriate knowledge and skills for care delivery. Staffing is discussed further in the context of human resource management in Chapter 7, and teamwork in Chapter 10. Furthermore, there are other associated issues that need to be considered, for example, account-ability and responsibility for care delivery and current debates such as the regulation of healthcare support staff as discussed in Chapter 5.

Educational Preparation of Care Professionals

To ensure that health and social care professionals – namely nurses, physiotherapist, midwives, radiographers, dieticians, social workers and so on – deliver patient or service user care safely and effectively, they must acquire the necessary knowledge and competence to do so. Each health and social care profession has its own specific breadth of knowledge and competence identified by its regulatory body (e.g. the Nursing & Midwifery Council (NMC), the Health and Care Professions Council (HCPC) and so on). In addition to competence in care interventions, professional competence also includes leadership and management competencies.

Educational preparation for competent care delivery by health and social care professionals is executed through pre-registration undergraduate university-based courses, and the professional competence acquired by individuals are referred to as 'standards', 'standards of proficiency' or 'competencies'.

Action point 1.4   Competence standards for your profession

Access via the Internet the published competencies for pre-qualifying preparatory edu-cation (often referred to as 'standards of proficiency' (SOP)), or national competencies, for your own health or social care profession, and then identify the competencies that specifically refer to organisation and management of care, and leadership.

The purpose of this Action point was principally for you to visit, or revisit, for yourself the current SOPs for your own profession as the minimum areas of exper-tise that are required for your professional group. Within the SOPs you should be able to easily identify the six groups of roles of DCMs identified in the introduction of this chapter, including organisation of care, management and leadership.

You may want to access job descriptions for qualified care professionals on different pay bands, in particular those of team leader/sister, and look at the differences between different levels of management and leadership skills required for those bands.

For pre-registration nursing education, the NMC (2010a) details a number of competencies that registered nurses will have acquired through their initial preparation. They are grouped under 4 'domains', namely (1) Professional values (2) Communication and interpersonal skills (3) Nursing practice and decision-making and (4) Leadership, management and teamworking. The fourth domain is the area predominantly addressed by this textbook.

Post-qualifying, registrants subsequently develop these skills further through continuing professional development (CPD) activities, informally as lifelong learners, or through attending post-registration university-based education programmes. For 'specialist' practice, however, the NMC (2001) indicates that specialist practice requires the exercising of higher levels of judgement, discretion and decision-making, focusing on four broad areas, these being: clinical practice; care and programme management; clinical practice development; and clinical practice leadership.

However, in addition to the mandatory competencies that pre-qualifying health and social care students must achieve (e.g. those set out by the NMC [2010a] for nurse education), pre-registration education is also influenced by paradigm shifts and evolving policies. As noted earlier in this chapter and in Box 1.2, in 2012 the newly appointed CNO at NHS England set out a strategy to incorporate 'a culture of compassionate care' within the NHS (DH, 2012b), and therefore as a concept within pre-qualifying educational preparation programmes. Even more recently, in response to the Francis Report (DH, 2013a) the government responded by making specific recommendations for pre-qualifying programmes, such as individuals intending to enter nurse education having to work for a year as a clinical support worker or healthcare assistant, as a prerequisite (Gov.uk, 2013).

As noted earlier in this chapter, HEE and LETBs have an important role to play in funding for education, training and CPD of health professionals. Post-qualifying learning activities are discussed in detail in Chapter 11 of this book.

Regulation of Care Professions, and Codes of Practice

Professional regulators of health and social care professions monitor the quality of health and social care delivered to patients and service users when alleged malpractice has been reported to them. Regulatory bodies include the NMC, HCPC, General Medical Council (GMC) and so on, and their work in turn is directed by various Acts of Parliament and is overseen by Professional Standards Authority for Health and Social Care (PSA). The PSA was previously known as the Council for Healthcare Regulatory Excellence (CHRE), which was instituted in 2003 in the United Kingdom in the wake of malpractice related to paediatric cardiac surgery at the Bristol Royal Infirmary during the preceding years.

The PSA is an independent UK health regulatory body that is funded by the DH and is answerable to Parliament; one of their roles is to co-ordinate standards and good practice amongst the bodies responsible for regulating health and social care professions. Alternatively, the CQC's role is to monitor the quality of services provided to recipients of health and social care in both NHS and the independent sector.

In addition to health and social care strategies, policies and legislation, daily care is also influenced directly by care professionals' *Code of Practice* for their own profession. All care professionals have to abide by their professions' codes of practice. For nurses and midwives, for example, the NMC (2010b) has published *The Code* and regularly promotes its content.

The management role of DCMs in nursing and midwifery includes their responsibility to ensure that all staff abide by *The Code*. Codes of practice are based on principles of ethics that advocate such edicts as no action or omission on the part of the healthcare professional should result in any harm to patients and service users.

Action point 1.5   Code of practice for your profession

Access and read through the latest edition of the code of practice for your own health or social care profession group – for example, the code of practice issued by the HCPC.

For nurses and midwives, for example, the most recent NMC code of practice is constituted in *The Code* (2010b). For social workers, the HCPC's (2012a) code of practice details the ethical practices for a number of health and social care professions. The HCPC code superseded the 2008 HCPC *Standards of Conduct, Performance and Ethics* for allied health professionals (AHPs) when the transfer of professional regulation for social workers to HCPC was completed in 2012.

Professional bodies and Royal Colleges

All healthcare professions also have their own professional bodies or Royal Colleges whose key roles include conducting research, providing educational packages, and developing guidelines for safe and effective practice. Healthcare profession colleges include the Royal College of General Practitioners, Royal College of Paediatrics & Child Health, Royal College of Psychiatrists, Royal College of Nursing, and the College of Social Work.

The Royal College of Nursing, for example, is a professional college which is set up and sustained by members' subscription, and their activities are collegial in that they build a body of knowledge for their profession through conducting research and through publishing guidelines constituted by experts on the actions to take when faced with specific issues.

Good practice guidelines for effective leadership and management in health and social care

The following points comprise good practice guidelines in relation to your knowledge of leadership and management in the current context of healthcare.

- As DCM, familiarise yourself with all relevant current legislation and policies, and how they relate to your practice.
- Ascertain ways in which national policies are implemented in your organisation.
- Become knowledgeable of the clauses in your health or social care code of practice issued by your professional regulator.
- Develop an understanding of your leadership and management competencies for achieving patient outcomes.
- Ensure that you are clear about the extent to which you engage in each of the six roles of the DCM as outlined at the beginning of this chapter.
- Have a working understanding of the roles and interrelationships of various organisations identified in the NHS structure (Figure 1.3) and how they relate to your role and organisation.

CHAPTER SUMMARY

This chapter started by examining the broader context of care management, which included considering a range of factors related to the contemporary social context in which care is delivered, and subsequently explored the various ways in which the DCM's leadership and management interface with these factors. This included identifying:

- instances of good practice in health and social care delivery, as well as incidents that comprise poor practice, and how these relate to the DCM's leadership and management roles;
- the roles, responsibilities and functions of qualified care professionals as DCMs, including specific activities that are undertaken in the course of daily duties, in relation to their leadership and managerial duties in practice settings;
- the prevailing social, demographic and economic context in which health and social care and treatment are provided, and their relevance to DCMs in their leadership and management roles;
- the current legislation, strategies and policies that underpin care delivery with current government policies guiding how healthcare organisations respond to the care needs of local communities; and
- the workforce for health and social care delivery, the educational preparation of care professionals for the delivery of competent, safe and effective care, as well as the regulation of care professions and the codes of practice that care professionals have to abide by.

Strong and effective management and leadership are required at all levels within health and social care. The DCM needs to have an understanding of the context within which contemporary health and social care is delivered, and to be able to translate this to their role within their individual practice setting. The various aspects of management and leadership will be explored in Chapters 2 and 3 respectively.

- The principles and values of the NHS in England, including the rights of patients, the public and staff, as well as the pledges that the NHS is committed to achieve, are all identified in *The NHS Constitution*. Service providers are required by law to take account of this Constitution in their decisions and actions. For further details, see:

NHS England (2013) *Updated NHS Constitution Published*. Available from: www.england.nhs.uk/2013/03/26/nhs-Constitution/.

- For scrutiny of the Health and Social Care Act 2012, see:

Department of Health (2012) *Health and Social Care Act 2012*. Available from: www.legislation.gov.uk/ukpga/2012/7/enacted.

- For details of similarities and differences in care provision between the four UK countries, see:

National Audit Office (2012) *Healthcare across the UK: A Comparison of the NHS in England, Scotland, Wales and Northern Ireland*. Available from: www.official-documents.gov.uk/document/hc1213/hc01/0192/0192.pdf.

- For details of the government's £20 billion efficiency savings by 2015, see:

Department of Health (2011) *Quality, Innovation, Productivity and Prevention* (QIPP). Available from: www.dh.gov.uk/en/Healthcare/Qualityandproductivity/index.htm.

- For details of social work reform conducted in the last couple of years see:

Social Work Reform Board or College of Social Work website (www.collegeofsocialwork.org/) for competencies for pre-qualifying social workers.

2

MANAGING EFFECTIVELY – THEORIES, ROLES AND STYLES

The DCM has a pivotal role in ensuring provision and delivery of the highest standards of care for patients or service users in their practice settings, whilst also ensuring optimal use of available resources. Having ascertained in Chapter 1 the contemporary social and economic context in which health and social care and treatment are provided in the United Kingdom, including codes of practice, this chapter now examines the theories, roles and styles that underpin effective management of care in health and social care settings.

More specifically, the chapter examines the day-to-day managerial duties of DCMs, the nature of healthcare management and care organisations, theories of management and how they apply to healthcare, styles of management along with specific ways of organising daily care, managerial communication and the interpersonal skills and personal qualities of DCMs; concluding with guidelines for effective management of care.

Chapter objectives

On completion of this chapter you will be able to:

- ascertain the specific day-to-day managerial activities that the DCM engages in, and management roles;
- demonstrate an understanding of organisations, recognise the importance of organisational structures of health and social care organisations, and where management fits into the organisation;
- distinguish between the key terms manager and management, and comprehend the various theories and styles of management that the DCM can draw on;
- demonstrate knowledge and understanding of how to apply significant theories of management to care settings, exploring the personal qualities required to be

a successful care manager and consider the development of your own personal managerial skills;

- analyse approaches that are available to DCMs for organising daily care, assess the strengths and weaknesses of the various modes of care organisation, and reflect on their relevance in different care settings; and
- determine the various ways in which the DCM communicates day-to-day care effectively in collaboration with relevant services, along with more specific management communication such as delegation, interviewing and so on.

The Day-to-day Activities of the Duty Care Manager

The end of the twentieth century saw varied questions and concerns raised about health and social care management. In particular, these were related to the amount of money being spent on health and social care services. Yet scientific advances will always uncover new and more effective ways of treating illnesses as health and social care needs continue to evolve, which in turn tends to cumulatively increase the costs of these provisions. The quality of care provision has also latterly been under the spotlight. Effective management is therefore an imperative to maintaining high quality care and to ensure these concerns are addressed.

At times managers might appear to be engrossed primarily in administrative duties such as 'doing the paperwork', or engaged in various meetings within or outside the department. At other times, they may appear to do no more than ensure that their employees are conducting their roles correctly, and intervene only when problems are anticipated or arise. Nevertheless, as the DCM may be the health or social care professional, as well as the ward manager/team leader in charge of a span of duty, they have to balance their care delivery duties with those of care management.

Action point 2.1   Care management activities

This Action point can be undertaken in small groups, in pairs or individually.

Identify and write down *all* 'real life' day-to-day management or managerial activities undertaken by the DCM in your workplace, and issues dealt with, over:

- a particular span of duty
- a 24-hour period
- a one-week period
- a period of one month, or a year.

The activities include dealing with routine as well as with unexpected events during different spans of duty.

Now list the reasons why you think managers engage in each of these activities.

Given more time, you may be able to add to the list of managerial activities that you have compiled in response to action point 2.1, especially when considering those that managers engage in over a period of one month, or a year. Your list of managerial duties may include many of those listed in the left-hand column of Table 2.1,

Table 2.1   The day-to-day managerial activities of the DCM, as identified by RNs and finalist pre-registration student nurses

Managerial activities identified by RNs and finalist pre-registration student nurses	Managerial components or roles
Workload management	Human resource manager
Doing the off-duty/self-rostering	
Staffing levels and skill-mix	
Dealing with staff shortages/crises	
Staff interviews and recruitment	
Identifying annual leave	
Sickness management	Promoter of staff welfare
Staff morale issues	
Acting as staff advocate	
Bed management	Capacity manager
Managing space, i.e. extra beds/patients on trolleys	
Budgeting	Effectiveness and efficiency monitor
Ensuring resources are available, e.g. equipment, collecting statistics	Planner and communicator
Delegation (of duties)	
Arranging and attending meetings	
Dealing with personality clashes, conflict between staff	Decision-maker and problem-solver
Bleep holder, deal with crisis	
Liaising with other agencies, e.g. education providers	
Dealing with/preventing complaints from staff/patients/their relatives	Quality assuror
Involved in audits	
Other clinical governance activities	
Dealing with child protection issues	Guardian of health and safety
Risk management	
Ensuring safety of patients, staff etc., deal with accidents	
Disciplining and handling grievance	Policy enforcer
Allocating study time/training	Staff trainer and educator
Checking staff training needs and statutory training	
Monitoring mandatory training	
Handling and moving; CPD, Fire – regular updates	
Appraisals (IDPR)	
Hands-on clinical care	Care giver and practice developer
Giving information	Leader and team worker
Mentor/supervise junior RNs	

which consists of management activities identified by RNs on management courses, and by finalist pre-registration student nurses, separately. The right-hand column groups the day-to-day care management activities as management roles.

The management roles grouping the day-to-day care management activities in the right-hand column of Table 2.1 form the basis for effective care management in care settings. Back in the earlier part of the twentieth century, Fayol (2012) conducted a much-quoted study that identified management activities (or functions) in five groups as planning, organising, commanding, co-ordinating and controlling (feedback), which was claimed to have universal relevance.

Although the 12 managerial roles in Table 2.1 are identified as discrete roles, more than one role may be fulfilled at any one time, such as being a 'Human resource manager' and a 'Decision-maker and problem-solver' at the same time. The table represents quite an accurate overall picture of contemporary managerial roles of DCMs. Further details of components that each role comprises of are presented in Table 2.2.

Table 2.2 Brief details of each managerial role

Managerial role	Further details or components
Human resource manager	Recruitment, staff retention, motivating the team, dealing with performance issues
Promoter of staff welfare	Knowledge of facilities and support that staff can draw on
Capacity manager	Ensuring skilled and competent staff provide and perform care interventions effectively
Effectiveness and efficiency monitor	Monitoring use of resources, both human and non-human resources
Planner and communicator	Communicating, delegating and negotiating plans and changes
Decision-maker and problem-solver	Making decisions at operational level; pre-empting/solving problems; conflict manager
Quality assuror	Monitoring informally and formally the quality of care provided to patients and service users (or care recipients); ensuring equality and supporting diversity
Guardian of health and safety	Ensuring that health and safety regulations, ethical guidelines and professional codes are adhered to
Policy enforcer	Ensuring that clinical policies and guidelines are adhered to; devising/adapting guidelines as necessary
Staff trainer/educator	Identifying, contributing to, and monitoring team members' professional development and learning
Care giver and practice developer	Managing change and innovation
Leader and team worker	Leader of the team; maintaining team cohesiveness, which can be multi-professional

This discussion on the activities of DCMs focuses attention on the practical aspects of their role during a typical span of duty, but their line manager may ultimately have ongoing responsibility and accountability for the care setting. There are of course various other ways of categorising management activities. Drucker (2007: 14, 11), for instance, categorises the jobs of management as managing the business, managing managers, and managing workers and work. He identifies five 'basic operations' in the work of the manager as setting objectives, organising, motivating and communicating, measuring, and developing people.

Alternatively, Mintzberg (1990) identifies management activities as 10 groups of roles (as discussed later in this chapter). Both examples illustrate how a wide range of managerial activities can be grouped into fewer categories of more generalised terms, although this can result in loss of detail of the multiple and complex activities that DCMs engage in during their work activities.

It is essential to appreciate that when engaged in the management activities (or managerial roles) that emerged from Action point 2.1, these are undertaken in the context of the overall health and social care organisational activities undertaken by various other departments in the organisation, professional and ancillary.

Management and Organisations

Table 2.1 identified the activities and roles of DCMs as many and varied. So what do the terms 'manager' and 'management' mean?

Managers and management

Most definitions of the terms 'manager' and 'management' refer to the activities and competencies of managers. For instance, Stewart (1999: 3) defines a manager as 'someone who gets things done through other people'. Armstrong (2012) suggests that a manager is someone whose main job is to organise their junior colleagues' time within an organisation in order to pursue the objectives of the organisation. Drucker (2007: 6) indicates that a manager is 'someone who directs the work of others and who does his work by getting other people to do theirs'.

In today's health and social care organisations, a manager is an employee who has been appointed specifically to ensure that the objectives in their span of remit are achieved effectively and efficiently. The DCM is a registered care practitioner with the knowledge and expertise required for the post that they hold, who therefore decides and prioritises the specific tasks or activities that are appointed to perform, and also then ensures that the tasks that they have delegated have been performed by appropriately skilled personnel to the required standard.

Managers often work in collaboration with other managers, who are either of similar status, more senior or junior to them. A group of managers could comprise a management team, which might include clinical directors, a general manager, modern matrons and consultant nurses.

According to Drucker (2007: 15), management in the context of a management team is 'a multi-purpose organ' that manages a business and its employees as individuals and teams, with the aim of accomplishing the objectives of the organisation. The analogy of an 'organ' in Drucker's definition implies that management is a live and dynamic entity that functions for specific purposes, can stretch its abilities, but can also be affected by problematic issues that need resolving. Care management comprises a team of qualified care professionals who are led by the DCM, and who fulfil the functions identified in Table 2.1, which includes that of care giver. Therefore, the term 'management' can be defined as a team of appropriately qualified individuals who engage in multiple activities aimed at effective and efficient achievement of the goals of the organisation.

Each healthcare trust is an organisation in its own right, and care interventions are carried out in the context of the particular organisation's specific function, which is to support the local population's health and social care needs. Organisations can span generations, and an individual employee may opt to leave at some point, but the organisation itself is likely to endure and outlive all individual employees by many years. That is, most organisations are very likely to continue existing long after current and subsequent managers have served their term and left for other posts or otherwise departed.

The organisation as a health or social care service provider

The aims and objectives of individual health and social care organisations are normally specified in their business plan, which also usually identifies its mission statement. Care organisations are service organisations. Organisations can be distinguished in terms of two generic groups: public sector organisations and private enterprise organisations. The distinction between the two is that public sector organisations do not have profit as their goal, they are 'owned' by taxpayers, and their main aim is to provide a service that is concerned with the wellbeing of individuals in the community in a defined geographical area. Private organisations tend to be owned and financed by individuals, partners or shareholders, and the main aim is of a commercial nature, that is, financial profit. However, the boundary between public and private sector is blurred to some extent with the prevalence of internal markets within healthcare and the advent of Foundation Trusts.

Thus, organisations vary according to the nature of the work they undertake. For example, contrasting a school with a car manufacturer, or a hospital with a public library, shows that each has distinct functions. These functions determine the people skills they require, how simple or complex they are, their size in the context of their output, the number of people they employ, and also the extent to which they use technology.

To achieve the aims of the organisation, a managing director, or in an NHS trust a chief executive, is appointed. The chief executive, in turn, is accountable to the chairperson of the appropriate trust Board, and NHS England, and then ultimately to the Secretary of State for Health. This is likely to change as NHS trusts move rapidly towards achieving 'NHS Foundation Trust' status that entails decentralisation of public services and devolution of decision-making from central government control to local organisations and communities so that they are more responsive to the needs and wishes of the local population (DH, 2007). NHS Foundation Trusts are accountable for their activites to the CCGs who commission their services, to CQC and Monitor, as well as to the local communities through the trust's members and governors.

The activities and performance of NHS Foundation Trusts are, however, regularly checked by 'Monitor', which is the independent regulator of Foundation Trusts. Monitor is responsible for authorising, monitoring and regulating Foundation Trusts to ensure that they are managed effectively, and are financially able to deliver 'excellent' health or social care. Monitor has the powers to intervene in the running of NHS Foundation Trusts in the event of failings in their healthcare standards or other aspects of their activities that amount to a significant breach of their terms of authorisation.

The structure of organisations

In addition to the building, or the complex of buildings that house a healthcare organisation, its staffing structure constitutes all individuals employed by the organisation, and the precise division of work, that is the allocation of individual tasks and responsibilities, for each employee. This entails establishing a structure of senior and junior staff with clearly demarcated duties, responsibilities and span of control, and may be hierarchical in nature. It also incorporates reporting relationships within the organisation, and the pattern of relationships between different posts and different employees, as well as the co-ordination of their activities that are directed towards achieving the organisation's aims and objectives. The hierarchical structure of employees is the mechanism through which the activities of the organisation are designated and monitored.

Within the structure of the organisation, various channels of communication are established to ensure they are effective. Team briefs, staff meetings, bulletins and email communications are just a few examples of modes of communication.

Organisational structures consist of a number of inherent common dimensions such as grouping of functions into sections and departments, with the objectives of each of these departments needing to be consistent with, and contribute to, those of the organisation as a whole. The work that needs to be done has to be clearly defined, and should be divided up appropriately amongst employees. Consequently, this constitutes the integration of the efforts and full participation of each individual employee. Motivation of staff through systems of appraisal and reward should also be established and implemented.

The allocation of individual tasks and responsibilities also comprises job definition and job specialisation. The degree of specialisation required to achieve the objectives of the organisation has to be delineated, and in nursing as well as in other health and social care professions in general there is increasing specialisation and demarcation of responsibilities that also identify their scope of accountability.

Every employee's functions in the organisational structure are important, as they impact on productivity as well as morale and job satisfaction. Another crucial factor is the frame of reference that takes account of the 'people factor', such as appropriate leadership and management styles. However, a good structure does not singularly guarantee success, as appropriate systems of work need to be in place, and effectiveness needs to be monitored and evaluated regularly.

Furthermore, in addition to the formal structure of the organisation that is precisely designed to fulfil a purpose and deliver a service, there is always an 'informal organisation', as also noted by Mullins (2010) and others. Every employee is an individual in their own right, with their own reasons for seeking employment in the organisation, and if any of the workings of the organisation causes them discomfort, they feel the need to verbalise their thoughts and feelings with someone who is usually of equal employment status as them, without jeopardising their post. Such an unofficial and informal mode of communication, including through social media, comprises the informal organisation.

The informal organisation essentially constitutes a sub-culture that: has different communication patterns; are led by personalities; involves underlying skills and knowledge; can incorporates political behaviour; and can also be in conflict with the formal organisation. Nonetheless, the informal organisation has important functions, in that it:

- satisfies members' social needs to communicate their thoughts and feelings
- provides additional channels of communication, e.g. through the 'grapevine' (and communicated quickly)
- gives a sense of personal identity and belonging
- is a feeling of stability and security
- is a means of motivation – through status, social interaction etc.
- can highlight deficiencies or weaknesses in the formal organisation.

Thus, the informal organisation has an important influence on the job satisfaction and performance of staff, their morale and motivation, and therefore the prevailing beliefs, assumptions and values (the culture of the organisation).

Hierarchical levels in the organisation

Varying levels of hierarchy exist within formal organisations. This could comprise a pyramidal structure, as illustrated in Figure 2.1.

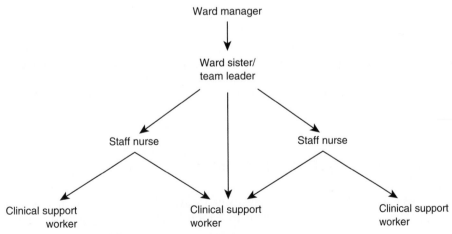

Figure 2.1 Pyramidal management structure

Action point 2.2   The hierarchy in your care setting

- Draw a diagram identifying the staffing structure within your team, department or organisation.
- How many levels of command are there, and what are the possible advantages and disadvantages of these particular levels of the hierarchy?
- Do you consider the management structure and levels of command within your care setting to be appropriate?
- What management structure do you consider to be ideal?

The current hierarchy of different levels of employees in any particular care setting or organisation could be functioning effectively, but due to continual changes influenced by internal and external factors (see Chapter 6 for more detail) problematic aspects could surface, and therefore the existing management structure needs to be regularly questioned to ascertain its effectiveness, and maybe efficiency.

Variations in the number of levels of management in the organisation and each manager's span of control can affect the effectiveness with which responsibilities are fulfilled. With pyramidal structures, for instance, care managers might choose to devolve certain functions to more junior members of staff. For example, rather than personally undertaking individual development and performance reviews (IDPRs) for all staff working within the team, the care manager might devolve those for CSWs to other senior care professionals. However, there is a danger that steep pyramidal structures could result in ineffective communication and relationships between the next-but-one level of management, which in turn could lead to misrepresentations and misunderstandings, such as when changes to work conditions are proposed.

Flatter structures

Flatter management structures, as illustrated in Figure 2.2, could resolve some of the issues related to pyramidal structures, and enable the organisation to meet the need for individual employees to achieve more autonomy and 'personal growth' within their posts.

Applying Management Theories

Numerous published theories of management are available to choose from, but before examining specific ones it is pertinent to establish what a theory is and what the

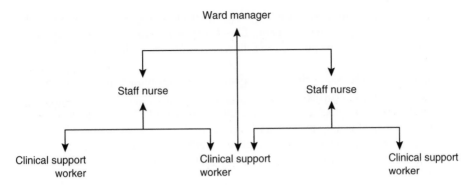

Figure 2.2   Flatter management structure

purposes of theories are. All human actions are based on some theory, that is, certain assumptions, hypotheses and generalisations. Theories tend to determine our prediction that if we do *a*, then *b* will occur; that is, it incorporates a 'cause and effect' type of relationship. A theory is a structure of ideas that seeks to explain a phenomenon, or underpin a way of working, that may be based around a number of principles.

Consequently, management theories (discussed next) also aim to fulfil such functions as describing, predicting and explaining the wherewithal of management of care settings. So, on which management theories can DCMs base their management activities? The theories available could be grouped under 'conventional management' theories and 'managerial role' theory. There are four main conventional management theories, namely the classical theory, human relations theory, systems theory and contingency theory. A subsequent theory referred to as post-modern theory has been mooted more recently.

Conventional Management Theories

The classical approach

The classical approach is one of the earliest management theories, but one that can be easily observed in bureaucratic organisations today. According to this theory, which was known as 'scientific management' in its early years, managers guide the organisation to improve efficiency. It constitutes the notion that if a formal structure is firmly established with regard to exactly which posts cover which tasks for the organisation, the technical skills that each post-holder needs to have to fulfil the job requirements, and a set of detailed procedures that they need to follow to do so, then the organisation would function effectively and efficiently. The formal structure is designed with the aim of achieving the organisation's goals. It includes a clear hierarchy of staff, with formal intra-organisational relationships, clear division of work and definition of duties and responsibilities, as well as established rules and procedures for various activities.

Scientific management theory was originally advocated by F. W. Taylor (1856–1917), based on his research on management. The theory was based on the belief that the organisation will achieve its aims if the following points are addressed:

- concern with improvements that are designed to increase productivity (i.e. the amount of work done during a particular shift);
- one 'best working method' to do a job, and this can be done by breaking jobs into discrete tasks and 'one best way' to perform each task;
- provision of monetary incentives as a motivator for high levels of output;
- making management a science by systematic selection, training and development of employees;
- co-operation with workers to ensure work is carried out in the prescribed way; and
- a clear division of work and responsibility between managers and workers.

This management approach was later referred to as the 'bureaucratic' method wherein employment is also based on technical qualification and skills. Some of the main features of the bureaucratic method are:

- specialisation in specific duties and responsibilities;
- a clear hierarchy of authority and precise stratification (as in the army or a factory production line); and
- specific relatively stable rules that are designed to provide efficient operation including clearly laid down appeal procedures against management decisions.

The likely strengths and weaknesses of the scientific approach are highlighted in Table 2.3.

Furthermore, within the scientific approach is the bureaucratic method of management, which in turn has its own weaknesses, including:

- over-emphasis on rules and regulations that can stifle growth and initiative, and lead to failure, frustration and conflict and stereotyped behaviours; and
- neglect of the employees' aspirations.

Furthermore, although scientific management methods can be applied to care management, the theory tends to overlook the post-holder's interpersonal needs,

Table 2.3 Strengths and weaknesses of the scientific approach of management

Strengths of the scientific approach	Weaknesses of the scientific approach
Better quality of management decisions	Bureaucratic i.e. structured rules, regulations,
Reduced employee turnover	templates
Less sickness and absenteeism	Managers ensure that rules are adhered to
Fewer accidents	May lack flexibility
Better labour relations	Can be impersonal

the benefits of interaction between employees, and post-holders' individual views on the functioning of the organisation. The method therefore often proves unacceptable to the employee and also managers. Subsequent theories of management, such as the human relations approach, emerged to overcome this major weakness in the classical approach by incorporating consideration of the personal and social experiences of individual workers.

The human relations approach

A landmark in the development of the human relations approach was the findings of the momentous Hawthorne experiments in the Western Electric Company in the United States during the period 1924 to 1932. One of the findings of the experiments was that productivity increased when people worked in groups, especially if these groups were self-selected. This approach consequently takes account of some of the psychological and social needs of the employees of the organisation, and can be configured into teamworking.

The human relations approach is also referred to as the 'behavioural' or 'informal approach', and later developments of this approach include neo-human relations theories, which includes concepts and theories developed by Maslow (1987), Herzberg (1974), McGregor (1987) (all three discussed in Chapter 10 in relation to staff motivation) and others. The work of these authors has direct impact on staff motivation because of their focus on human needs as discussed in Chapter 10 in relation to teamwork.

The human relations theory is clearly the most appropriate approach for managing health and social care staff, primarily because the whole ethos of health and social care services is founded on caring and promoting the holistic wellbeing of people. Some of the ways in which the DCM could effectively implement this approach are presented in Box 2.1.

Box 2.1   Ways in which the human relations theory could be effectively applied by DCMs/care managers

- Taking into account each individual member of staff's personal prospects in relation to their post, e.g. personal and professional development needs, forming new alliances etc.
- Attending to social factors by encouraging staff to socialise during short breaks etc.
- Encouraging groups of staff to work as teams, rather than as separate individuals.
- Monitoring how new members of staff are 'fitting in' with the existing team, and guiding them if appropriate.
- Showing an appropriate level of interest in the employee's family, their birthdays, wedding, new baby etc.
- Maintaining a structure that provides sufficient availability of clinical supervision and peer support for individual members of staff.

Action point 2.3   Implementing the human relations approach

Think of various instances when managers who you know, or those in your workplace, demonstrate the human relations approach by adopting features like those identified in Box 2.1.

How feasible it is to implement all these features depends on several other factors. For instance, certain provisions might not be in place due to resource constraints, levels of employees' motivation and their knowledge and competence. It could also be said that it is difficult to please all staff, all of the time. These issues will be explored further under the management of change (in Chapter 6). However, dedicating excessive time using the human relations approach at the expense of scientific methods could also negatively affect productivity.

Additionally, new mechanical equipment and electronic medical devices that facilitate health and social care workers' daily duties have evolved over the years, with new ones emerging all the time requiring regular re-learning by staff. The 'systems approach' to management takes into account the use of these necessary aids.

The systems approach

The systems approach to management recognises organisations as comprising a number of systems and sub-systems, and subsumes the advantageous aspects of classical and human relations' approaches. This approach sees organisations as: (1) open systems, with multiple channels of interaction internally and with the broader external environment; and (2) socio-technical system, which recognises the relationship between social and technical variables within the organisation. The socio-technical system not only heeds the increasing need to use new technologies to accelerate and improve the quality of organisational outcomes, but also advocates heeding the effect this might have on individual employees.

The systems approach is clearly visible in care settings where medical technology is required for care interventions, diagnostic technologies that enable a wide range of pathology laboratory investigations and those that enable results to be communicated more speedily to care staff. In other team structures, non-medical practitioners can be involved in undertaking minor surgical or endoscopic procedures. The recognition of the role that these facilitative devices play to support the delivery of care, treatment and communication by managers form the basis of this approach. The widespread, almost universal, use of computers today, and even hand-held devices in places, obviously contribute to health and social care delivery and management.

The contingency approach

The three management theories briefly discussed above evolved over several decades in the order presented, but the more recent and widely adopted theory is referred to as the 'contingency approach'. The contingency approach, which is also referred to as 'situational management', stipulates that there is no one optimum state in an organisation, and therefore the management approach used, and its success, is dependent (or 'contingent') upon the nature of the task that needs to be undertaken, or situation to be dealt with, at a particular point in time and under prevailing environmental circumstances.

The contingency approach therefore comprises the belief that there is no one best and universally applicable management theory as there are a large number of variables and situational factors which directly influence organisational performance. It is seen as an 'if–then' form of relationship. 'If' a particular situation exists, 'then' the scientific approach might be the most appropriate, such as if a newly qualified health or social care professional is learning new procedures, then he or she must follow the organisation's procedure or clinical guidelines. In other situations the human relations approach might be more appropriate, such as when dealing with a patient who has expressed concern regarding the standard of care received. Consequently, over particular periods of time, the DCM might well choose to use an appropriate combination of the three approaches. Box 2.2 presents a summary of conventional theories of management.

Box 2.2   Summary of conventional theories of management

Classical management theory involves having:

- clearly defined goals
- formal hierarchical management structures
- common procedures and policies
- minimal or no consideration of employees' views.

Human relations theory incorporates consideration of:

- social factors in the work setting
- formal groups and emerging sub-groups

(Continued)

(Continued)

- appropriate leadership
- personal matters.

Systems theory builds on:

- classical and human relations approaches, and further develops them
- up-to-date technological aids
- the organisation vis-à-vis its external environment.

Contingency theory stipulates that:

- there is no one best management theory
- the management approach taken is based on the nature of the situation at that point in time.

The Post-modern Approach

Beyond conventional management theories, the post-modern approach to management has also been advocated. This approach is based on post-modern philosophies and beliefs about society in general (e.g. Petersen and Bunton, 1997; Rolfe, 1999), which suggests that every situation requires a rethink of all alternative approaches or avenues available every time as there could well be other unprecedented, or more than one appropriate, acceptable and effective approach to resolve a situation.

For instance in healthcare, the NHS Institute for Innovation and Improvement (NHS III) (2008a) promoted 'lean' thinking as a management system, which refers to the least wasteful way of providing care, which also maximises the use of resources, and reduces delays. Castle (2007) suggests that lean methods are implemented by top-level managers by devolving quality assurance and various other responsibilities to teams of employees who are skilled in a variety of tasks, and by reduced individual specialisation.

Brookes (2011: 16) indicates that strengthening the leadership component of management theories, with emphasis on bringing out 'the best in people, organisations and communities', through taking a 'possibility centric' approach, rather than problem-centred thinking, can lead to improved team performance and care on a paediatric ward. Leadership as a key role of managers is also identified by Mintzberg (1990) – which is discussed briefly in the next section, and in detail in Chapter 3.

Managerial Roles Theory

This section focuses on management theories from another angle, which is that of managerial roles theory. Table 2.2 identifies 12 managerial roles of the care manager, which are illustrated in Figure 2.3. These roles reflect a comprehensive approach to management in health and social care.

Another managerial roles theory was proposed earlier by Mintzberg (1990), whose research identified 10 key role areas for managers:

1   Figurehead – represents the care setting formally.
2   Liaison – deals with peers and outsiders in order to exchange work-related information.
3   Leader – staffs the care setting and motivates employees.
4   Monitor – gathers and interprets necessary information.
5   Disseminator – passes on to subordinates information not otherwise available.
6   Spokesperson – passes on appropriate information to external agencies.
7   Entrepreneur – initiates change and innovation.
8   Disturbance handler – intervenes when disruptions occur.
9   Resource allocator – decides where and how resources will be deployed.
10 Negotiator – deals with outsiders whose consent and co-operation is required in care provision and delivery.

Mintzberg's 10-role theory is therefore an alternative framework that the DCMs can use to analyse and fulfil their management functions in care settings.

Figure 2.3   The managerial roles of care managers

Action point 2.4   Your own managerial roles

Recall and jot down several managerial tasks that you have recently undertaken, and consider how these relate to the managerial roles in care management identified in Figure 2.3. Then:

- Using the format below, examine specific ways in which you get directly involved in each of these managerial roles.
- After you have completed the second column, rate the extent of your skill and self-confidence with each role from 1 to 5, where 1 represents low skill and self-confidence and 5 represents high.
- How effective do you feel in each of the roles you undertake?
- Ask your line manager, or another manager whose views you value, how effective they believe you to be in each of these roles.
- Consider self-development opportunities to enhance your effectiveness in each of these roles.

Management roles	My specific involvement in management roles	Skill rating	Self-confidence rating
Human resource manager			
Promoter of staff welfare			
Capacity manager			
Effectiveness and efficiency monitor			
Planner and communicator			
Decision-maker and problem-solver			
Quality assuror			
Guardian of health and safety			
Policy enforcer			
Staff trainer/educator			
Care giver and practice developer			
Leader and team-worker			

The actions suggested above might have overlapped to a fair extent with that of Action point 2.1, but will nonetheless have enabled you to identify your own areas of strengths as a manager, as well as those of deficit, and those in which you wish your management role to develop further.

Styles of management

In addition to theories of management, another dimension to managing people is the notion of management styles. The word 'style' refers to the individual characteristic or manner in which the person expresses himself in social situations, and therefore also performs his managerial tasks, and this also applies to the DCM. It incorporates how managers, being in positions of authority, conduct themselves and their tasks towards their juniors, to the general public and to their seniors.

One of the most prominent perspectives on styles of management has been advocated by Blake and McCanse (1991), who, based on research on behavioural leadership styles in the 1970s and 1980s, developed a grid that identified the manager's style as reflecting 'concern for people', that is, their employees, or 'concern for productivity', in other words the amount of work completed (also discussed in Chapter 3 under leadership). High 'concern for people' is consistent with a democratic style of management, as opposed to an autocratic style, or the human relations approach to management. High concern for productivity indicates that the manager performs his tasks with the principal focus being on how much work gets done, which is largely a feature of the classical approach.

Another popular style of management was advocated even earlier by Odiorne (1979), and also by Drucker (2007: 103), which is known as 'management by objectives' (MBO), and directly affects contemporary management in health and social care. In this style of management, the manager endeavours to juxtapose the organisation's objectives with those of the individual employee's, along with the latter's development needs. Odiorne (1979) described MBO as a mechanism whereby a manager and each employee jointly identify goals that are common to the employee and to the organisation, and define the individual's major areas of responsibility in terms of results. MBO is consequently founded on: (1) defining specific areas of responsibility, setting objectives and targets, and criteria of performance, and the continual review and appraisal of results; and (2) the professional development needs of the employee.

MBO has been widely used in both private and public sectors and focuses on people's strengths enabling their further development, rather than concentrating on their weaknesses. When reviewing performance, the manager concentrates on the tasks that the employee has completed, but does not treat completion or non-completion as a feature of their character or personality. The focus is on the achievement of objectives.

Consequently, the MBO style of management incorporates the use of IDPR. However, the individual employee's objectives and targets are not imposed but established and agreed through discussion between them and their line manager. Thus, within agreed limits and the policies of the organisation, employees are given some freedom of action to decide how best to achieve their objectives and targets. MBO can be contrasted with the more autocratic management style that is based on direction and control.

One possible drawback of MBO is that it could focus too much on the job and reflect the scientific management approach; another is that it also assumes that there will be complete alignment between individuals and the organisation's goals.

Applied to health and social care organisations, MBO tends to figure in the organisation's business plan in the form of strategic and operational objectives. Annual

IDPRs for health and social care professionals working in care settings in the NHS is specified as the skills framework and review in the *NHS Knowledge and Skills Framework (NHS KSF)* (DH, 2004a). This document provides a structure that directly links the care organisation's skill needs for the achievement of corporate objectives with the individual employee's self-determined responsibilities and professional development needs. Accordingly, employees need to identify their competence and development needs in six core dimensions:

1 Communication
2 Personal and people development
3 Health, safety and security
4 Service improvement
5 Quality
6 Equality and diversity.

There are further 'specific dimensions' identified, along with specified levels for each dimension, that correspond with *Agenda for Change* (DH, 2004c) pay bands. The *NHS KSF* is a fully structured framework for facilitating performance reviews for most healthcare practitioners, and includes the requirement to develop personal and professional development plans. For social care professionals, the Social Work Reform Board identifies the 'Professional Capabilities Framework' outcome statements under nine domains or areas that, on qualifying, social workers should be capable of performing competently (College of Social Work, 2012).

Communication will be explored shortly, but before that the options available to DCMs for ways of organising daily care is examined.

Approaches to Organising Daily Care

Having identified the numerous health and social care factors that impact on ways in which care is delivered to patients and service users, the remainder of this chapter returns to the role and activities of the DCM in the organisation of daily care, and in communicating care.

In the context of the activities identified in Action point 1.1, when the DCM begins a span of duty they not only have to deliver care but also organise the care of all patients or service users whom they are accountable for. The care is provided collaboratively with doctors and AHPs, and as already mentioned is influenced by various legislation, codes of practice, policies, guidance and benchmarks. There are a number of ways in which the DCM can organise and deliver care as they aim to achieve the highest quality care and outcomes for patients or service users. They also have to take into account the resources that are available to them.

A number of factors shape the choice of the preferred methods of care delivery that individual teams or organisations employ. They include the patient group and available skill mix (registered to non-registered staff ratio – discussed in Chapter 7) and the level of supervision and the developmental needs of junior staff and learners. The care delivery method can be eclectic rather than singular, and therefore combined in response to the prevailing circumstances within the span of duty.

Choosing how to organise care

Care delivery is organised in different ways by care managers in different care professions. Social care professionals tend not to deliver care, but generally commission care, with the aim of promoting service users' independence, by using such approaches as personalisation and personal budgets. In nursing care, a number of models of organisation of care are available.

The models of organisation of care address principles such as which member of staff provides care for which patient, and who has responsibility for decision-making and managing the care delivery process. The various models reflect issues such as staffing, skill mix, clinical speciality and patient group. Some care delivery models are specific to nursing, and the scope of their application is limited to the institutional setting, while others have relevance for other health and social care professions and can be applied within primary care settings.

Team leader

Within the team leader approach to organising care, there is a skill mix of team members such as a Band 6 registered practitioner, a Band 5 registered practitioner and CSWs. The team is led by a registered practitioner referred to as the 'team leader', and the team collectively provides care for a group of patients during the span of duty. The team leader plans, co-ordinates, monitors, supervises and evaluates the care that is delivered and is responsible for assigning patients based on the competencies of the staff members within the team. The underlying philosophy of this approach is the achievement of goals and outcomes through collaborative teamwork.

The team approach facilitates the supervision of more junior team members while capitalising on individual expertise and competencies. This approach can also foster staff and patient satisfaction as it supports the delivery of holistic care. The team leader has a fundamental role within this approach and needs to be familiar with the care needs of all patients or service users being cared for by their team.

Named nurse

A registered nurse who is identified as responsible for a particular patient or service user's nursing care is known as the 'named nurse'. This method gives the nurse responsibility for designated patients, and ensures continuity of care for them. They are responsible for the planning and co-ordination of the patient's nursing care from admission (or before) through to discharge and follow-up, and are actively involved in the delivery of some of that care. Shift patterns such as 12-hour shifts and part-time working can prove challenging to this approach, as continuity of care can be affected for patients. This approach has relevance for short episodes of care within the patient journey, such as that delivered within outpatient departments and day surgery units.

Total care or patient allocation

With total care or patient allocation, which is also referred to as the 'case method', a practitioner is responsible for all aspects of care required by one or more patients, for the duration of the span of duty. This method is typically used in areas requiring a high level of expertise and intervention such as in intensive care units (ICUs) and the community. This approach is patient-focused and encompasses clear lines of accountability. Total care fosters a more pronounced holistic approach to care delivery. However, it is not considered to be cost-effective, with registered practitioners engaging in all aspects of patient care when some of the essential care needs could be met through delegation to CSWs, for instance.

Task allocation

Task allocation, also known as the 'functional method', is where the organisation of care is based on the division of labour. Tasks are allocated according to the qualification, currency of their knowledge and skills and the competence of the care practitioner. The assignment of tasks is predominantly hierarchical in nature, in that a senior practitioner, for example, may manage the unit, while CSWs may be allocated to the less complex skills such as making beds and feeding patients. This approach can be compared to that of an assembly line with the combined interventions of a number of individuals, each of whom has a component part. Within this approach, the DCM can allocate tasks and can easily check if they have been completed, as there is limited margin for overlap.

This approach was prevalent in the mid-twentieth century, although it continues to hold some value for contemporary practice in relation to efficiency, particularly where shortages of staff are experienced. Some specialist areas, such as renal dialysis units and aspects of theatre nursing, might use this approach as it lends itself to the technical nature of care delivery and the high patient turnover.

Case management

Case management is also known as the 'care organisation method', in which a named care practitioner assesses a particular patient or service user on first referral or visit, and takes on responsibility for their ongoing care. This method is used in the care of patients with ongoing mental health problems, and those with learning disabilities, in which the practitioner maintains contact with the patient until intervention is no longer required. As the prime manager of the patient or service user's care needs, the DCM arranges and ensures that all required care is delivered along the planned pathway.

Primary nursing

Primary nursing encompasses accountability for 24-hour care by one qualified nurse for a group of patients throughout the duration of their hospital stay. Primary nursing is both a philosophy and a system, and is associated with high levels of patient satisfaction. The achievement of primary nursing, however, can be challenging when the primary nurse is away from the care setting. This method is also resource intensive and its popularity in acute care settings is limited.

Managed care

The managed care method is a multi-disciplinary path of care determined for each patient specific to their medical diagnosis. The path is the critical pattern of events and progress that should be achieved for that patient, from the point of diagnosis to the expected date of discharge. The co-ordination of the path to ensure that all the actions are carried out by the relevant healthcare practitioners is often completed by an RN.

Key working

There are differing interpretations of the term 'key working', but in the context of the organisation of care, the key working method entails an identified person being charged with defined responsibility towards a specific group of patients. This method has application for use with clients who have learning disabilities and is also used within mental health. It has relevance to the community setting, and the scope of the model extends from meeting healthcare needs to addressing social needs.

Triage

Triage is a process by which a patient is assessed at the point of contact with the care team, to determine the urgency of the health problem and to designate appropriate healthcare resources to attend to the identified problem. Patients are therefore not seen on a 'first come, first served' basis, but on the basis of the identified urgency of their health problem. This approach tends to be used in emergency care settings.

Strengths and weaknesses of different ways of organising care

Particular ways of organising care have their advantages, but can also be problematic. A study by Gullick et al. (2004), for instance, compared four models of organisation or care, namely patient allocation, team nursing, primary nursing and task allocation. Seventy-eight per cent of respondents taking part in this study expressed a preference for patient allocation, with 47 per cent characterising 'responsibility' and 'control' as positive features for this approach.

Action point 2.5   Advantages and disadvantages of different approaches to organising care

With regard to organisation of care in care settings, for each of the following approaches, identify and record two advantages and two likely disadvantages:

Approach	Advantages	Disadvantages
Team leader		
Named nurse		
Task allocation		
Total patient care		
Case management		
Primary nursing		
Managed care		
Key working		
Triage		

For task allocation, for instance, several decades ago Menzies (1960) identified problems with this method of care organisation, describing how task-orientation to care alienates patients from staff, demotivates staff and is counter to the philosophy of holistic care, which is a concept and practice that tends to distinguish nursing activities from those of other care professionals.

The nature of healthcare for many service providers is that it is provided 24 hours per day, 7 days a week, 52 weeks of the year. It is therefore important for the approach adopted to be evaluated in relation to a number of key indicators, such as:

- Patient satisfaction (complaints, commendations, patient surveys).
- Family/carer satisfaction (complaints, commendations).
- The achievement of outcomes (clinical audit, quality metrics, research).
- Cost effectiveness (budget).
- Multi-disciplinary team (MDT) satisfaction (sickness statistics, morale, staff surveys).

Integrated care pathways

Integrated Care Pathways (ICP) are evidence-based, multi-professional plans of care, treatment and therapy based on the patient's journey through health and/or social care systems from initial contact with care professionals to ultimate conclusion (i.e. full recovery, or death). They constitute a structured plan of health and social care, and offer a more integrated approach to patient management and the achievement of outcomes. The success of ICPs is dependent upon collaborative teamwork in the development, implementation, monitoring and evaluation of this approach. Care practitioners need to identify evidence-based practice and reach consensus in relation to the patient management requirements for a particular condition, need or speciality. ICPs also provide patients with greater opportunities for involvement in their care, as the care they should receive is clearly identified within timelines set out in the ICP.

Integrated record-keeping is an integral element of ICPs, with all members of the team sharing and documenting within the same record system. ICPs can also feature in-built strategies to monitor patient outcomes in the form of provision for the analysis of variances and clinical audit. They promote a more standardised approach to care delivery than previous ways of organising care, and are designed to lead to a reduction in inconsistencies and inequalities in care delivery. Wales (2003) distinguishes ICPs from other approaches to care delivery in that ICPs encompass integral features that record, track and use variances to enhance care delivery.

ICPs, however, can initially be resource intensive to develop in relation to staff time, although long-term benefits include a reduction in time spent on documentation. Some critics of this approach argue that ICPs promote 'cook-book' medicine, reducing professional autonomy and are therefore not conducive to the delivery of individualised care. Conversely, Middleton and Roberts (2000) assert that members of the multi-professional team can opt not to follow the pathway in individual instances where reasonable justification for this deviation can be provided.

ICPs are developed around an agreed timeframe that can be expressed in minutes, hours, days or even weeks, depending upon the focus of the pathway. A stroke pathway, for example, may contain distinct phases such as acute care and rehabilitation, with the duration of the pathway expressed in terms of weeks. Interventions can be mapped out in terms of when they should be performed, together with the anticipated outcomes. Table 2.4 provides a simplistic representation of an ICP; key areas of intervention are highlighted in the first column with a timeframe included in this instance from pre-operative assessment, through to post-discharge and outpatient follow-up. The blank boxes will detail an agreed plan of intervention mapped out against the timeframe for the duration of the pathway. Box 2.3 lists key steps that are identified from the literature as being integral to the successful development of an ICP.

Table 2.4 Exemplar format of an ICP for day surgery

Intervention	Pre-operative assessment	Day of surgery	Out-patient department
Assessments			
Consultations			
Investigations			
Observations			
Medication			
Pain			
Nutrition			
Health education			
Therapy			
Psychosocial			
Discharge planning			

As suggested above, ICPs incorporate health as well as social care, and healthcare professionals from different professions input care as appropriate at different stages of care (i.e. assessment and intermediate care and long-term care as required).

Box 2.3   Key steps in the development of an integrated care pathway (ICP)

1   Identify a chosen pathway for a medical condition/need/speciality.
2   Configure a multi-professional working group to develop the ICP; this may include representation from other departments, services, sectors, agencies etc. dependent upon the timeframe for the pathway.
3   Obtain examples of ICPs from other organisations.
4   Consider and action the most appropriate strategy in involving patients in the development of the ICP.
5   Select a timeframe for the pathway, i.e. pre-operative, rehabilitation etc.
6   Audit current practice to identify both the optimum timeframe and interventions for the ICP.
7   Use sources of evidence to reach consensus on evidence-based interventions (National Guidelines, National Standards, etc.).
8   Agree a timeframe for the ICP and identify outcomes.
9   Develop inclusion/exclusion criteria for the ICP.
10   Identify variances and how they will be monitored.
11   Agree who will co-ordinate the ICP.
12   Provide staff training and pilot the ICP.
13   Undertake audit.
14   Amend the ICP according to the outcomes of the pilot and the audit results.

This section of the chapter has defined what an ICP is and explored the essential features of this approach for care delivery. To apply some of the processes involved in developing an ICP, complete Action point 2.6.

Action point 2.6   Developing an integrated care pathway

First, identify a patient condition to form the basis for your pathway:

• Select a timeframe for your pathway.
• Develop a format for your pathway using the exemplar outlined in Table 2.4.

- Consider the interventions provided by your own discipline and record these at appropriate points within the pathway.
- Consider the interventions provided by members of the multi-professional team and record these at appropriate points within the pathway.
- Identify and record anticipated outcomes for the interventions included within your pathway.

Second, reflect upon the steps that you have engaged in:

- If you were to develop an ICP, list six challenges that may present themselves in terms of its development.
- For each challenge identify strategies for how you could both prevent this from becoming a problem and also, should it occur, how you can overcome it.

When an ICP has been formulated and documented, it needs to be communicated to all care practitioners who will be involved in the delivery of the identified care interventions. Successful organisation of patients and service users' care requires collaboration and effective communication, which is explored next.

Communicating Day-to-day Care, and the Inter-personal Skills of DCMs

As identified in Table 2.1 under managerial activities, and also as just noted in the *NHS KSF* (DH, 2004a), a crucial component of care managers' roles is that of 'planner and communicator' of care requirements to their juniors, as well as to their seniors and equals as appropriate (see Figure 2.5). This is to ensure that care is delivered as intended in the care plan or pathway, ensuring that this is done safely and effectively.

Communication is inevitably the most significant vehicle for exchanging information related to care and treatment. All care interventions that health and social care practitioners undertake require effective communication. Care, treatment and illness prevention would be impossible without the DCM and colleagues communicating patient information with each other. The information includes continuous information gathering, deciding on actions and communicating them to colleagues. Communication is also a crucial element of teamworking, which is examined in Chapter 10.

On a broader level, communication between human beings is essential for both the survival and the development of society. Humans have an instinctive penchant towards gregarity, and Ellis et al. (2003), for instance, suggest that the effectiveness and happiness of adults is directly linked to this. In the context of health and social care provision and delivery, effective communication is both a requirement and a necessity.

How communication occurs

Communication can be defined as an interchange between individuals and groups to impart and receive information. It is a process in which two or more parties endeavour to make their intentions known and adjust their messages at each step of the interaction, and in effective communication, a common understanding of the messages is shared throughout. Three sets of modes of communication can be identified, namely:

- Written: typed or word-processed, handwritten, emailed, faxed, texted on mobile phone etc.
- Oral: speaking with an individual or small group face-to-face, speaking by telephone, shouting, video conferencing, lecturing etc.
- Non-verbal: listening, gestures, posture, tone of voice etc.

Oral or spoken communication is generally accompanied by non-verbal messages, which is often a more accurate reflection of the sender's feelings, and is usually easily detected by the receiver.

Thus, the sender of the message, the message itself and the receiver of the message are essential components of communication. In reality, effective communication between two parties entails a number of necessary events, or steps, as illustrated in Figure 2.4. It starts with the thoughts and ideas that one person wishes to impart to another, which he formulates and sends. The listener or receiver receives the message and might decide to respond, whereupon they formulate and send their own message. However, communication can be influenced by various predisposing factors, such as previous experience in similar situations and each person's aims of the communication. Figure 2.4 indicates that communication comprises, and is influenced by, several significant impinging components.

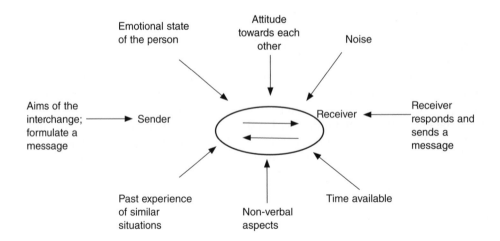

Figure 2.4   Events and factors influencing effective communication

The DCM's role in communicating care delivery

DCMs communicate with several individuals including their subordinates, managers, peers, medical staff, other health and social care professionals, patients and their families/carers, and social care staff. Furthermore, the directions of communication (see Figure 2.5), formal and informal, can be:

- Downward: manager discussing with, or instructing, a subordinate about what needs to be done, and how.
- Upward: to provide senior management with information for decision-making.
- Lateral: between peers of the same hierarchical level; for information sharing/ negotiation.
- Diagonal: between individuals or departments at different hierarchical levels; i.e. for requesting and giving information.

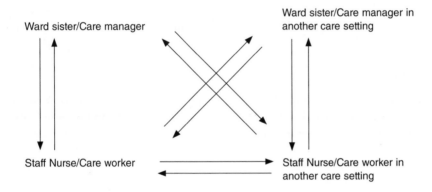

Figure 2.5 Directions of communication between care managers, staff nurses and care workers

More specific reasons for effective and efficient communication by managers are to:

- establish and disseminate the aims and specific objectives of the health or social care organisation;
- develop plans for achievement of the objectives;
- organise human and other resources efficiently;
- select, develop and appraise post-holders in the organisation;
- lead, guide and motivate employees of the organisation; and
- ascertain the effectiveness of care interventions.

Some communication can take place in challenging circumstances, such as when a complaint has been received or when breaking bad news. Instances or types of communication that are specifically management communication activities include:

- Delegation of duties
- Arranging and conducting meetings
- Conducting IDPR
- Team-building exercises
- Report writing
- Negotiation
- Making presentations
- Staff interviews, e.g. for recruitment and problem-solving
- Motivational activities
- Counselling.

Going by the above list, and the various managerial roles of the DCM discussed in the next chapter, it is obvious that all management functions include communication. The mechanics of the first item in the above list – delegation of duties – is now explored as an example of how each of these avenues or functions comprises several facets.

Delegation

An essential responsibility and function of the DCM is to delegate the work that needs to be carried out to appropriate members of the care team. Curtis and Nicholl (2004: 26) note that delegation is becoming increasingly important because of changes, such as:

- the falling number of nurses;
- issues around skill mix;
- restructuring how care is delivered; and
- the expanding role of nurses.

In their guidelines on delegation of care interventions to nurses, students, CSWs and assistant practitioners, and associated accountability, the Royal College of Nursing (2011) notes that tasks need to be delegated appropriately. For example, whoever the task is delegated to must have the skills and abilities to perform the task competently in the first place. The NMC's (2012a) guidance on delegation indicates that a nurse or midwife should only delegate an aspect of care to a person who has had appropriate training and whom they deem competent to perform the task, and that nurses and midwives are accountable for the decision to delegate care.

The following points should be considered by the DCM to ensure effective delegation:

- Ultimate accountability for all work rests with the registered professionals, and therefore what to delegate to non-registered staff needs careful consideration.
- Awareness that delegation can provide subordinates with opportunities to learn, and can support their career development.

- Staff morale can improve through the responsibility that goes with delegation.
- All delegation involves some risk, but can be minimised by measured coaching and effective supervision.
- Despite careful preparation mistakes can occur, and the DCM should be able to learn from them rather than stop delegating.

The various stages for effective delegation are as follows:

1 Assessment of tasks that need to be completed.
2 Matching tasks to competencies of delegates.
3 Assigning tasks.
4 Tasks are completed by delegates.
5 Supervising and monitoring task completion.
6 Evaluation and feedback as appropriate.

It should be noted that steps 4 and 5 are usually undertaken simultaneously rather than as separate entities. However, some managers tend to be reluctant to delegate care tasks, believing that juniors are unlikely to perform them as competently. As part of the delegation process managers need to consider the importance of the task and the consequences if it is not completed effectively. Managers can use a number of strategies to support the delegation process, such as coaching, and have a contingency plan should any problems be experienced.

Communication is fundamental to all aspects of the role of the DCM. Each type of management communication listed earlier in this section can be unpacked to ascertain its various component parts. Each can be defined, the reasons for the type of communication examined, the issues surrounding each explored, and how they can be operationalised ascertained. For instance, arranging and conducting meetings can comprise:

- Types of meetings
- Membership and terms of reference
- Functions of different types of meetings
- Mechanics of meetings
- Seating positions and impact on the meeting's outcomes
- Reasons for attending meetings
- Chairing a meeting – managing time, the process, the people
- Involving group members in the meeting
- Constructing task subgroups
- Communicating outcomes.

Communication problems

A further important perspective to consider in relation to communication is how it can be improved. There are a number of 'barriers' to communication and the various reasons for communication breakdown need to be considered to enable the DCM to be an effective communicator.

Action point 2.7   Communication breakdown

Think of a situation where a communication breakdown has occurred within your care setting. This could be communication between colleagues, or between a practitioner and a patient. Consider the reason(s) for this breakdown of communication and identify ways in which this could have been avoided.

Communication breakdown could mean that the individual feels that necessary information (the message) being imparted was markedly misunderstood or misinterpreted. Communication can be classified as effective, ineffective and persuasive. Furthermore, as Yoder-Wise (2010) suggests, poor communication can lead to conflict, which is a reality in organisations, but which presents opportunities for change and progress, as discussed in Chapter 4.

Different forms of communication have application in different situations ranging from basic to more specialist communication skills. Basic communication skills are those used in straightforward brief encounters when communicators exchange light greetings, or superficial neutral comments, and more specialist communications are those used in lengthier interactions (e.g. when interviewing for a post, and in counselling). Specialist communication skills are developed over several years of training and experience. It includes using particular communication frameworks such as Heron's (1989) 'Six-category intervention analysis', which constitutes a model of counselling with six possible interactions that are started by the initiator of the communication. These are:

1   Authoritative interventions:

- ○ *Prescriptive*: giving advice on correct action to take.
- ○ *Informative*: giving concrete factual information.
- ○ *Confrontational*: challenging perceptions expressed.

2   Facilitative interventions:

- ○ *Supportive*: accepting the person, giving time and reflective learning.
- ○ *Cathartic*: enabling to express emotions.
- ○ *Catalytic*: being as neutral and as unbiased as possible.

Effective communication underpins all aspects of management and leadership and is an essential skill for the DCM. Communication in the context of teamwork is further discussed in Chapter 10.

On examining theories and styles of management that DCMs could adopt in their care settings, it becomes obvious that care managers' personality and personal qualities are also important ingredients of how they are perceived by those they interact with, and manage. Calpin-Davies (2000) reports on a study that explored the key characteristics and the necessary personal skills of nurse managers. Her findings are summarised in Box 2.4.

Box 2.4   Key characteristics and personal skills of nurse managers

Key characteristics of nurse managers	Personal skills of nurse managers
• Being service oriented	• Communication skills
• Radiating positive energy	• Ability to motivate people
• Believing in other people	• Ability to influence others
• Leading balanced professional lives	• Adaptability
• Seeing professional life as an adventure	• Ability to respond positively to change,
• Being synergistic	both planned and unplanned
• Exercising professional self-renewal	

Additionally, Calpin-Davies (2000) suggests that the nurse manager should also be able to self-manage, and supports Covey's (1992) suggestion that managers should also develop the 'seven habits' or characteristics of highly effective people, which are:

1 Be proactive: planning ahead as opposed to merely reacting to events.
2 Begin with the end in mind: determine the outcomes in full prior to deciding on the strategies to be used for achieving them.
3 Put first things first: prioritising what needs doing.
4 Think win/win: being aware of situations that warrant mutual benefits.
5 Seek first to understand, and then to be understood: use of empathy.
6 Synergise with others: developing two-way communication and negotiating.
7 Sharpen the saw: adequate rest and relaxation leading to better functioning.

Box 2.5 summarises the personal qualities of the successful DCM.

Box 2.5   Qualities of the successful DCM

• Has good social skills	• Forward thinking
• Shows understanding	• Lifelong learner
• Communicates effectively	• Able to motivate
• Creative	• Articulate
• Emotionally resilient	• Nurturing
• Self-aware	• Adaptable
• Solves problems	• Energetic
• Proactive planner	• Analytical but decisive
• Has command of basic facts, knowledgeable	• Sensitive to events

Action point 2.8   Enhancing your managerial effectiveness

A comprehensive range of aspects of care management have been discussed in this chapter. Based on areas such as the roles and qualities of effective managers, reflect on the management component of your role, and identify how you will apply what you have learnt in this chapter to your everyday management practice together with your personal development needs.

You may find it helpful to compile an action plan, remembering that action plans include 'achieve by' dates, as well as identifying personnel and other resources that will help to achieve the objectives in the action plan. Therefore, reflect on the content of this chapter and identify your current managerial strengths and development needs using the format below. Some suggestions for 'Human resource manager' are given as an example for guidance on how action plans could be constituted.

Managerial role development	Objectives	How I will achieve them and who can support me	Review and achieve by date
Human resource manager	Develop knowledge and competence in the performance of IDPRs	• Attend in-house course for preparation as reviewer • Shadow my manager conducting an IDPR review • Discuss opportunities to conduct IDPRs for junior colleagues within the team • Complete a reflective account of an IDPR I have completed	Two months
Promoter of staff welfare			
Capacity manager			
Effectiveness and efficiency monitor			
Planner and communicator			
Decision-maker and problem-solver			

Managerial role development	Objectives	How I will achieve them and who can support me	Review and achieve by date
Quality assuror			
Guardian of health and safety			
Policy enforcer			
Staff trainer and educator			
Care giver and practice developer			
Leader and team worker			

It should be noted that objectives identified in action plans and personal development plans need to be SMART: Specific, Measurable, Achievable, Realistic (or relevant) and Time-bound. It also needs to be acknowledged that all management components identified above are underpinned by the necessary communication skills, with specific communication skill warranted by different situations, clinical specialisms and purposes, as discussed above.

Guidelines for Effective Management in Care Settings

This chapter has examined theories and styles of management and the roles and personal qualities of care managers. The term 'effective' is an adjective, which refers to being able to achieve or accomplish results. To 'effect' is to 'accomplish', and the noun 'effect' refers to 'something attained or acquired as the result of an action'. The closely related term 'efficient' also refers to being effective, but with the use of the least amount of effort and resources. Therefore, the effective and efficient DCM is one who achieves results of a pre-determined standard, and does so without waste of available human and non-human resources.

A number of strategies have been suggested to enable the DCM to reflect upon and self-assess their effectiveness as a manager. The managerial roles theory suggested in Figure 2.3 is one, Mintzberg's (1990) role theory is another, as is Fayol's (2012) groups of management activities (or functions). Different guidelines for effective management practice are required, which comprise being proficient in the activities identified in Figure 2.3 as they are extracted from contemporary management practice. Guidelines for effective management practice are presented next.

Guidelines for effective management practice – actions for success

Good practice guidelines for effective management are:

- Work with people, and see your team members as your most valuable resources.
- Create appropriate mechanisms that enable employees to meet their social and psychological growth needs.
- Act as a role model, lead by example and endeavour to empathise with your staff.
- Take into account your employees' expectations of their employment, and what motivates them.
- Use an eclectic model that draws upon various theories to support how you manage.
- Ensure that each person feels important, and let them know that you appreciate them, and recognise their expertise and contribution to the team's objectives.
- Be accessible.
- Help individuals achieve their aspirations, as their success is reflected in yours.
- Distribute workload, responsibilities and new opportunities equitably.
- Treat people fairly but according to merit.
- Delegate duties responsibly and in line with professional accountability.
- Monitor and supervise duties that you delegate to ensure that they are completed to the required standard.
- Be knowledgeable of current health/social care policies and guidance, and your profession's code of practice, for the effective organisation of care delivery,
- Organise daily care delivery based on the patients and service users' care needs, and shift attitude to care delivery based on integrated health and social care provision.
- Allocate patients and service users to staff with the appropriate skills to ensure the best use of skill mix.
- Ensure that all plans and actions are communicated fully, appropriately and effectively to all concerned.

CHAPTER SUMMARY

It was noted early in this chapter that it is through the process of management that the activities of employees are co-ordinated and directed to ensure achievement of health and social care organisations' goals. Management is consequently the launch pad and bedrock for organisational effectiveness, and is therefore concerned with appropriate use of resources, human and non-human, in the provision of a service. The next chapter explores leadership theories and styles, a concept that is complementary to management.

This chapter has examined management theories roles and styles that should enable the DCM to manage care settings effectively, and constituted discussions on:

- day-to-day management activities of DCMs, their roles, styles and personal characteristics, as well as effective care management; a pragmatic approach in examining the extent to which existing knowledge on management can be applied to care settings at the practical level, as well as taking an analytical stance;
- managing an area of the organisation, including managers and management, the structure of organisations and hierarchical levels within them;

- conventional management theories such as the classical approach, the human relations approach, the systems approach, the contingency approach and post-modern approaches as well as managerial role theory; it also examined management styles of health and social care managers;
- approaches to organising care delivery, including integrated care pathways, together with an assessment of the strengths and weaknesses of each approach discussed;
- the reasons, nature and modes of communication used by DCMs, which included the role of communication in management and leadership, effective communication, types of management communication, followed by problems of communication;
- the personal qualities and inter-personal skills of health and social care managers; and
- being an effective manager in the care setting, followed by management principles and guidelines.

- Scrutinise the British *Journal of Nursing Management* or *British Journal of Healthcare Management* for research articles on various components of management.
- For developments in the ways in which the NHS is managed, see the news sections of the *Health Service Journal*.

RECOMMENDED
FURTHER READING

3

LEADERSHIP AND
THE CARE MANAGER

Effective leadership is essential for driving health and social care delivery, despite continuous new directives, policy changes and public expectation, some of which were discussed at the beginning of Chapter 1. As the lynchpin of care delivery, the DCM therefore needs to have the ability to exercise the leadership skills that are required in their job role for effective and efficient management of care. These skills, in turn, are skills that can be developed through leadership development programmes. This chapter delves into the wide range of research and concepts in the leadership literature, and focuses on those leadership skills that are most applicable to health and social care managers.

Chapter objectives

On completion of this chapter you will be able to:

- identify the reasons for studying leadership in health and social care;
- distinguish between the concepts leadership and management;
- demonstrate comprehensive knowledge of available theories and styles of leadership, and how DCMs can develop them;
- give an account of the ways in which power is a component of leadership, as well as the nature of power exercised in care settings;
- cite some of the more significant research studies on leadership, and some of the current leadership development programmes.

Why Study Leadership?

One of the reasons for exploring the leadership role of the DCM is that it comprises one of the essential roles of managers as identified in the managerial role framework presented in Figure 2.3.

Action point 3.1   Leaders and their attributes

Think of well-known leaders in health and social care in the following domains:

- Historical, e.g. Florence Nightingale.
- Within your own care organisation.
- An international leader.

Now think about the attributes you consider they have that make them good leaders, and jot them down.

In response to Action point 3.1, you may have identified that health and social care leaders as role models have to first and foremost be health or social care practitioners who inspire colleagues and juniors, and lead by example, who therefore actively engage in delivering competent care, and who are usually available to listen to suggestions for more effective and efficient ways of working. They might be more senior post-holders such as care managers, nurse (or AHP) consultants and practice facilitators. They would be health and social care practitioners who sincerely have the interests of their patients and their profession at heart.

Clegg (2000) notes that managers' styles of leadership in part determine staff satisfaction at work. Botting (2011), and previously Almio-Metcalf (1996), amongst others note that leadership style and organisational culture are also associated with staff satisfaction, as well as with an increase in productivity, as also noted by Ford (2009) in the context of the 'productive ward' (see Chapter 5). Manley's (1997) work concluded that in healthcare there is a strong correlation between effective leadership and the quality of patient care and staff morale, as also noted by the DH (2012b: 20).

An organisation's success or failure is dependent upon its leaders, and all care professionals can be considered to be in positions for taking the lead in some certain aspects of care. Furthermore, there does not seem to be any evidence that leadership qualities are inherited, or belong to one particular type of person. Research (e.g. Cunningham and Kitson, 2000; Kouzes and Posner, 2012) has indicated that leadership comprises competencies that can be learned through appropriate development programmes. All DCMs, therefore, have the potential to be effective leaders within their care setting.

The importance of leadership development has been emphasised in various policy publications including *The NHS Plan* (DH, 2000b), *High Quality Care for All* (DH, 2008a), and *Compassion in Practice – Nursing, Midwifery and Care Staff Our Vision and Strategy* (DH, 2012b); the *NHS Change Model* (Medical Directors' Bulletin, 2012); and publications by other institutions such as the NHS III (e.g. Mortlock, 2011). Various leadership development programmes are available for health and social care professionals from a number of providers.

What is Leadership?

Distinguishing between leadership and management

The concept management and roles of managers were explored in Chapter 2, but are there any differences between the concepts management and leadership?

> ## Action point 3.2   Similarities and differences between leaders and managers
>
> Who are the leaders in health and social care, and what do they do? Based on your own experiences of management and leadership in care settings, consider the notions of being a manager and being a leader, and make notes on what you consider are the similarities and differences between these roles.

Various terms such as 'manager', 'leader', 'supervisor', 'head of department' and even 'administrator' are at times used interchangeably. However, management and leadership in particular are distinct entities, albeit with overlapping functions.

As noted in Chapter 2, 'management' refers to activities and competencies of managers, while the term 'manager' refers to the person who has been appointed to plan, organise, co-ordinate, supervise, negotiate, evaluate and integrate health and social care with the use of resources that are made available to them by the organisation. Managers are given responsibility to ensure that the organisation's objectives are achieved and that all activities are fully co-ordinated and progress smoothly through the day. Managers need to communicate effectively, exercise interpersonal skills and authority in this endeavour, and be accountable for their actions.

'Leadership' is defined by Buchanan and Huczynski (2010: 596) as 'the process of *influencing* the activities of an organised group in its efforts towards goal-setting and goal achievement'. Mullins (2010) sees leadership as a relationship through which one person *influences* the behaviour or actions of other people.

These are fairly standard definitions that indicate that leaders are individuals who exert *influence* and authority over others. In the context of the DCM's role, leadership comprises the ability to influence the behaviour of the workforce, to motivate, inspire and energise individuals, and to achieve the health and social care goals of the care setting. To disentangle the term 'leadership' further, it is important to note that leadership is a noun that can have four possible meanings, namely:

1 The activity of leading.
2 The body of people who lead a group.
3 The status of the leader.
4 The ability to lead.

It is also possible to distinguish between managers and leaders, in that leadership is one of the roles of managers, as identified in Table 2.1 and Figure 2.3, and is therefore a subset of management. The overall distinctions between leadership and management are that management is about monitoring and measuring performance against pre-determined planned outcomes of care, ensuring adherence to policies and procedures, maximising outputs and productivity, working within allocated resources, and controlling and organising necessary structures and systems. Leadership is about being visionary, showing the way forward, anticipating developments, innovating, seeing the bigger picture, as well as focusing on the development of individuals. In health and social care, like managers, leaders are also usually post-holders in the organisation, though do not have to be.

Leadership is thus a dynamic two-way process based on a leader–follower relationship. McGregor (1987), a well-known researcher in leadership and staff motivation (see Chapter 10), suggests that leadership is a dynamic form of behaviour with a number of variables affecting the leadership relationship, namely:

- characteristics of the leader;
- attitude, needs and other personal characteristics of the followers;
- nature of the organisation, such as its purpose, its structure, the tasks to be performed; and
- social, economic and political environment.

Hollingsworth (1999) suggests that managers can learn leadership development from the armed forces. He suggests that there are six fundamental differences between managers and leaders:

1 Managers administer – leaders innovate.
2 Managers maintain – leaders develop.
3 Managers focus on systems and structure – leaders focus on people
4 Managers rely on control – leaders inspire trust.
5 Managers keep an eye on the bottom line – leaders have an eye on the horizon.
6 Managers do things right – leaders do the right things.

Such suggestions indicate that managers are more concerned with ensuring that the organisation functions smoothly, and achieving organisational or departmental aims and objectives, whereas the leaders usually demonstrate interest in the thoughts, interests, aspirations of the individuals they lead, as well as in their ongoing personal development. Leaders are therefore more people-oriented or staff-oriented, which signifies having shared goals between the staff and the organisation, which is at times referred to as 'people-oriented' management.

Furthermore, Gratton (2000) suggests that the very nature of management methods is currently changing, and has moved away from an emphasis on getting results by close control of the workforce towards an environment of coaching, support and empowerment: that is, leading. Note however, the DH's (2012g) gradual implementation of 'payment-by-results', which is briefly discussed in Chapter 7 in the context of 'resources' for the NHS. Leaders are accountable for their followers' performance, which they achieve by helping them to be efficient, and to develop their abilities and strengths (Murphy, 2005).

Whose Leadership?

Moving on from different meanings of the term 'leadership', and distinguishing between managers and leaders, there are also different types of leadership. The key types are delineated in Box 3.1.

Box 3.1   Different types of leadership

Traditional leadership: When authority or power rest on an established belief in the sanctity of traditional and historical leaders, such as a prince. Family traditions and social ties directly influence the continuity of this form of leadership.

Formal leadership: Practised by the individual with *legitimate authority* conferred by the organisation and described as an aspect of the approved position. This could be a *formally* appointed care manager or a project leader, for instance. It is also referred to as legal/rational leader.

Informal leadership: Is exercised by a staff member who does not have a specified management role but has knowledge, personal status and skills in influencing and guiding others in specific organisational activities.

Attempted leadership: Where an individual in a group attempts to exert influence over other members of the group.

Successful or effective leadership: Brings about the behaviour and results that were intended by the leader, and in the achievement of group goals.

Naturally emerging or charismatic leadership: Leads through natural charm.

Political leadership: When the individual takes a strong lead in favour of one specific preference or party.

Shared leadership: Such as when two or more band 6 RNs share leadership in a practice setting because they are of equal status.

Elected leadership: For example the prime minister.

Imposed leadership: An individual (or small group) who is appointed as manager, but also adopts the leadership role.

All health and social care professionals should be able to easily identify various types of leadership in different care settings. For instance, in the context of nursing, the notion of shared leadership can be found in teams with several employees on the same pay bands such as in a community mental health team, or band 7 RNs working in an ICU. However, a leader is not a leader unless they have followers, and people who they provide guidance and support to.

Action point 3.3   Leader and follower

Think of aspects of your work in which you are a leader, and aspects in which you are a follower. Consider the ways in which your approach to your work varies depending on your follower or leader role.

Being a keyworker for a particular aspect of care such as 'moving and handling' or infection control and so on, are ways in which healthcare professionals can take a leadership role in the practice setting.

Theories and Styles of Leadership

Several theories of leadership have emerged over the years endeavouring to comprehend this important function more fully, and make its practical applications more impactful. As suggested in Chapter 2, a theory implies that if a certain action is taken in a particular way, then a certain predictable effect can be expected.

Action point 3.4   Effective leadership

Prior to delving into established theories of leadership, consider the following, and its significance for care provision. Think of a senior care professional in your organisation who is a good leader, and decide what it is about them that makes them a good leader. Contrast this to someone whom you consider to be a poor leader. Complete columns A and B as illustrated below:

Column A: An effective leader is	Column B: An ineffective leader
• An effective communicator	• Does not share information effectively
• Approachable	• Is inaccessible and unapproachable
• ...	• ...
• ...	• ...

The purpose of Action point 3.4 was to sensitise you to published theories of leadership. Over the years, leadership theorists have viewed the subject from different perspectives, and four prominent groups of theories can be identified (see Box 3.2). Wisely, contemporary leadership theories do not discard previous theories, although some theories are still at experimental stages and might not have gained wide acceptance within social sciences yet.

Box 3.2   Prominent leadership theories

There are four main groups of leadership theories:

1	Trait theories	• Characteristics of leaders
2	Functional theories	• Action-centred leadership
3	Behavioural and style theories	• Leadership styles
		• The managerial grid
4	Contemporary theories	• Charismatic leader
		• Connective leadership
		• Servant leadership
		• Transactional leadership
		• Transformational leadership

The chapter will now focus on analysing these competing theories.

Trait theories

By the 1950s, hundreds of studies had already been conducted exploring the specific characteristics of effective leaders (e.g. Handy, 1993). These studies were aimed at ascertaining the characteristics of people who are leaders, so that subsequently such characteristics can be developed in others, and also differentiating them from non-leaders. Thus trait theories, which are also known as 'great man' or 'great woman' theories of leadership, attempt to identify inborn traits of successful leaders. Subsequent studies elicited significant correlation between leadership effectiveness and the following traits:

- Intelligence
- Supervisory ability
- Initiative
- Self-assurance
- Individuality.

Based on several research studies, Bass (1990) developed a profile of traits that are evident in successful leaders. These are categorised in three areas as:

- *Intelligence:* including judgement, decisiveness, knowledge, fluency.
- *Personality:* including adaptability, alertness, integrity, nonconformity.
- *Ability:* including co-operativeness, popularity, tact.

The trait approach has both its proponents and its critics. The key problems with trait theories are that:

- traits are difficult to define accurately or understand fully;
- there are many exceptional leaders who do not possess all the identified traits of successful leaders;
- possession of most or few of these traits does not mean that a person is a better or worse manager or leader; and
- it is questionable whether an individual could have all the traits identified in different studies.

Another difficulty with the trait approach is that if individual traits or characteristics are seen to be responsible for effective functioning as leaders, then the question arises of whether people are born with these traits or characteristics; that is, whether they are 'born leaders' or whether they have learned them, through either diligent reflective actions or through attending courses.

However, despite the emergence of several other leadership theories over the years, trait theories have not been discarded. For instance, Wright (1996) suggests that some leadership traits can be ascribed as unique to nursing leadership positions, including being a care expert, a change agent, and a centred human being who uses 'head and heart'. Presently, based on extensive ongoing research over several years, Kouzes and Posner (2012) conclude that 'Admired Leaders' tend to elicit specific characteristics, whereupon 50 per cent or more respondents specify these characteristics to be:

- Honest (approximately 89%)
- Forward looking (approximately 71%)
- Competent (approximately 69%)
- Inspiring (approximately 65%).

Of the respondents, 26–45 per cent (i.e. a lesser number) tend to specify 'intelligent, broad-minded, fair-minded, dependable, supportive, straightforward, co-operative and determined' as specific characteristics of effective leaders; less than 25 per cent of respondents specify 'courageous, ambitious, caring, loyal, imaginative, mature, self-controlled and independent'. However, there is no universal agreement on the nature and essential characteristics of a leader, nor on what an effective leader is, as leadership can be an attribute of position (e.g. appointment to a post), or of knowledge or wisdom; or it can be based on personality functions or in terms of the ability to ensure that effective work performance is achieved by followers.

Furthermore, the Myers Briggs Personality Types (Team Technology, 2012) provides a widely used typology for identifying the personality traits of individuals who aspire to team leadership positions. It comprises assessment of the individual on four spectrums – namely, extraversion and introversion; sensing and intuition; thinking and feeling, and judging and perceiving – which are dimensions of individuals' qualities and can be used for self-assessment and for subsequent development of these qualities.

Functional theories

Subsequent to trait theories of leadership, the functional (or group) approach to leadership was developed, which focuses on the functions of the leader (as opposed to their traits), and which in turn bypasses the overlapping concepts of appointed versus naturally emerging leader. It indicates that in either case the leader can learn to elicit the right functions at the right time. Kotter (2009) suggests that by concentrating on the functions of the leader, their performance can be improved by training and thereby developing their leadership skills further, and perfecting them. Kotter (2009) also indicates that organisations should not wait for leaders to come along, but 'grow' their own by identifying employees with leadership potential and enabling them to develop those skills. This approach therefore also supports the notion that several members of a professional group can have scope to develop their leadership potential and exercise leadership skills.

Adair's action-centred leadership

One widely accepted function-related leadership theory is Adair's (2005) action-centred leadership (ACL), according to which, the leader functions by paying attention to three sets of needs of the organisation: task needs, individual needs and team maintenance needs. The effectiveness of the leader is dependent upon meeting these three areas of need within the work group. Too much concern for any one of these three areas can cause imbalance, and can interfere with the productiveness and effectiveness of the group. This could consequently affect the quality of the outcomes, the morale of the group, its motivation and accomplishment.

In health and social care organisations, leaders need to pay attention to all three sets of needs, immaterial of whether the leadership position is attained through appointment or through natural emergence.

> ## Action point 3.5 Applying ACL
>
> Consider the DCM's activities as the care leader from Adair's ACL viewpoint. Then, make notes on how the DCM can endeavour to meet the needs of those who are led effectively within your care setting, categorising their actions under task, individual and team needs.

The DCM can use Adair's (2005) ACL in various ways that are applicable to most organisations. Briefly, for meeting task needs, they can ensure that the objectives of the work group are achieved, resources are allocated as appropriate and they delegate according to individuals' capabilities. For meeting team or group needs, they can hold appropriate team meetings, make themselves approachable and available, and give feedback. For meeting individual needs, they can conduct IDPRs regularly, and be aware of any conflict and potential problem areas in interpersonal relationships within the team.

To ensure leadership effectiveness, all three sets of needs, task, group and individual have to be met. It may appear that some items in a particular set of needs also apply to another set, but this is immaterial as the main purpose of ACL is to ensure an integrated approach to one's leadership functions.

Behavioural and style theories

The third group of leadership theories focus on styles of leadership, some of the more widely accepted of which include traditional leadership styles and the managerial grid style. 'Leadership style' refers to the ways in which the leader carries out their functions; that is, the way in which the leader is perceived as typically behaving towards their followers. Such leaders develop their styles through education, training and life experiences, assuming that effective leaders acquire a pattern (or style) of learned behaviours. Therefore 'style' refers to how, as leaders, we behave on a day-to-day basis, because we know or have learnt from previous experience that the way we do things works.

Traditional leadership styles

There are many ways of categorising leadership styles, the traditional classification being authoritarian, democratic, permissive and bureaucratic (see Box 3.3).

Box 3.3   Traditional leadership styles

Authoritarian or autocratic	• Focuses on power and need for authority and approval of status by others • Exercises control and directive behaviour • Makes decisions alone and expects obedience of instructions • Uses undertones of coercion
Democratic or participative	• Formally seeks the views of all relevant parties • Displays a wish to consult and work with individuals and teams • Uses the human relations approach (discussed in Chapter 2) • Engages in open two-way communication • Encourages collaborative teamwork
Permissive or laissez-faire	• Uses few established rules and policies • Monitors performance from a distance, and therefore might appear detached • Permits individuals and teams to work autonomously
Bureaucratic	• Follows established policies and rules to the letter • Power is exercised by applying fixed and inflexible rules • Communications are impersonal • Only makes new decisions based on norms

Despite the approving and disapproving overtones of each of these styles of leadership, it is useful to ascertain more clearly what the likely merits or weaknesses of each style might be.

Action point 3.6   Merits and drawbacks of different styles of leadership

Based on your experience of professional leadership, consider and make brief notes on both the strengths and the weaknesses of each of the four styles of leadership:

• Autocratic
• Participative

- Laissez-faire
- Bureaucratic.

Now consider care situations where each of these styles can be used appropriately by DCMs.

Parish (2006) reports on a study of 22 acute hospital wards, whereupon different styles of leadership are identified as directive, visionary, affiliative, participative, pace-setting and coaching leadership. The study concluded that high-performing ward managers are able to choose from and use a wide range of leadership styles, while lower-performing managers choose from a limited range of styles.

Many of the positive effects and drawbacks of each style were identified just before Action point 3.6. Leadership styles can also vary according to specific care circumstances. Following on from your responses to Action point 3.6, for example, in a situation where an unexpected episode of aggression occurs in say a mental healthcare setting, or a team of paramedics dealing with an emergency situation, the leadership style may be more directive (or autocratic). In situations where there is no immediate risk to individual safety, more democratic (or participative) styles may be adopted. Other leadership styles can be considered and developed based on those identified in Box 3.1, including political leadership.

The managerial grid style of leadership

Based on the preceding discussion, 'leadership style' refers to certain particular ways in which individual leaders conduct themselves in leadership positions, that is specific ways in which the leader is perceived as typically behaving to influence the activities of the personnel he or she leads. In addition to the leadership styles just discussed, an alternative perspective on leadership styles is presented by Blake and McCanse (1991) who suggest that there are five identifiable leadership styles based on the extent to which the leader manifests 'concern for the people whom they lead, plotted against their 'concern for productivity' in their area of responsibility. The concept of concern for people versus productivity was also briefly discussed in Chapter 2 as a style of management, but as a style of leadership Blake and McCanse (1991) suggest that:

- High 'concern for people' and high 'concern for productivity' is the most effective style, as most work gets done and staff are content.
- High 'concern for people' and low 'concern for productivity' results in the leader being popular, but less work gets done.
- Low 'concern for people' and high 'concern for productivity' results in substantial work getting done, but staff feel ignored.
- Low 'concern for people' and low 'concern for productivity' is the least effective style.
- Medium 'concern for people' and medium 'concern for productivity' is unsatisfactory for both parties.

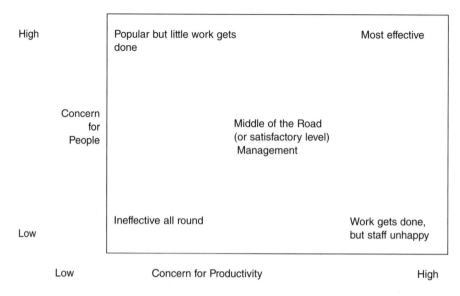

Figure 3.1 'Concern for people' or 'concern for productivity'

These leadership styles are learned behaviours that will have been developed through previous experiences of leadership either as a leader or as a follower, or through education or training. On analysing the effect of each of these styles of leadership on the team of which you are a member, and you are likely to deduce that although any of the five styles could prevail in the team, a leader being able to demonstrate having 'high concern for people' as well as 'high concern for productivity' would be the most effective in your care setting, as simply illustrated in Figure 3.1 (for more detailed discussion please access Blake and McCanse's (1991) work which is included in the references list at the end of this book).

Contemporary theories

Evolving from the trait, functional and behavioural theories just discussed, are the more current theories that are referred to as 'contemporary' theories of leadership. To a good extent, these contemporary theories represent further developments from the earlier leadership theories, and instead of dismissing them, take into account the prevailing social, political and organisational factors. The most prominent contemporary leadership theories are:

- Charismatic
- Connective

- Servant
- Transactional
- Transformational.

Charismatic leadership

Charm, persuasiveness, personal power, self-confidence, extraordinary ideas and strong (often unconventional) convictions are the main personal qualities that characterise charismatic leaders. The leader's personality arouses affection and emotional commitment, first to the leader, and second to the beliefs and aims of the organisation that the leader espouses. However, charisma as an individual quality is difficult to define and has not been scientifically tested adequately, and because it is not acquired through training or education, the theory goes against the current belief that leadership skills can be developed or learned (DH, 2000c), but has not been discarded.

Connective leadership

As a theory in its own right, connective leadership recognises the role of leaders in fostering collaborative intra-organisational and inter-organisational working relationships in the pursuit of achievement of organisational goals. Lipman-Blumen (2000) indicates that the connective leadership model emphasises various modes of working with and through other people instead of bowing to authoritarianism, and includes creating 'coalitions' for enterprises to which those led want to commit themselves.

This theory suggests that the activities of contemporary leaders must include the ability to create inter-connections between and across practice settings, the purpose of which is to better co-ordinate and integrate patient and service user care services in a caring, non-competitive, collaborative manner.

Earlier on, one of the key advocates of connective leadership, Charns and Tewksbury (1993) explained that the process of creating connections and fostering integration requires that the leader:

- identifies actual and potential collaborators;
- communicates and sells a potential shared vision to those in varied settings and in disparate conditions;
- describes the value each collaborator could bring to the endeavour, both to the individual and others;
- facilitates communication by sharing information, preparing for interactions and follow-up on communication exchanges;
- builds and maintains social interactions and comfort;
- defines and sells roles and assignments;
- tracks and rewards contributions;
- formalises an integrated effort at the right time.

However, this theory seems limited as a complete leadership theory because being appropriately connected with similar other experts or individuals with similar interests, through networking and so on, is already a recognised essential attribute of most effective leaders in current day health and social care.

Servant leadership

As another distinct leadership theory that tends to be advocated as contemporary is servant leadership, which constitutes being a leader primarily because of the wish to do good for one's followers (e.g. Greenleaf, 2003). It therefore entails taking an altruistic stance, and is based on the premise that leadership originates from a desire to serve, and not so much because one's job role includes being a leader or for any other reasons. It could be argued that politicians take on servant leadership roles because they choose to serve the public.

Howatson-Jones (2004) commends the use of servant leadership theory in healthcare, noting that this approach incorporates the leader endeavouring to ascertain the followers' perspectives as a better way to promote effectiveness. The servant leader can lead care practitioners by empathising with them, taking into account their job roles, views and aspirations. Servant leadership is therefore about serving the needs of the followers and empowering them, and thereby includes a stewardship element. The likely weakness with the servant leadership approach is that if the organisation's purpose and task needs are considered as secondary, then the amount of work done (i.e. productivity) could suffer.

Furthermore, Waterman (2011) identifies various advantages and disadvantages of servant leadership, suggesting that the term 'servant' is ancient and has religious connotations and might not be acceptable to nurses, and that the term implies humility, which can be perceived as weaknesses.

Transactional leadership

Based on the presumption that one doesn't have to be a natural leader to manage, nor a manager to lead, transactional leadership theory relates to leading by virtue of the management position held by the incumbent in the organisational hierarchy. This approach is closely related to the achievement of organisational goals, which in health and social care organisations constitutes attending to the health of the local population, with pre-determined objectives or outcomes. Transactional leadership is founded on the proviso that leaders are successful or effective to the extent that they aim to maintain equilibrium and harmony by fulfilling their roles according to policies and procedures, and by use of incentives to enhance employee loyalty and performance (Bass and Riggio, 2006).

Although this approach supports and maintains the status quo, and has firm elements of predictability, it can also be criticised for lacking in vision for the enhancement of organisational provision, and strategic longer-term aims being seen as low priority.

Transformational leadership

Transformational leadership is currently a widely advocated leadership approach for health and social care professionals. It entails aspiring to effect revolutionary changes (Bass and Riggio, 2006; Kouzes and Posner, 2012), and focuses on merging the goals, desires and values of leaders and followers into common goals. It refers to 'the ability of leaders to influence others by transforming their behaviour without necessarily being in a position of authority' (Morgan, 2005:27). The objective of transformation is to generate employees' commitment to the organisation's vision and ideal, in conjunction with their own individual aspirations and aims for the organisation.

Murphy (2005) suggests that transformational leaders are visionary, balanced, self-aware and confident in breaking professional boundaries to develop a multi-disciplinary team approach to patient care. Using transformational leadership, the leader enables individuals to consider their personal beliefs regarding health and social care, and fosters followers' innate wishes to pursue higher values. Transformational leaders encourage others to exercise leadership, and inspire followers by instilling a belief that the followers have the ability to achieve exceptional aims. The transformational leader demonstrates the ability to stimulate growth and development, and to discourage dependence. Consequently, the transformational leader acts as a catalyst for creativity and innovation in care organisations

Botting (2011) notes that transformational leaders focus on transforming others by creating significant change in the lives of their followers and organisations. While acknowledging that the key elements of leadership are leaders' personal characteristics, their interpersonal relationships, teamwork and being role models, it can be deduced from the above-mentioned points that the transformational model of leadership is most appropriate for health and social care, which concurs with the current notion of continuous improvement and enhancement of care provision and delivery.

A systematic review of transformational leadership conducted for the Joanna Briggs Institute (2011) provides a useful summary of the nature of this style and theory of leadership. It identifies transformational leadership as comprising intellectual stimulation by encouraging new ideas, individual consideration of followers, inspirational motivation, stimulating creativity, transmitting optimism and significance for tasks at hand, providing a sense of direction in attaining organisational goals, providing example of performance (i.e. role models), and instilling pride and motivation.

Leading by example is one of five 'key practices' of exemplary leaders, which Kouzes and Posner (2012) identify following their research on leadership, these key practices being:

1 Modelling the way (i.e. leading by example, etc).
2 Inspiring shared vision.
3 Challenging the process.
4 Enabling others to act.
5 Encouraging the heart.

Action point 3.7   The vision in transformational leadership

The term 'transformational' implies being visionary; that is, having ideas and aspirations of how things could be different for the better, and then implementing those visions. Such concepts directly apply to all health and social care professionals and to care settings in the quest for continually raising standards of care. What is your vision of how care can be delivered, organised or led better in your own care setting, and in your health or social care organisation?

Thus transformational leadership is widely advocated for the attributes just identified, but it is worthy of note that transformational leaders display substantially more energy and enthusiasm than those around them, which their followers might not have done over time, and consequently may sometimes be seen as pushy by the latter.

Alternatively, an organisation's vision for its future can be contrasted with Blake and McCanse's (1991) styles of leadership, which warns of the risk of a dichotomy between 'concern for people' and that of 'concern for production' ('production' refers to care provision), as discussed earlier in this chapter. A comparison of a leader who uses the transformational approach to one who uses transactional theory of leadership is presented on Table 3.1.

Table 3.1   Comparison of transformational and transactional leadership approaches

Transformational leadership	Transactional leadership
Merges own and followers' goals, aspirations and values with those of the organisation into a common goal	Aims to maintain equilibrium and status quo
Generates employee commitment to the vision	Is task-centred and orderly
Inspires and instils a belief in followers that they have the ability to do exceptional things	Performs tasks strictly according to current policies and procedures
Stimulates growth and development by discouraging dependence	Has a short- or medium-term focus
Challenges subordinates	Coaches and fosters prescribed learning
Rewards informally and personally	Uses extrinsic rewards
Is emotional, passionate about the organisation's existing and new ventures	Has high self-interest, and interested in current organisational commitments
Sees home and work on a continuum	Sees home and work as separate entities

The two approaches are therefore different in that while transactional leadership is predominantly about managerial 'transactions' between the manager and the managed, transformational leadership is about endeavouring to make more radical changes that can present challenges and growth for all (transforming). Transactional leadership thus constitutes the orderly breaking down of tasks, although this can often be limited in vision and energy. Transformational leadership constitutes keeping a strategic or 'helicopter view' of the whole.

Furthermore, on examining transformational approaches to leadership, Govier and Nash (2009) discuss the three constants that provide stability in times of uncertainty: ways of responding and adapting to change; choosing how to respond to stimuli; and working with principles that reflect a 'whole person' approach, which in turn governs growth and prosperity.

The five contemporary theories of leadership relate to existing knowledge of leadership, and in particular research on transformational leadership (e.g. Joanna Briggs Institute, 2011; Lipley, 2004) for care settings suggests that this is the most useful theory for healthcare professionals, and therefore for DCMs. For more useful implementation of some of the other contemporary leadership theories, further research through structured empirical studies is needed to firm up their application potential in different care settings.

Leadership and Power

Most definitions of leadership incorporate the 'influence' of the leader over those they lead. Leadership influence is thus also dependent upon the type of power that the leader exercises over those they lead. Power can be defined as the capacity to produce or prevent a specific change. Various types of power can be identified, as illustrated in Box 3.4.

Box 3.4 Types of power

Personal power:

Expert (or profession) power is based on the profession or occupation of the individual, together with possession of the unique knowledge and expertise associated with their role; seen as competent; usually limited to narrow, well-defined specialism.

Referent (or ascribed/status) power is based on the perceptions of others, admiration and respect for an individual, and identification with the leader; the leader with

(Continued)

(Continued)

perceived reputation, charisma and attractiveness; has position in society, e.g. wealth.

Connection power is based on the individual's formal and informal links to influential or prestigious persons within and outside an area or organisation.

Organisational power:

Reward power is based on inducements such as pay, promotion, praise and recognition that the leader can offer group members in exchange for co-operation and contributions towards the achievement of the group's objectives.

Punishment or coercive power is based on penalties that a leader has ability to impose on an individual or a group such as withdrawal of support, invoking disciplinary procedures and withholding promotion.

Authority or legitimate power is based on the position (or job and rank) that the individual holds within the hierarchy of the organisation; stems from the leader's right to make requests because of their authority in the organisation's hierarchy, not so much on personal relationships.

Information power is based on access to valued information.

Action point 3.8   Power

Taking into account all of the care practitioners who have input into care delivery in your practice setting, try to identify individuals who actually exercise power of one or another of the seven types of power identified in Box 3.4.

Leaders are individuals who stand out from others in the degree of influence that they have on others' thinking, motivation and activities. In response to Action point 3.8, you are likely to have identified individuals who have one or more forms of power detailed in Box 3.4. As a minimum the DCM has legitimate power, and possibly other types such as referent power.

Guidelines for the effective use of these different forms of power in organisations have been suggested by Yukl (2002); those for two types are presented in Table 3.2. Similar guidelines can be constituted for the other types of power identified in Box 3.4.

Table 3.2   Guidelines for effective use of two types of power in organisations

1 Using legitimate power or authority	2 Using reward power
Use politeness and clarity when making requests	Offer the type of rewards that people desire
Explain the reasons for requests	Ensure that rewards are fair and ethical
Do not exceed your scope of authority	Do not make promises of more than you can deliver
Verify authority if necessary	Identify and publish simple criteria for giving rewards
Follow agreed organisational channels	
Follow up to ascertain compliance	Provide rewards as promised when requirements have been met
Insist on compliance if necessary	Use rewards symbolically (not in a manipulative way).

Research on Clinical Leadership

A fair range of research has been published on clinical leadership. Earlier research on leadership has tended to be directed at particular aspects of leadership such as:

- Leadership attributes/skills
- Leadership traits (not attributes)
- Style and effect of leadership
- Effective leadership.

With a laissez-faire behavioural style, the least amount of work gets done. On exploring leadership effectiveness, Goleman (2000) concludes that the most effective leaders tend to combine different leadership styles for different situations, as they consider appropriate, as reported by Parish (2006). However, there are several variables that can affect the effectiveness of the leader in the workplace. These variables include a range of aspects of management such as availability of resources (namely, equipment and materials), the relationship between the manager and employees, and external influences such as specified annual objectives for the post, legislation and pressure groups.

Specific to care settings, Cook (2001) used the grounded theory approach to explore the concept of effective leadership of clinical nurse leaders, which he suggested also applies to leaders in other care professions. The five key attributes of effective leaders and associated 'facilitative factors' identified by Cook are:

1   Highlighting, e.g. willingness to negotiate, questioning attitude encouraged, willing to learn from others.
2   Respecting, e.g. empathy and understanding, self-motivation.

3 Influencing, e.g. motivating others, instilling confidence, proving oneself in the field of practice.
4 Creativity, e.g. able to prioritise, planning ahead.
5 Supporting, e.g. time for planning, empowered to adapt the working environment to improve practice.

Clegg (2000) reported on a study of the successful application of transformational leadership on team performance and the quality of patient care in a community trust, the results of which are said to be encouraging as they could clearly demonstrate an improvement in the quality of the care they deliver evolving from their quest for excellence. Lipley (2004) reports on an extensive study conducted by the University of Sheffield that suggests that a mix of transformational leadership and transactional leadership is better than the laissez-faire approach to making staff more enthusiastic about their jobs.

Burns (2009) explored clinical leadership development for general practice nurses, and concludes that role development opportunities play a very significant part in this, as do the structure and culture of the organisation.

Opinion and guidance literature on leadership in healthcare abounds, and new research in the field will no doubt appear in the future. Furthermore, effective leadership is linked to mentoring in that on researching effective mentoring for health profession students, Webb and Shakespeare (2008) conclude that the promotion of facilitation of learning in care environments is dependent upon the leadership skills of ward managers, as also concluded by Fretwell back in 1980.

A number of recent studies on leadership, however, are related largely to leading research on key initiatives or projects on the management of specific medical conditions or health education, not to researching leadership styles or approaches to, or theories of, leadership as such.

Current Leadership Initiatives and Skills Development Programmes

Policy documents by the DH (2000c) and the general literature on clinical leadership suggest that all health and social care professionals may be in positions where they take the lead in some way, and can be leaders in different components of care provision, and at different levels in the management hierarchy. The DH (2012b) indicates that a national leadership development programme that underpins the nursing, midwifery and care staff vision for compassionate care in daily activity is available. The programme leads to a nationally recognised qualification gained by working through placements during which specific skills are practiced. These skills include change management, building coalitions of support and communications and engagement with staff, patients, service users, carers and other stakeholders. Healthcare professionals on the development programme are supported by mentorship for aspiring leaders.

Therefore, for the development of one's own leadership skills, individuals might need to attend appropriate courses or workshops based on self-assessment of knowledge and skills and identifying self-development areas to work on. Various other leadership development programmes are available. The development of the titles 'clinical leader' and 'team leader' have emerged, both comprising leaders at the practice edge of care provision. One of the more prominent nursing leadership development courses for nurses, for instance, is the Royal College of Nursing's (RCN) (2012a) Clinical Leadership Programme (CLP) that has been available for some years now.

Byrne (2007), however, observes that leadership development programmes are often seen by nurses as not directly relevant to the real world of practice, and recommends leadership coaching (see Chapter 11) as an alternative with strong potential. Existing knowledge of leadership thus needs to be built on by application of theories to current care provision contexts. It is advocated by many, though, that team leaders need ongoing development programmes together with the managerial support to fulfil these roles (Anonymous, 1998; Binnie, 1998). Care professionals are being encouraged to become lifelong learners, a concept that has fast become a substantive and unavoidable component of care provision (Gopee, 2001; Davis et al., 2013) and a core skill for leadership development for health and social care professionals.

The preferred leadership theory base adopted by many development programmes is primarily transformational leadership, as it challenges autocratic unilateral leadership approaches, and because other leadership theories implicate inborn leadership qualities. Transformational leadership is also preferred to transactional leadership theory as the latter tends to be related to management functions, which is to 'get the day-to-day job done', and could imply 'imposed leadership' (Cook, 2001). An extensive range of qualities and abilities are cited in leadership literature on effective transformational leadership. Those identified by Murphy (2005) are:

- Being a visionary.
- Being a futurist.
- Being a catalyst for change.
- Exercising persuasive and captivating communication.
- Stimulating fervent emotions.
- Influencing beliefs, attitudes and behaviours.
- Promoting motivation and commitment through interpersonal communication.
- Displaying honesty, integrity, commitment and credibility.
- Encouraging staff to become independent, responsible and autonomous in their decision-making.
- Possessing high self-esteem, self-regard and self-awareness.

Several leadership self-assessment and skill development tools are available in textbooks (e.g. Marriner Tomey 2004; Kouzes and Posner, 2012), journals articles (e.g. McNichol and Smith, 2001; Murphy, 2005) and via the Internet (e.g. Mortlock, 2011). McNichol and Smith (2001), for instance, report on a leadership effectiveness analysis (LEA) psychometrically validated instrument, which constitutes 22 leadership behaviours as 128 statements that can form the basis for self-assessment of strengths and developmental needs. Subsequently, appropriate learning actions can be taken.

Another well-publicised personality type test is the Myers-Briggs Type Indicator (Ashridge Psychometrics, 2012). This test, which can be purchased online or adapted versions accessed online, assesses individuals' preferences on four facets of personality, namely: extraversion or introversion; sensing or intuitive; thinking or feeling; and judging or perceiving. After assessing their personality type, individuals can explore and understand their leadership in terms of facets of their personality that they wish to develop, and not use those aspects which are not helpful in their leadership roles.

Guidelines for effective care leadership

A number of leadership theories, styles, competences and attributes have been examined in this chapter, from which it can be concluded that ultimately it is the specific skills of the performance and leadership styles displayed and exercised by health and social care professionals in leadership positions that determine their effectiveness.

Action point 3.9   Effective leadership

Various activities undertaken through this chapter will have facilitated greater insight into leadership traits, functions, styles and theories. For this final Action point, focus on the characteristics of effective leaders. Draw 3 columns and 12 rows on a sheet of paper as illustrated in Table 3.3, and record Kouzes and Posner's (2012) practices of more effective leaders in the left-hand column, which are to:

- create higher-performing teams;
- generate increased sales and customer satisfaction levels;
- foster renewed loyalty and greater organisational commitment;
- enhance motivation and the willingness to work hard;
- more successfully represent their units to upper management;
- facilitate high patient-satisfaction scores and more effectively meet family members' needs;
- promote higher degrees of involvement in schools;
- enlarge the size of their religious congregations;
- increase fundraising results and expand gift-giving levels;
- extend the range of their agency's services;
- increase retention, reducing absenteeism and turnover; and
- positively influence recruitment rates.

These practices also comprise a comprehensive range of skills of an effective care leader. Perform a self-assessment on these 'practices', making notes in the second and third columns on how you see yourself as a leader now, and your aspirations as a leader, respectively.

Table 3.3 Construing leadership

Characteristics of an effective leader	Me as I am now	My ideal self as a leader

Table 3.3 can clearly be used to identify areas of self-development as a leader in health and social care. When you have completed these columns, you may choose to discuss them with colleagues of senior, junior and equal status to obtain external views of your abilities and development plans, a concept and exercise referred to as '360-degree feedback' (Faugier and Woolnough, 2003; Kouzes and Posner, 2012). With 360-degree feedback it is essential that a supportive medium is created, possibly by using an external facilitator so that the receiver of the feedback does not feel over-criticised.

Guidelines for good leadership by care managers

- Always consider the effectiveness of your leadership in the achievement of your organisation's mission and goals.
- Be fully conversant with the different styles of leadership, and thoroughly aware of the styles that you portray, and be comfortable with it.
- Be genuine in your intentions to enable all your 'followers' to self-develop in ways that are mutually beneficial to them as well as to the organisation you are all working for.
- Always consider the extent of 'transformation' of others being achieved by your leadership.
- The 'power' and influence that you can exercise as a leader must only surface when action has to be taken for the benefit of the team that you lead.
- Identify opportunities and support team members to develop their own leadership skills in aspects of the organisation's goals.
- Obtain 360 degree feedback periodically when appropriate opportunities present themselves.
- Regularly, identify your own self-development needs, and take action to maintain and enhance your leadership skills and activities.

CHAPTER SUMMARY

Providing leadership in the effective delivery of health or social care to individuals and teams of care professionals is an inherent component of the management of care. A number of leadership development programmes have emerged mainly because of limited evidence of leadership activities and role models. They are largely based on piloted projects, and opportunities are more widely available to health social care professionals with the ultimate view being to achieve consistency in the highest quality of care within the NHS. In this context, this chapter has explored:

- the reasons for requiring effective leadership in care provision and delivery;
- definitions and the exact nature of leadership, that is, what it is, types of leadership, and ways in which leadership and management are different but overlapping concepts and activities;
- the various theories and styles of leadership that can be applied to lead effectively in health and social care, including trait theories, the functional approach such as action-centred leadership, behavioural theories and styles of leadership, namely, leadership styles, the managerial grid style of leadership and contingency styles of leadership;
- the significance of different types of power as an aspect of leadership, and guidelines for effective use of power in organisations; and
- research on leadership, and a number of recent and current initiatives and programmes on clinical leadership skill development.

RECOMMENDED FURTHER READING

- For the Myers and Briggs self-assessment leadership tool, see:

Ashridge Psychometrics (2012) *Myers-Briggs Type Indicator.* Available from: www.ashridge.org.uk/Website/Content.nsf/wELNPSY/Psychometric+Instruments+-+Myers-Briggs+Type+Indicator+(MBTI)?opendocument.

- For details of the implementation of a framework of leadership, see:

Mortlock S (2011) 'A framework to develop leadership potential'. *Nursing Management*, 18 (7): 29–32.

- For the leadership self-assessment tool published by the NHS Institute for Innovation and Improvement, see:

NHS Institute for Innovation and Improvement (2011) *Leadership is for Everyone: Take the Leadership Challenge with the New Self Assessment Tool.* Available from: www.institute.nhs.uk/index.php?option=com_content&task=view&id=4330&Itemid=3834.

4

DECISION-MAKING AND PROBLEM-SOLVING IN CARE SETTINGS

The theories and principles of management and leadership in health and social care were examined in Chapters 2 and 3, along with how they are applied in care settings. Both functions involve care professionals and DCMs making several decisions and resolving issues during the course of their day-to-day work. In recognition of these crucial management activities, this chapter focuses on the concepts and practice of decision-making and problem-solving in care settings.

Incorporated in this analysis are the theoretical knowledge, skills and systematic approaches to decision-making and problem-solving that DCMs can apply, as well as using their repertoire of personal and professional experience and intuition. Conflict of preferences and values can be a feature of care management, and therefore how conflict is managed and resolved is also explored.

Chapter objectives

On completion of this chapter you will be able to:

- identify a wide range of decisions made by health and social care professionals and analyse the significance of these decisions;
- explain the exact nature of, and distinctions between, the terms 'decision-making' and 'problem-solving';

(Continued)

(Continued)

- explain the basis on which health and social care decisions are made, and the systematic approaches that can be used in both making decisions and solving problems in care settings;
- enunciate the nature of conflict and how conflict in care settings can be managed and resolved successfully; and
- feel prepared to engage in opportunities to practise professional decision-making and problem-solving skills with a view to ensuring new learning and creativity.

Day-to-day Personal and Professional Decisions and their Significance

Day-to-day decision-making

Action point 4.1   Day-to-day decisions

1   Consider the actual decisions that you make in both your personal and professional life, and compile a list of:

   ○ personal decisions made from the point that you woke up this morning, such as which clothes to wear; and
   ○ decisions made over the course of a particular span of duty (professional decisions), such as specific tasks to delegate to particular members of staff.

   Allow 5 to 10 minutes for this part of the Action point and note these instances of decisions on a plain sheet of paper, leaving a 5-cm margin on the right-hand side of the paper for stages 2 and 3.

2   Consider which of these decisions were made consciously, and which were made subconsciously.
3   Now decide which of these decisions were in fact problems being solved, and write 'PS' against them; then write 'DM' against those that were not problems being solved.

On reviewing the items in the list, you will appreciate that we make numerous decisions, small and big, during the course of time, minute-by-minute and day-by-day. Some of the professional and personal decisions identified by care professionals studying on management modules are listed in Table 4.1.

Table 4.1 Personal and professional decisions

Personal decisions made so far today	Professional decisions made over a particular shift/span of duty or two
Whether to reset snooze/sleep button	Whether to discharge a patient (or service user)
What to have for breakfast, which cereals to eat	Whether to have a word with a colleague who was a little abrupt with a student
What to wear	Patient allocation to staff members
Whether to call course peer	What dressing to use
Whether to put the washing out	Whether to apply for the new post/job
How to spend lunch break	What to tell a relative regarding the condition of a patient
What to cook for tea	
Whether to telephone teacher regarding daughter	Whether to go to a meeting on a new care package
Whether to have another cup of coffee	Ensure that the next shift is covered
How to get son to swimming lessons at 4 p.m.	Whether to give more time to a particular patient

One of the aims of Action point 4.1 was to start to distinguish between the activities that involve decision-making and those that involve problem-solving, as they are different concepts (see Box 4.1).

Box 4.1   Is it decision-making or is it problem-solving?

What to have for breakfast/which cereals to eat	*Decision-making*
How to get son to swimming lessons at 4 p.m.	*Problem-solving*
Walk to work or go by car	*Decision-making*
Whether to put the washing out	*Decision-making*
Whether to attend a lecture	*Decision-making*
Whether to call a course peer	*Problem-solving*
Whether to apply for the new post/job	*Decision-making*
Which patient or service user to allocate to which staff	*Decision-making or problem-solving*
Which patients to visit (Community)	*Decision-making*
Whether to discharge a patient	*Decision-making*
Whether to give more time to a patient	*Decision-making and problem-solving*
Which dressing to use	*Decision-making*
Whether the next shift is covered	*Problem-solving*
Which staff to send on a patient transfer	*Decision-making*
What to tell a patient regarding the condition of their ill baby	*Problem-solving*

You will have noted no doubt that some of the activities listed in Box 4.1, such as patient allocation to individual members of staff, can entail either a decision being made and a problem being solved, or both simultaneously, depending on whether the decision was made because of a sudden shortage of skilled staff or just a routine activity.

Decision-making and Problem-solving as Important DCM Functions

The DCM's role as decision-maker and problem-solver is one of the 12 managerial roles in care management identified in Figure 2.3. Previously, Mintzberg (1990) identified 10 key managerial roles, four of which (entrepreneur, disturbance handler, resource allocator and negotiator) are grouped as 'decisional roles'.

Decision-making in relation to care delivery is a function of all health and social care professionals involved in care provision by sheer virtue of their contract of employment and their professional body's code of professional practice. For the more junior care professional, the decision might be when to report a patient observation to the doctor, for instance, and for a more senior care professional, this may involve deciding at which point to increase the dose of a particular patient's medication.

What is Decision-making and What is Problem-solving?

Definitions and distinctions

So what is decision-making and what is problem-solving, and what, if any, are the similarities and differences between them? As noted in Action point 4.1, some decisions are clearly decisions being made and not problems being solved. Other situations are clearly problems being solved. Additionally, a decision being made can entail taking action to prevent a potential problem occurring.

For instance, ensuring safe staff:patient ratios when a colleague telephones in sick is a problem being solved. This can be done by reviewing the workload and patient dependency to establish if cover is required, and asking a team member to do a split shift or borrowing a staff member from another care team. In another instance, the DCM could be invited to attend a meeting to discuss a new record-keeping system. This would be a decision that they have to make because by attending the meeting they would contribute towards the design of new documentation on the one hand, but on the other they are also being taken away from care delivery.

Consequently, decision-making entails considering several components of the situation and ultimately selecting one specific course of action. However, a straightforward act as it might sound, decision-making often entails making a number of smaller but crucial sub-decisions. It requires accessing and collecting appropriate facts which lead to the final action. An open mind is often needed, which allows a total view of the situation to be gained. It is also important to consider the availability of evidence, previous experience and the use of professional judgement.

The notion of problem-solving is different in that there is clearly a problem involved or that something is about to go wrong, and that some action needs to be taken to resolve or avert it. Indeed, dictionaries define the word problem as 'a doubtful or difficult matter, or a seemingly insoluble quandary' (Brown, 2002: 2353). A decision-making situation does not always include a problem. Nonetheless, the two notions tend to be treated jointly and even used interchangeably. Problem-solving usually requires making decisions, and, as became apparent in Action point 4.1, some activities encompass both notions. However, there are distinctions between the two terms, as illustrated in Box 4.2.

Box 4.2   Distinctions between decision-making and problem-solving

Problem-solving	Decision-making
• Involves diagnosing a problem and solving it through a set of decisions • May entail one or more correct solutions	• May not involve a problem, as a number of decisions are made routinely without seeing them as problems • Always involves selecting one specific decision and related actions • Often decision-making is a subset of problem-solving, i.e. a decision is made on how to solve or avert the problem

---

Micro- and macro-decisions

Decisions, like problems, can be small or big. That is, some decisions are straightforward and simple in that very few variables are involved, while others are more complex as many more variables have to be considered in reaching the decision. Nonetheless, most health and social care decisions involve a number of smaller or micro-decisions. For instance, consider how many sub-decisions the care professional has to make when administering an intravenous bolus of antibiotics. Box 4.3, although not an exhaustive list, identifies a number of these micro-decisions, which are akin to reflection-in-action (Boud et al., 1985; Ghaye 2011), and which involves continuous thinking about every single action being taken, in conjunction with justifiable rationales for them, and any associated evidence base.

Box 4.3   Micro decisions and reflection-in-action when administering intravenous bolus antibiotics*

Am I competent to administer this IV drug? - No ➔ (take action as appropriate)
- Yes
⬇
Do I know why is it being given (e.g. wound infection)? - No ➔
- Yes
⬇
Is it prescribed correctly? - No ➔
- Yes
⬇
Is the medication in stock? - No ➔
- Yes
⬇
Expiry date checked? - No ➔
- Yes
⬇
Draw prescribed amount in correct syringe, tray etc.
- Yes
⬇
Check correct patient, drug, dosage, route, time etc. - No ➔
- Yes
⬇
Patient's consent/permission obtained? - No ➔
- Yes
⬇
Access site healthy? - No ➔
- Yes
⬇
Administer over x minutes
⬇
What conversation should I engage patient in?
⬇
State of surrounding tissue when administering.
- OK
⬇
Patient reaction?
- OK
⬇
and so forth.

*Please note that this is not a comprehensive list of micro-decisions and does not include all aspects of infection prevention, etc.

Similar sets of micro-decisions are made in other areas of healthcare, whether it involves enabling an agitated youngster in an adolescent unit to relax; enabling a woman with a complicated pregnancy to give birth safely; supporting a suicidal patient or service user to avoid self-harm; or a practice nurse helping a group of patients to give up smoking. Many of these micro-decisions are made in seconds in the course of the care intervention. Other decisions are more major and can be classed as macro-decisions, such as setting up an outreach service, or withdrawing an existing provision, or changing over to a new way of organising care. Macro-decisions tend to involve and affect more people, and take longer to complete.

Box 4.4 illustrates the decision-making process in social care related to making life-changing decisions with people with impaired mental capacity, incorporating the Mental Capacity Act 2005 (Legislation.gov.uk, 2005), based on the following case study.

Making life-changing decisions with people with impaired mental capacity, incorporating the Mental Capacity Act 2005

CASE STUDY

Mrs M is a 79-year-old woman living alone in her own home, where she has lived for the last 40 years. A care plan was put in place two years ago when her daughter noticed that she was forgetting to take her medication, was not eating regularly and struggling with her personal care. Concerns have now been raised by the carers who feel there has been deterioration in Mrs M's memory, and on two occasions when the carers have called she has not been at the house and later found at her local shops presenting as distressed and confused. Mrs M's daughter took her to the GP who referred Mrs M for psychiatric assessment, where she was diagnosed as suffering from dementia. Her daughter feels that Mrs M is no longer safe living alone and wants her to be moved to a care home.

Box 4.4   The decision-making process in social care

Is there a decision to be made to move the
individual to a care home? - No   ⟶
- Yes
↓

Is there a question about the person's ability
to make the decision?- Yes   ⟶
- No
↓

(Continued)

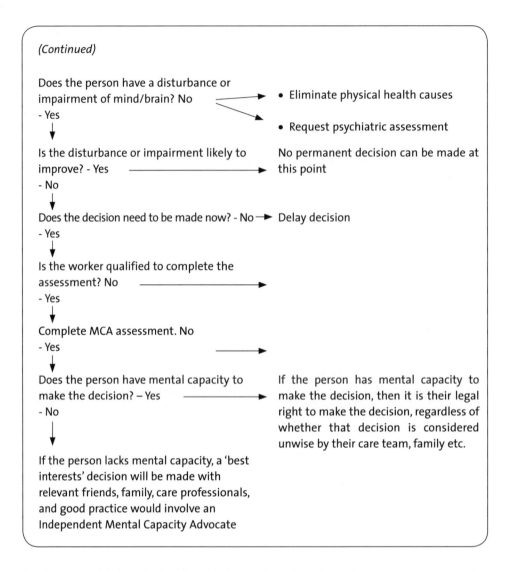

(Continued)

Does the person have a disturbance or
impairment of mind/brain? No ⟶ • Eliminate physical health causes
- Yes
                                 • Request psychiatric assessment
↓

Is the disturbance or impairment likely to   No permanent decision can be made at
improve? - Yes ⟶ this point
- No
↓

Does the decision need to be made now? - No → Delay decision
- Yes
↓

Is the worker qualified to complete the
assessment? No ⟶
- Yes
↓

Complete MCA assessment. No
- Yes ⟶
↓

Does the person have mental capacity to   If the person has mental capacity to
make the decision? – Yes ⟶ make the decision, then it is their legal
- No   right to make the decision, regardless of
                                                  whether that decision is considered
↓   unwise by their care team, family etc.

If the person lacks mental capacity, a 'best
interests' decision will be made with
relevant friends, family, care professionals,
and good practice would involve an
Independent Mental Capacity Advocate

In the case of Mrs M, the risks of her living alone have become apparent and a decision has to be made about whether she needs to move house so she can have a higher level of support. She has a diagnosis of dementia and as this is a degenerative disorder, the impairment is unlikely to improve (and is likely to worsen over time) so the decision can be made now. Due to her confusion and memory impairment her social worker must first determine whether she is able to make this decision, using the principles and guidance of the Mental Capacity Act 2005.

Yet another consideration in decision-making is *ethical* decision-making, in which the five basic principles of ethics (the value of life; goodness and rightness; justice and fairness; truth telling and honesty; and individual freedom) need to be heeded.

These principles and concepts are examined in detail in most books (e.g. Thiroux and Krasemann, 2011; Wheeler 2012) on care ethics, and they explain in detail how they are applied. Briefly they mean:

- *The value of life:* enhancing patients' or service users' health and social wellbeing.
- *Goodness and rightness:* actions that are socially seen as doing good, and what is right, for those in their care.
- *Justice and fairness:* being fair and just towards all patients and service users, and ensuring that they are justly protected from incompetent practice.
- *Truth telling and honesty:* ensuring that correct practices are transparently transmitted.
- *Individual freedom:* promoting choice.

Creativity in decision-making

Each instance of decision-making and problem-solving could present opportunities for growth and development, because although problems may be encountered with relative annoyance at first as they disrupt the planned sequence of events, they may also present scope for developing new knowledge and skills, or even changing attitudes. Under the significance of decisions made by care professionals, it is clear that several decisions have interpersonal implications.

Where decision-making and problem-solving involve dealing with novel situations, novel actions may be required, which would involve thinking creatively. There are different and sequential ways of being creative. Marriner-Tomey (2004) suggests that being creative entails five stages:

1 *The felt need to be creative:* in relation to a decision or problem situation.
2 *Preparation:* involves exploring several possible solutions.
3 *Incubation:* a period for pondering over solutions after all potential solutions have been identified.
4 *Illumination:* when the most logical or preferred solution emerges.
5 *Verification:* when the solution is implemented, tested, monitored, refined and evaluated.

The preparation stage can entail group or teamwork where appropriate, and uses group techniques such as information sharing, focused case analysis, ideas-generation exercises and SWOT analyses (see Chapter 6). Whether situations are dealt with individually or in groups, we also need to be aware of various factors that can either encourage or block creativity in care settings.

Creative people tend to view problems as new challenges that provide scope for learning, they are always open to alternative views and lines of action, are much more flexible and adaptable, and are enthusiastic about novel ventures and openings. They do not see authority as the final, definite and only perspective, and are keen to be part of new developments. How the roles of individual team members combine for effective decision-making in care delivery is discussed in

Chapter 10 under team roles in the context of inter-professional and inter-agency working.

Systematic Approaches to Decision-making and Problem-solving

Following on from the notion that novel decision-making and problem-solving situations in particular can also present scope for being creative, it therefore follows that some decisions the DCM makes might involve innovative actions. Consequently, decisions can be seen as innovative-type decisions, otherwise they might be routine decisions or adaptive decisions.

Types of decisions

Brief details of the above-mentioned three types of decisions are:

> *Routine decisions* involve using established rules, policies or procedures, such as what to do if a member of staff makes a drug error, a complaint is received, or a mental health patient who is detained under the Mental Health Act goes absent without leave, as for these there is a specific policy or guidelines to follow. Routine decisions are often made by more junior managers as the actions to take are well-established.

> *Adaptive decisions* are made when both problems and alternative solutions are somewhat unusual or only partly understood, such as a patient admitted with an unknown identity, or with a health problem that does not normally occur at a certain age. Ways of dealing with similar previous situations may be adapted, and their effects monitored continuously.

> *Innovative decisions* are made when problems are unusual, unclear or unprecedented and creative novel solutions are required, such as how to cater for the health or social care needs of the increasing number of over-85s in a particular locality or for a new group of immigrant workers living in the area.

Managerial decisions include both individual and organisational processes, as the decisions made affect both staff and systems within the organisation. For example, if it is decided that a dietician should set up a weight self-management programme for obese patients at a general practitioners' surgery, then both organisational and individual actions have to be considered. At organisational level, there will be a need to establish the availability of necessary resources, such as salary for the dietician, rooms where they can meet the patients on a regular basis, probably administrative support, a referral system for the practice nurse and the general practitioner to refer patients to the dietician, and details of anticipated patient outcomes. At individual level, they need to ensure that they have full knowledge of the physiological and psychosocial interface of obesity, and the skills to run the programme.

Action point 4.2 Routine, adaptive and innovative decisions

Refer back to the list of decisions that you made in response to Action point 4.1, and consider which of the decisions were routine decisions, which were adaptive decisions, and which were innovative. Mark them as 'R', 'A' or 'I' accordingly. Consider the processes that you have used to reach the final decisions.

Systematic approaches to decision-making entail ascertaining the types of situations being encountered and the decision-making techniques used, along with group decision-making, as well as exploring the implications of non-decisions.

Probability analysis

With flattening management structures, increasingly, more decisions and accountability are devolved to individual health and social care professionals. However, although several decisions are made with the expectation of a high degree of certainty of achieving the anticipated outcomes, there is almost always some risk of the outcome not being achieved. Thus routine decisions made by care professionals and DCMs should present a 'high certainty' of being the correct decision, and low risk of being incorrect. Decisions are made under conditions of certainty when alternatives and conditions surrounding alternatives are known, and when therefore decisions can be made with a fairly good knowledge of the likely consequences.

DCMs make decisions in expectation of particular outcomes. The likelihood of achievement of the particular outcomes might be high, medium or low. If a patient is suspected of having an infection, then the decision may be to administer an appropriate course of antibiotics in the expectation that it will clear the infection. However, despite research evidence, it is not guaranteed 100 per cent that this outcome will be achieved as various other variables might come into play. In social situations, the likelihood of the achievement of outcomes may again be high but would be even less certain. The degree of certainty of outcomes of decisions is referred to as 'decision based on probability' (Hellriegel et al., 2007), and involves probability analysis before making the decision. For every decision made, the DCM needs to weigh-up or endeavour to gauge the probability of the decision achieving the anticipated goal, and the risks being taken.

Adaptive decisions involve moderate degrees of certainty and risk. Innovative decisions can involve high uncertainty and high risk. A number of care management decisions, such as staffing the unit for the next 24 hours, are based on probability estimates (expressed as a percentage), generally made under conditions of some risk that the actions might not succeed.

In the above examples, the decisions based on research and facts and figures can be referred to as having 'objective probability', and therefore more likely to be the right decisions; and those based on less empirical evidence as having 'subjective probability', as they are often based on individual personal judgement.

Hellriegel et al. (2007) note that in situations where decisions involve more objective probabilities, as in routine decisions, there is more certainty of that being the right decision, but where they are made with subjective probabilities, as in innovative or adaptive decisions, there would be less certainty. Decisions are made under conditions of uncertainty when all alternative options, the attendant risks and likely consequences of each option are not known (also known as 'limited control decisions': Shoup, 2000). Figure 4.1 illustrates the interface between risks and certainty of decisions being correct ones.

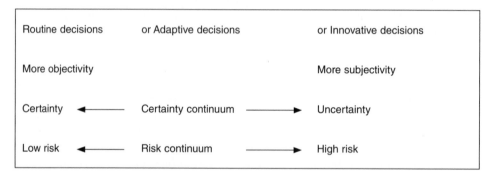

Figure 4.1   Types of decisions based on risk and certainty

Other types of decision-making include 'delayed action decisions' (Shoup, 2000: 115), such as awarding a pay rise but delaying payment by six months. They can be 'provisional decisions', which implies decisions contingent upon certain prerequisite, such as booking annual leave 12 months in advance – the prerequisite being, for example, that staffing and the amount of work remain stable.

Box 4.5 lists the types of decisions discussed in this section and the next.

Box 4.5   Various types of decisions

- Limited control decisions
- Routine decisions
- Adaptive decisions
- Innovative decisions
- Delayed action decisions
- Provisional decisions
- Logical decisions
- Optimum decision-making approach
- Pessimistic approach
- Political decision-making model

Approaches to decision-making

There are a number of alternative approaches to the decision-making process. For instance, rational decision-making is a decision-making model based on logical, well-grounded rational choices that maximise the achievement of objectives. It constitutes what can be considered to be logical decisions. For example, if the road is very busy, then the pedestrian may decide to cross the road at the designated crossing point; if an in-patient who is undergoing a structured rehabilitation programme requests permission to spend the weekend at home, then the decision to grant this will be based on a number of factors, which may include consulting all appropriate personnel.

Another perspective is the optimum decision-making approach, which constitutes selecting an approach that aims to produce the best possible outcome for all parties involved. Otherwise, a pessimistic approach to decision-making can be taken whereby the worst possible outcomes for each alternative are compared and the least objectionable one is chosen. For instance, if the choices of decisions between admitting an older person with a fractured neck or femur from the accident and emergency (A&E) department to a hospital 25 miles away, or waiting in an admission unit on a trolley for a bed to become available at the same hospital, or admitting to a mixed-sex unit with a reasonable level of privacy at the same hospital, the third alternative might be the least objectionable. This is decision-making through screening out the unacceptable options and choosing the more acceptable ones from those conjectured. Personal choice, impact on others, achievement of national policy/targets and so on must also be considered within the decision-making process.

Another approach is the political decision-making model, which is a process in which the particular interests and objectives of powerful stakeholders or allies influence the decisions made by individuals.

Decision-making based on knowledge and intuition

Action point 4.3   Basis for decisions made

Refer back to Action point 4.1, and consider item 2 with regard to whether the decisions were made consciously or subconsciously. Then think of the basis on which each of the decisions were made. More specifically, were the decisions based on thorough knowledge of facts, or were they based to certain extent on intuition?

Hamm (1988) suggests that we make decisions about a situation based somewhere on a continuum that has knowledge from empirical studies at one end and intuition at the other. It depends also on the time available, and therefore if, for instance, when less time is available as in a critical situation, then intuitive approaches are also relied upon (see Figure 4.2).

In health and social care, decisions are based predominantly on knowledge from cognitive modes 1 to 4 on Hamm's cognitive continuum; that is, on research evidence, quasi-experiments (e.g. clinical audits) and system-aided judgement (e.g. by receiving and using pathology laboratory results available electronically and accessed directly from the care setting's computer). These components generally apply to what Hamm refers to as 'well-structured' situations. The 'analysis' mode is a slower process, consisting of careful scrutiny of available knowledge, conscious and consistent, usually quite accurate, and using organisational principles. Analysis involves breaking things down into small components for greater understanding, whereas intuition retains wholeness.

For less structured situations, peer-aided judgement and intuition tend to be used. It is suggested that experienced professionals use 'intuitive judgement' more often, and with more self-confidence. The intuitive mode involves rapid unconscious information processing (Thompson, 1999) that combines and averages the available information, is low in consistency and is moderately accurate.

Hamm (1988) indicates that a rational intuitive approach to decision-making is primarily determined by: the complexity of task structure; the ambiguity of the task; and the nature of presentation of the task. If the task is complex, unfamiliar

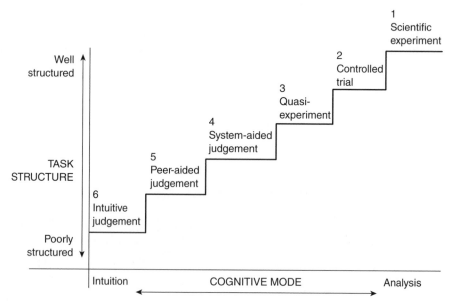

Figure 4.2 Hamm's (1988) cognitive continuum

Source: Hamm R M (1988) 'Clinical intuition and clinical analysis: expertise and the cognitive continuum' in Dowie J and Einstein A (eds) *Professional Judgement: A Reader in Clinical Decision Making*. Milton Keynes: Open University Press.

and the time available is limited, then intuitive approaches are used (Thompson, 1999). When ample clues about the situation are available, which is therefore less ambiguous, and the situation can be addressed as sub-tasks, then analytical approaches can be taken.

In problem-solving, on the other hand, problems can be solved using knowledge (including information), experience and intuition. Clearly, DCMs have to base as many of their care decisions on research knowledge as possible. Looking back at Action point 4.1, consider the nature or types of knowledge base on which you made your decisions. Professional knowledge can also be viewed from Carper's (1978) patterns of knowing perspective, each of these 'patterns' being seen as equally important for care delivery and for developing further knowledge. These patterns of knowing are:

- *Empirical knowledge*: from traditional science viewing reality as something that can be measured, tested and authenticated.
- *Ethical knowledge:* based on morals and philosophy, and that which cannot usually be tested.
- *Aesthetic knowledge:* based on sensitivity and intuition.
- *Personal knowledge:* knowing of oneself in influencing one's practice.

In a study exploring whether nurses use research to inform decision-making, Thompson (2002) found that although colleagues are the more immediate source of information on which to base decisions, they are also a source of research knowledge and useful networks. However, decisions made by DCMs are also influenced by experience and intuition, which are in fact based on the care professional's own accumulated repertoire of knowledge and mastery over its production and application, as previously identified by Schon (1995) and Dearlove (1997).

Intuitive knowledge is related to patterns of personal knowledge, and tends to refer to sudden perceptions or realisation of a pattern, or 'cause and effect' in an apparently disjointed set of situations. Furthermore, Benner (2001) suggests that novices tend to prefer to use rules and guidelines (i.e. practical knowledge) while 'expert' care professionals tend to use intuition more.

Group (or consensus) decision-making

Another systematic approach to decision-making is *group* decision-making. When a decision is made to choose from and implement (e.g. a health clinic for asylum seekers or an evening clinic for all patients), then such a decision is better taken as a group after the appropriate discussions, as co-operation by all staff may be required.

Of course decisions that are made at strategic level are made by structured committees. However, although group decision-making is generally preferred because of its democratic element, consensus and increased commitment, it might also have its limitations or drawbacks in that they are more time-consuming and can lower the decisiveness that leaders are expected to manifest. Furthermore, as Alexander (1997) has noted, professional decision-making is becoming increasingly complex and anxiety causing for care workers, as the needs of individual patients have to be balanced against resource constraints, the increase in litigation, and consumer awareness and expectation.

Moreover, referring to the contingency model of leadership discussed in Chapter 3, decision-making approaches are also dependent upon leadership styles as to whether they are autocratic, consultative or laissez-faire, for instance.

Another aspect of decision-making is related to the quality of decisions. On evaluating the decision chosen for a particular situation, the DCM might decide that it was not the best decision, which could have been due to shortage of time and resources, for instance. Marquis and Huston (2012) identify the critical elements of decision-making as choosing and acting decisively, defining objectives clearly, gathering data carefully, generating many alternatives, thinking logically and using an evidence-based approach. Defining objectives is also directly linked to IDPRs (2012: 546) and is also an important component of MBO (p. 552–4).

Problem-solving methods

As problem-solving is a slightly different concept from decision-making, there are distinct methods of solving problems to choose from. Those related to such problems as staff conflict will be discussed shortly. Consider in the meantime the following situations:

- While performing a medical intervention, a new doctor is being rude to a member of your team.
- You arrive on duty and find that one of your colleagues who should be on duty has just rung in sick.

What are the processes that the DCM would go through to resolve the issues, and what are the factors that determine the final solution(s)? In management, problem-solving involves taking a systematic set of actions that involve careful consideration of all variables to resolve or to avert a problematic situation.

Thus, on encountering a problem, the DCM may identify a range of actions to choose from to solve it. For instance, if the problem is outside their competence or responsibility, the DCM may pass the problem on to relevant other personnel. Alternatively, they may need to seek expert advice (i.e. further knowledge) before taking further action. They may decide to share the issue with the team to explore the problem and suggest the most suitable solutions. Past experiences and intuition can be used to resolve problems, whereupon previously successfully used problem-solving methods might be used.

Yet another alternative is that the DCM may decide to delay any action to resolve a less-serious problem (depending on its significance), in the expectation that it will solve itself. Problems at times solve themselves when they have run their natural course. For instance, a mentor may decide not to formally assess a student who is struggling to meet his/her practice outcomes as the student may already be aware of this problem, and already taking actions to achieve the outcomes. However, problems being solved on their own are rare, as usually some action has to be taken by some-one to resolve it. Therefore this is a dangerous problem-solving strategy, and in the example provided, delayed action could result in other repercussions.

At times, the trial-and-error method may be used by DCMs with lesser manage-ment experience, whereupon they try different solutions until one works. However, the traditional problem-solving method, as identified by several authors (including Bond and Holland (2010) and Marquis and Huston (2012: 7)) and which can also be represented as a uni-directional path or as a problem-solving spiral, involves:

1 Identifying the problem.
2 Gathering data to analyse the causes and consequences of the problem.
3 Exploring alternative solutions.
4 Evaluating the alternatives.
5 Selecting the appropriate solution.
6 Implementing the solution.
7 Evaluating the solution.

Nonetheless, further consideration of problem-solving reveals that it requires identifying and defining the problem in the first place, and thereafter using decision-making strategies. In problem-solving, the DCM can also take into account the plan-do-study-act (PDSA) cycle (NHS III, 2008a), which is an action-orientated learning method that comprises implementing new actions by planning, trying it out, observing the results and acting on what has been learnt. This method is also discussed in the context of quality assurance in Chapter 5, and the management of change in Chapter 6.

However, 'experimentation' is another alternative problem-solving method sug-gested by Sullivan and Decker (2013), which entails taking a more rigorous approach that involves empirical testing of a theory, hypothesis or hunch to determine the most appropriate solutions, including pilot projects.

Competing Challenges and Conflict in Practice Settings

The decision-making and problem-solving managerial roles of DCMs include pre-empting problems, and taking action to avert or resolve them when they do occur. The DCM needs to recognise these challenges, that there are times when things do not go smoothly, and that there can be disagreements between individuals or groups. Such disagreements or alternative strong views can manifest themselves as open disturbances, or as latent conflict situations.

Conflict in care settings – what are the causes?

Conflict is part of normal organisational life. There are several reasons for conflict, not least because of the numerous decisions that are continually being made by differ-ent care professionals in the day-to-day provision of care in various departments.

Another perspective is that each employee and sub-group in the organisation is in some way different from one other, and each have their own beliefs, perceptions, thoughts, expectations and aspirations about the employing organisation, and therefore there are likely to be situations when views differ markedly, and now and again clash with one another. These can lead to disagreements that require attention to restore equilibrium. For instance, some employees may be given 'term time contracts' under *Improving Working Lives Standard* (DH, 2000d), and therefore are away from work during summer, for instance, but this may be resented by those who do not have young families and yet would also like to take extended time away from work during summer.

The word 'conflict' originates from the Latin word *confligere*, which means 'clash, contend, fight or struggle' (Brown, 2002: 484). It could mean 'don't agree', argument, different priorities, different attitudes, different perceptions, ineffective or lack of communication, for instance.

Marquis and Huston (2012: 467) define conflict 'as the internal or external discord that results from differences in ideas, values or feelings between two or more people', and as deliberate behaviour intended to obstruct the achievement of some other person's goals (Mullins, 2010). Conflict therefore can be based on the incompatibility of goals of two or more parties, and arises from opposing behaviours. It can occur at individual, group or organisational level, and there can be negative or positive outcomes from any particular conflict.

Incidence and sources of conflict

Examples of conflict that could occur in care settings include:

- two members of staff wanting to be nominated for the same next professional development course;
- staff being told by their managers that they must do internal rotation between day and night shifts, but this clashes with several individuals' domestic lives;
- discontinuing overtime pay;
- being asked to lead a form of therapy for which you have not had training;
- an older patient is kept in hospital for social rather than ill-health reasons; and
- a manager wants a patient discharged home quickly so that the bed can be free for use by a patient waiting in the A&E department, but the care professionals feels that more time is needed for certain facilities to be in place to ensure a safe discharge.

Various potential sources of organisational conflict can be identified. They can be caused by differences in perception; limited resources; departmentalisation and specialisation; or inequitable treatment, as also noted by Mullins (2010). Furthermore, conflict can occur at different levels, such as between:

- two employees of almost equal status;
- an employee and their line manager;
- informal subgroups (informal organisation – discussed in Chapter 2) and the formal organisation;
- different departments or teams/groups within the organisation;

- the employee's beliefs and the organisation's objectives;
- an employee and the employing organisation;
- the workforce and the organisation.

Action point 4.4   Potential sources of organisational conflict

Think of real-life examples of sources of conflict in your own care setting for each level of organisational conflict identified above, and make some notes on this in the grid format below.

Instances of potential sources/levels of conflict in my care setting
Between two employees
Between employee and their line manager
Between informal subgroups and the formal organisation
Between different departments or groups
An employee's beliefs and the organisation's
The workforce and the organisation
Other

You should have been able to think of a few examples of sources of conflict in your care organisation. The different levels of conflict just discussed can also be referred to as interpersonal conflict (between individuals), intergroup conflict (between groups), intrapersonal conflict (within the individual) and intra-group conflict within a group, for instance. Conflict can also be competitive conflict, or disruptive conflict.

However, conflict does not have to be a bad thing, as although it can have negative effects, it can also produce growth, depending on how it is managed. On the other hand, too little disagreement could result in organisational stasis, but too much conflict can reduce the organisation's efficiency and effectiveness (see Glossary for explanation of these terms).

The Conflict Process

How does conflict progress from the time it is initially felt by one or the other party? Filley (1975) identified six stages of the conflict process, which can be represented diagrammatically as shown in Figure 4.3.

Figure 4.3   Six stages of the conflict process

Antecedent conditions refers to the pre-existence of persisting *latent conflict*, such as when staff shortage or budget cuts persist and conditions are 'ripe' for conflict. During the *perceived* or *substantive conflict* stage, issues start to be explored, and if there is substantial disagreement between the two parties, then *felt conflict* is experienced. At this stage the conflict is emotionalised, and hostility, fear and mistrust prevail. In the *manifest* or *overt conflict* stage, action has to be taken to *resolve* or *suppress* the conflict. In the *conflict resolution aftermath* stage, positive or negative outcomes ensue for the two parties.

When there is conflict in a care setting, this is detectable by the personnel in the setting as symptoms of (potential or actual) conflict such as: irritability, mistrust, low morale, suspiciousness, raised voices or shouting, lack of communication, some staff being absent or 'off-sick' frequently and staff being unapproachable.

Responding to and resolving conflict

Action point 4.5   Response to conflict: case study and alternative approaches

Case study

You are an experienced band 5 care professional, and you are encouraged to apply for the band 6 vacancy that has been advertised. You have the required experience in the specialism and know you can do the job. You apply, get interviewed, but the job is given to someone else who is external to the organisation, has fewer years' experience but has a university degree, which you do not have. You feel you have been 'led up the garden path', and furthermore, you have been asked to help the new person settle in.
   From this case study:

- Identify your initial reactions.
- Think of alternative approaches to the situation.
- Consider what are the possible positive outcomes, and the possible negative outcomes of the particular conflict.

Your initial reaction to the situation might be resentment towards your employer, or a philosophical reaction such as 'some you win, some you lose'. Nonetheless, the likely negative outcomes of conflict might include feeling defeated and demeaned, with consequent lowered self-esteem, creating a cold social atmosphere of mistrust and suspicion, loss of motivation, sickness, and even leaving the employment, resulting in an increase in employee turnover. There can be a loss of self-confidence, for instance whether to apply for a similar position. Employees might find it difficult to take orders or instructions from the other person, there could be resistance to teamwork, and individuals and groups might become more self-interested.

There are various likely positive outcomes from the Action point 4.5 case study. To start with, the vacancy is filled, and therefore the unit is back to a full complement of staff. Both parties could learn new skills or knowledge from each other and gain new perspectives. It is also an opportunity to identify CPD needs based on why you did not get the job, and enable you to seek support for further professional development courses, or guidance on contemporary ways of presenting your curriculum vitae. Both have the opportunity to network and make a new professional acquaintance. You can apply for a different job, and see this application as useful interview experience. You could go for post-interview counselling to receive constructive critique of your performance at the interview and suggestions on how you can learn from the experience.

General positive outcomes of conflict that could ensue include:

- increased problem-solving ability through being forced to search for new approaches;
- other underlying problems being brought to the surface and getting resolved;
- individuals' views getting clarified and protocols being established;
- stimulation of interest and re-motivation; and
- an opportunity to test own abilities further.

However, conflict tends to cause stress, hardening of attitudes and a tendency to be rigid as individuals, and we also tend to develop habitual ways of reacting to conflict situations.

Resolving conflict – goals and strategies

Pedler et al. (2007) note that where there is conflict between two parties, the mode (or style) of conflict resolution depends upon the two basic dimensions of conflict situations:

1 How assertive or unassertive each party is in pursuing their own goals.
2 How co-operative or unco-operative each party is.

The extent to which each dimension is adopted by each party determines one of five particular modes, or styles, of conflict resolution, namely: competing, collaborating, compromising, avoiding and accommodating, viz:

- Both parties assertive but unco-operative results in 'competing'
- Both parties assertive and co-operative results in 'collaborating'

- Both parties partly assertive and partly co-operative results in 'compromising'
- Both parties unassertive and unco-operative results in 'avoiding'
- Both parties unassertive but co-operative results in 'accommodating'

Therefore, if both parties are highly assertive and highly co-operative, then they will be using the 'collaborating' mode, and the conflict will be resolved to both parties satisfaction. But if both parties are highly unassertive and unco-operative, then they are likely to 'avoid' facing the conflict, and might be pretending that it does not exist. However, if both parties are highly assertive but unco-operative, this reflects a 'competing' (battling) style which will cause the conflict to linger on unresolved for some time.

Resolving conflict is usually interactive in that the style or mode of conflict resolution adopted by each party tends to be mutually reciprocal, which implies that the style of conflict resolution that you adopt is likely to affect the style your opponent adopts, and vice versa. Disjunction and difficulty in resolving conflict also occurs if one party is, say, in 'competing' (assertive and unco-operative) mode while the other is in 'avoiding' mode.

Action point 4.6   My reaction to conflict

Use Pedler et al.'s (2007) concept of modes of conflict resolution through assertiveness and co-operativeness dimensions, identify how you have personally reacted to a particular conflict situation in which you have been involved. Did you react assertively or unassertively, co-operatively or unco-operatively? How did the other party react? Furthermore, was your eventual response the same as your initial reaction?

Thus the style of resolving conflict varies with such factors as the nature of the current interaction between you and the other party. It may be affected by background or contingent issues such as need to exert power, urgency of the situation, and clarity of goals. However, by identifying any habitual responses you may have in certain situations and observing the responses these produce in others, you can gain further insight into yours' and others' modes of conflict resolution, and change if you wish. Furthermore, after identifying your own style(s) or modes and the responses generated in others, you still have scope to select the response you feel is the most appropriate.

Managing conflict

On encountering conflict situations, DCMs can draw on various available strategies, such as the modes or styles of conflict resolution suggested by Pedler et al. (2007)

noted above. Sullivan and Decker (2013) suggest that other strategies for conflict management are:

- *Negotiation:* the conflicting parties discuss the issues, and give-and-take on particular elements.
- *Confrontation*: the problem is openly discussed by all parties involved.
- *Win–win strategy:* a strategy that focuses on goals or the welfare of both parties, and attempts are made to meet the needs of both parties; also known as 'joint-welfare choice'.
- *Win–lose strategy:* one party is determined to win, and the other has to submit or lose.
- *Lose–lose strategy:* strategy in which neither side wins, nor settlement reached, and is unsatisfactory for both sides.
- *Partisan choice:* attending to the needs of only one party.

For conflict to be resolved successfully, it is essential that each party is clear about their goals and objectives. If the goals of the two parties are diametrically opposed to one another, then a mutually beneficial (i.e. joint-welfare or win–win) outcome might be more difficult to achieve.

Care managers realise that conflict is a natural and inevitable process in organisations, and often it is also a precursor for change. Conflict can be seen as the cutting-edge of change (Yoder-Wise, 2010). Resolving conflict is an interactive and dynamic process, and can be positive or negative. Responses to conflict situations include resolving them by analysing a variety of alternatives as positive opportunities, by identifying goals and particular strategies, and not seeing them as negative obligations.

Overall, dealing with conflict is also related to coping strategies, which can be facilitated through clinical supervision, for instance, which is discussed in Chapter 8. Care professionals must not allow themselves to feel stressed by conflict situations, but to treat them as challenges that provide opportunities for learning from events.

Guidelines for effective decision-making, problem-solving and conflict management

The following constitute guidelines for effective decision-making, problem-solving and conflict management in care settings:

- Accept decision-making, problem-solving and conflict management as normal management encounters, and see them as challenges and opportunities for positive outcomes and learning.
- Do not delay decision-making, problem-solving and conflict management unduly, as delays can lead to unnecessary complications such as further resentment.
- Use systematic approaches to decision-making, problem-solving and conflict management whenever possible.
- Be clear about the goals of each situation prior to taking interventional actions.
- Allow plenty of space and scope for individual and teams to develop creativity when faced with issues.

CHAPTER SUMMARY

This chapter has explored the decision-making and problem-solving function of DCMs. Key components of these concepts were examined, which include:

- day-to-day personal and professional decisions and their significance, including instances of decisions that health and social care professionals make during the course of a day, and why decision-making and problem-solving are important care management functions;
- what decision-making and problem-solving are, together with distinctions between them, micro- and macro-decisions, and creativity in decision-making;
- systematic approaches to decision-making and problem-solving, including types of decisions, probability analysis, approaches to decision-making, decisions based on knowledge or intuition, group decision-making, and problem-solving methods;
- competing challenges and conflicts in care settings, including what they are, incidents and sources of conflict, and the conflict process;
- responding to conflict, and resolving conflicts through goal-setting, and using strategies of conflict management; and
- guidelines for effective decision-making, i.e. applying the principles of effective decision-making and problem-solving.

RECOMMENDED FURTHER READING

- For further discussion on Hamm's cognitive continuum related to decisions based on analysis against those based on intuition, see:

Hamm R M (1988) 'Clinical intuition and clinical analysis: expertise and the cognitive continuum' (Chapter 3), in Dowie J and Elstein A (eds) *Professional Judgement: A Reader in Clinical Decision-making*. Milton Keynes: Open University Press.

- For a critique of how student nurses learn decision-making skills when using early warning scoring (EWS) systems, see:

McCallum, J, Duffy, K, Hastie, E, Ness, V and Price, L (2013) 'Developing nursing students' decision making skills: are early warning scoring systems helpful?'. *Nurse Education in Practice*, 13(1): 1–3.

5

ENSURING HIGH QUALITY CARE

The provision of high quality care is becoming increasingly challenging with rising consumer expectations, increasing technological advances, demographic changes and budgetary constraints. Healthcare providers need to be competitive to attract patients and ensure the financial viability of their respective organisations. The DCM has a vital role in maximising the use of resources and ensuring the best outcomes for patients in their practice setting. Quality in healthcare encompasses ensuring safety and that the patient comes to no harm, while also ensuring that a high standard of care is achieved and the patient has a positive experience of their care. This chapter focuses on quality, patient safety and the patient experience. Quality concepts will be explored together with a number of models and quality assurance tools.

Chapter objectives

On completion of this chapter, you will be able to:

- define and distinguish between quality, quality assurance and related concepts;
- review and analyse various models, tools and frameworks that are available to support quality improvement and assurance, and evaluate their significance for the DCM;
- explore the principles of customer care and how you can apply them within your practice setting;
- discuss various strategies for quality improvement and quality monitoring and their application within your practice setting.

Policy Reasons for Quality Consciousness

The implementation of *The NHS Plan* (DH, 2000b) saw a period of investment and growth in both NHS staffing and facilities. Coupled with reform, this led to the NHS realising reduced waiting times and ongoing improvements in efficiency, including hospital throughput and reduced lengths of patient stay. *High Quality Care for All* (DH, 2008a) aimed to build on the achievements made from the implementation of the *NHS Plan* and set out a vision of an NHS with 'quality of care at its heart'. The definition of 'quality' encompassed three interrelated areas, namely care that is clinically effective, personal and safe.

High Quality Care for All set out the requirement for the publication of 'quality accounts' and also introduced Commissioning for Quality and Innovation (CQUIN), which enables commissioners to reward excellence by linking a proportion of English healthcare providers' income to the achievement of local quality improvement goals. Quality improvements achieved included, amongst others, a reduction in healthcare associated infections such as Clostridium difficile (C. diff) and Methicillin-resistant Staphylococcus aureus (MRSA) bacteraemias.

More latterly, the publication of *Equity and Excellence: Liberating the NHS* (DH, 2010a) identified the strategic priority of the NHS as 'to ensure that health services in England achieve quality and outcomes which are among the best in the world'. It also set out how the Secretary of State for Health would hold NHS England to account for delivering better health outcomes through a national NHS Outcomes Framework. The intention of which was to move away from simply measuring process outputs to ensuring the measurement and subsequent improvement of clinical outcomes. This has been followed by the publication of the NHS Outcomes Framework (DH, 2010e), which contains a number of indicators that are intended to: provide an overview of how well the NHS is performing; provide an accountability mechanism between the Secretary of State for Health and NHS England; and act as a catalyst for driving up quality throughout the NHS by encouraging a change in culture and behaviour.

Indicators in the NHS Outcomes Framework are set out across five domains (see Figure 5.1), which define the national outcomes for improvement across the NHS with a focus on improving health and reducing inequalities.

In addition to the NHS Outcomes Framework, there are also outcomes frameworks for adult social care and public health. The frameworks are intended to support all parts of the health and care system to work collectively to support people to 'live better for longer'.

The need for clear responsibilities and accountability for care quality and assurance have been further emphasised in light of high-profile failings in healthcare such as the Mid Staffordshire NHS Trust and Winterbourne View scandals, and subsequent findings and recommendations from the associated investigations and inquiries.

Significant changes initiated within the NHS that will also have an impact on the quality agenda include:

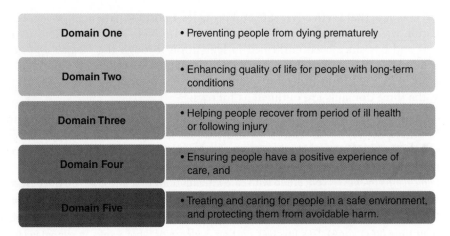

Figure 5.1 Five Domains of the NHS Outcomes Framework (DH, 2010d)

- the transfer of health commissioning responsibilities to NHS England and local Clinical Commissioning Groups;
- the expansion of providers within the healthcare market through initiatives such as 'any qualified provider' (AQP) processes;
- a strengthened role for the Care Quality Commission as a quality inspectorate;
- developments to the role of Monitor;
- developing a stronger partnership with Local Authorities through the establishment of Health and Well Being Board and Healthwatch, who provide additional scrutiny to the quality of services;
- The role of National Institute for Health and Clinical Excellence (NICE) in developing quality standards for services.

The chapter will now define 'quality' as a concept and explore cultural dimensions and human factors in relation to quality and patient safety.

Defining Quality

It is often stated that quality as a concept is difficult to define as it is subjective and individuals have their own interpretation of its meaning. High quality care provision is care delivery that meets a certain standard of excellence that is acceptable to both staff and patients. There are a plethora of definitions in existence, but they are dependent upon two sets of factors: intrinsic and extrinsic; the former relates to values, beliefs, attitudes and self-knowledge, and the latter to time, money, people and other resources. As mentioned in the introduction, the definition of quality in the NHS is care that is effective, safe and provides a positive patient experience. This definition was borne from *High Quality Care for All: NHS Next Stage Review* (DH, 2008a) and has since been enshrined in legislation through the *Health and Social Care Act* (DH, 2012a). The three interrelated domains are outlined in Figure 5.2 and all need to be present in order for quality care to have been achieved. As an overview, the three domains are outlined as follows:

- *Patient safety* relates to 'doing no harm' to patients. This can be achieved through provision of a clean and safe environment together with taking steps to reduce avoidable harm, e.g. pressure ulcers, healthcare associated infections and medication errors (DH, 2008a).
- *Clinical effectiveness* is concerned with care interventions that are based on the best available evidence and applying them to real-life conditions to deliver the best outcomes. Clinical effectiveness is doing the *right* thing in the *right* way for the *right* patients at the *right* time (RCN, 1996). This involves getting *evidence* of what works in everyday clinical practice and evaluating its effect on patient care through outcome measures such as mortality, complication rates and patient-reported outcome measures (PROMs).
- *Patient experience* relates to the quality of care from the perspective of the patient. This includes the degree to which the patient has been treated with compassion, dignity and respect (DH, 2008a).

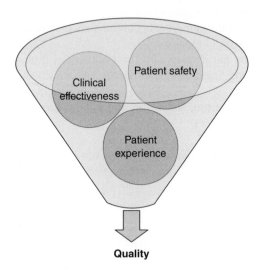

Figure 5.2   The three interrelated domains of quality

Based on the definition of quality set out in *High Quality Care for All: NHS Next Stage Review* (DH, 2008a)

Outcomes that could illustrate the achievement of high quality care in practice are provided in Figure 5.3. The example provided is based around the scenario of a patient admitted to hospital for a knee replacement.

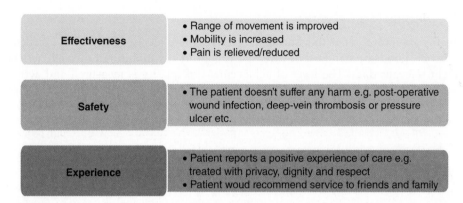

Figure 5.3   Outcomes to demonstrate quality of care for a patient who has a knee replacement

Action point 5.1   What high quality care means to me

Consider what 'high quality care' means to you. If a close family member became a patient within your practice setting, what type of service would you like them to receive? Focus your thoughts around the three domains of quality as outlined in *High Quality Care for All – NHS Next Stage Review* (DH, 2008a):

- Clinical effectiveness
- Patient safety
- Patient experience.

In achieving quality care it is necessary to agree on both the definition of quality and how to measure quality. The chapter will now address quality assurance, and the monitoring and evaluation of quality.

Quality Assurance Frameworks

There are several published frameworks or models of quality assurance that can be used for measuring and monitoring quality assurance. These include:

- The NHS Quality Framework
- Energise for Excellence
- Clinical governance
- Maxwell's elements of quality
- Donabedian's structure, process and outcome model.

NHS Quality Framework

'Quality assurance' refers to assuring the receiver of an identified degree of excellence of service, goods or standard of care that is continually monitored through actively sought relevant data. The level of achievement of quality is measured and actions are taken to correct identified deficiencies. *High Quality Care for All* (DH, 2008a) set out a seven-step framework for systematically addressing how to improve quality, as set out in Figure 5.4.

Figure 5.4   The NHS Quality Framework

Based on the seven steps of quality outlined in *High Quality Care for All* (DH, 2008a) and updated in *Quality in the New Health System* (DH, 2012h)

An overview of the steps included within the NHS Quality Framework is outlined below:

1   *Bring clarity to quality:* being clear about what high quality care looks like in all specialities and reflecting this in a coherent approach to the setting of standards.
2   *Measure quality:* measuring and understand exactly what we do in order to work out how to improve. Ensuring a quality measurement framework at every level.
3   *Publish quality performance:* making data on how well we are doing widely available to staff, patients and the public to help the understanding of variation and best practice and to focus on improvement.
4   *Recognise and reward quality:* The system should recognise and reward improvement in the quality of care and service. This means ensuring that the right incentives are in place to support quality improvement.
5   *Leadership for quality:* Quality is improved by empowered patients and empowered professionals. There must be a stronger role for clinical leadership and management throughout the NHS.
6   *Innovate for quality:* continuous quality improvement requires health services to search for and apply innovative approaches that are consistently and comprehensively applied across the system.
7   *Safeguard quality:* patients and the public need to be reassured that the NHS everywhere is providing high quality care and that essential standards of safety and quality are maintained.

Energise for Excellence

Energise for Excellence in Care (E4E) (DH, 2012c) is underpinned by 'social movement thinking' principles and provides a quality framework for nursing and midwifery that aims to support the delivery of safe and effective care, creating positive patient and staff experiences that build in momentum and sustainability. E4E brings together a number of improvement initiatives such as: High-impact Actions, Productive Care, Safety Express, and the Essence of Care. A number of these initiatives have been available for some time; however, E4E supports a pick-and-mix approach which offers healthcare providers a portfolio of tools to support improvement work in the five domains as shown in Figure 5.5. E4E now sits within the Chief Nursing Officer of England's Compassion in Practice Strategy.

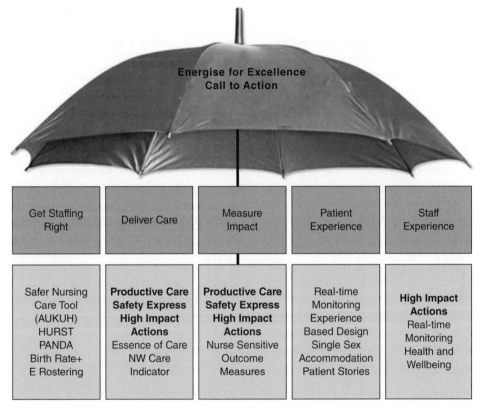

**Energise for Excellence
Call to Action**

Get Staffing Right	Deliver Care	Measure Impact	Patient Experience	Staff Experience
Safer Nursing Care Tool (AUKUH) HURST PANDA Birth Rate+ E Rostering	**Productive Care Safety Express High Impact Actions** Essence of Care NW Care Indicator	**Productive Care Safety Express High Impact Actions** Nurse Sensitive Outcome Measures	Real-time Monitoring Experience Based Design Single Sex Accommodation Patient Stories	**High Impact Actions** Real-time Monitoring Health and Wellbeing

Figure 5.5   Energise for Excellence (DH, 2012c)

Clinical governance

Clinical governance describes the structures, processes and culture needed to ensure that healthcare organisations and staff are continuously focusing on continuous improvement and can assure the quality of the care they provide (DH, 2011d). Clinical governance was developed to ensure accountability for the safe delivery of healthcare and can be viewed as an umbrella term for a number of key components that collectively combine to facilitate the delivery of safe, high quality care. The component parts are all equally relevant while also having an interdependent relationship. As identified by the Clinical Governance Support Team (2013), the component parts of clinical governance include:

- *Patient, public and carer involvement:* analysis of patient–professional involvement and interaction, and strategy, planning and delivery of care, as discussed in Chapter 9.
- *Strategic capacity and capability:* planning, communication and governance arrangements, and cultural behaviour aspects, as discussed in Chapter 1.
- *Risk management:* incident reporting, infection control, prevention and control of risk (discussed later in the chapter).
- *Staff management and performance:* recruitment, workforce planning, appraisals, as discussed in Chapter 7.
- *Education, training and CPD:* professional re-validation, management development, confidentiality and data protection, as discussed in Chapter 11.
- *Clinical effectiveness:* clinical audit management, planning and monitoring, learning through research and audit (discussed later in the chapter).
- *Information management:* patient records and other data (discussed later in the chapter).
- *Communication:* patient and public, external partners, internal, board and organisation-wide, as discussed in Chapters 1, 9 and 10.
- *Leadership:* throughout the organisation, including board, chair and non-executive directors, chief executive and executive directors, managers and clinicians, as discussed in Chapter 2.
- *Teamworking:* within the service, senior managers, clinical and MDT, and across organisations, as discussed in Chapter 10.

All these components are examined either in this chapter or in other chapters in this book as indicated. Key component parts of clinical governance such as audit, risk management, information management and benchmarking are discussed later in the chapter in the section on service improvement tools.

Maxwell's elements of quality

Maxwell (1984) identified six elements of quality as a quality assurance framework that should be contained within a quality monitoring cycle. Maxwell's model comprises three 'A's and three 'E's, whereupon once one quality cycle is completed a further cycle should begin straight after. The model comprises:

- *Acceptability:* providing a service that meets the reasonable expectations of the patients and stakeholders.
- *Accessibility:* the ease with which care interventions and services are accessible to the patient. Constraints to access may include distance, time and lack of knowledge.
- *Appropriateness:* providing a service which the individual or community actually needs.
- *Effectiveness:* the extent to which the intended benefits for the individual have been achieved.

- *Efficiency:* closely related to effectiveness and considers how resources are used.
- *Equity:* ensuring that everyone has equal access to the service being provided.

At clinical level, this framework can be used, say, in pain management. If, for instance, the care standard is that all patients should be pain-free within 10 minutes of complaining of pain, then Maxwell's model can be used to monitor whether:

- this standard is acceptable to the patient and the staff;
- they have access to the healthcare practitioners to obtain pain-relieving interventions;
- the means of pain relief is appropriate;
- the method of pain relief is effective and acceptable to both parties;
- the pain relief is administered efficiently; and
- all patients are afforded the *same standard* of care.

Donabedian's structure, process and outcome model

Another quality assurance framework devised by Donabedian (1988) is one that consists of three sets of criteria: structure, process and outcome. The Donabedian (1988) model is also discussed as a model of evaluation of change in Chapter 6.

Structure criteria

The setting in which care takes place include the people, equipment and the environment (resources), and therefore comprises:

- the physical environment and buildings;
- ancillary services – laundry, pharmacy, paramedical services, catering, laboratory services;
- equipment;
- staff numbers, skill mix, training, expertise;
- information – agreed policies and procedures, rules and regulations; and
- organisational system.

Process criteria

'Process refers' to the care given by healthcare practitioners, and therefore involves the actions of assessment, planning, implementation and evaluation (in partnership with patients and relatives where appropriate). It encompasses the knowledge held by the practitioner in:

- the assessment techniques used, and methods of delivery of care and intervention;
- the healthcare organisation's procedures and clinical guidelines;
- methods of patient, relative and/or carer education and information giving;
- methods of documenting; and
- ways in which resources are used.

Outcome criteria

The specific benefits or positive results experienced by the patient, which encompass indicators of patient outcomes such as health status, wound healing, patient satisfaction, immunisation uptake, patients' knowledge of their condition, behaviours such as successful use of equipment by patients, as well as evaluation of the competence of staff delivering care.

Quality Improvement

Quality improvement, applied to healthcare, encompasses adopting a systematic approach through the use of improvement methodologies and tools with the aim of improving outcomes related to clinical effectiveness, patient safety and patient experiences of their care. The various approaches are based on similar principles that are outlined in Box 5.1.

Box 5.1   Quality improvement principles

Current state: Looking at how things currently work and what the issues are.

Future state: Identifying how things might look in the future.

Tools: Selecting the improvement methods and tool/s.

Resources: Identifying and agreeing the other resources required to support the improvements in practice, e.g. staff and patient engagement.

Evaluation: Evaluating and measuring the impact of the change.

Sustainability: Monitoring the change to ensure outcomes continue to be achieved.

There are a range of quality improvement methods for the DCM, health and social care professionals and managers in healthcare to draw upon; from Total Quality Management – which was a favoured approach a few years ago – to more contemporary approaches such as Lean and Six Sigma, which have been adopted more recently from the manufacturing industries. Boaden et al. (2008) assert that the success of quality improvement is less dependent on the methodology and more dependent on the process of improvement itself. They identify that having an improvement model or method can make a significant difference to improving outcomes, but conclude that analysis of 'failure to deliver' improvements is less likely to be an issue with the tool or approach, but more a 'human dynamics' or 'leadership system'. When the DCM is leading a service improvement, therefore, it is important to both adopt a systematic approach to improvement through the application of a method and to focus on 'leading' the improvement.

Total quality management

Total Quality Management (TQM) provides a holistic approach to long-term success which aims to radically transform an organisation through progressive changes in attitudes, practices, structures and systems (BusinessDictionary.com, 2012). It does this by focusing on the customer; and through effective communication and involvement of all employees, it integrates quality within the activities and culture of the organisation. It is synonymous with continuous quality improvement and in a mature TQM organisation:

- everything is driven by its customers' needs;
- a highly trained and motivated workforce continually seeks better ways of working;
- change is based on measured fact and monitored in a continuous cycle of improvement;
- errors are relentlessly traced and eliminated; and
- hands-on management drives the quest for quality.

Quality improvement tools

As previously stated, a current priority for healthcare is to achieve high quality and efficient services. NHS Improving Quality (NHS IQ) has a central role to build improvement capability at scale across the NHS to enable delivery of transformational change. NHS IQ brings together elements of five former improvement organisations (National Cancer Action Team, National End of Life Care Programme, NHS Diabetes and Kidney Care, NHS Improvement, and the NHS Institute for Innovation and Improvement). The priorities for NHS IQ include supporting both the Outcomes Framework and the work of NHS England's Five Domains:

1 Prevention
2 Long-term Conditions
3 Acute Care
4 Patient Experience
5 Safety.

The Institute for Healthcare Improvement (IHI) is an independent, not-for-profit organisation based in Cambridge, Massachusetts, and is a leading innovator in health and healthcare improvement worldwide. IHI works in collaboration with improvement partners to invent and promulgate ideas that improve patient care. The IHI website contains information about a range of improvement tools, which can be accessed at www.ihi.org. Examples of service improvement techniques will now be explored.

The Plan, Do, Study, Act (PDSA) Cycle

The PDSA cycle, also known as the Deming Cycle, is a continuous quality improvement model based on sequences of four steps as illustrated in Figure 5.6 (also discussed in Chapter 6 as a model of implementation of change). The steps include:

- *Plan:* how you will implement the change and break it down into steps.
- *Do:* implement the plan.
- *Study (check):* study the results and outcomes.
- *Act:* standardise or further improve the process.

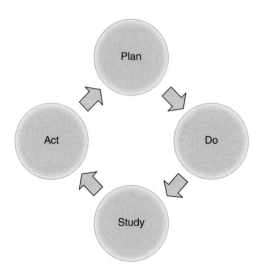

Figure 5.6   The PDSA cycle

Process mapping

Process mapping uses a workflow diagram to represent a process or series of parallel processes. The resultant process map can provide a clear picture of the activities performed, where they are undertaken and by whom. This enables the identification of bottlenecks that can be re-engineered to improve the process. Using the example of discharge planning, the process-mapper will develop a diagram that illustrates the various steps in the process. This enables the identification of delays; for example, the prescribing or dispensing of tablets to take out (TTOs). Re-engineering of the process could be achieved in a number of ways, such as the implementation of non-medical discharge, the use of a discharge lounge or the operation of a traffic light discharge system so that staff are aware of the discharge status of the patients within their care.

Metrics

Metrics provide parameters for quantitative assessment of the outcomes of a process in order to facilitate comparative analysis of results; for example, the number of patients who receive a Care Programme Approach (CPA) assessment within a defined period of time, or the number of patients who sustain a fall or pressure ulcer whilst in an in-patient setting.

Health and social care providers can identify their own metrics as part of their quality monitoring and quality assurance function. Quality metrics are also of importance to commissioners and form part of contract monitoring. Quality dashboards can be agreed that include a number of metrics to monitor the achievement of organisational performance and quality. Metrics employed within a quality dashboard could include:

- number of clinical incidents, e.g. falls, medication errors etc.;
- number of complaints; or
- percentage of patients who would recommend the service to family and friends.

Challenges can include deciding on what to measure and identifying metrics that will provide the best assurance regarding the quality of service delivery. Another challenge relates to data collection and minimising bureaucracy and impact on clinical time. Electronic clinical records can facilitate data collection and reduce the need for retrospective case note analysis for some metrics.

Benchmarking

Benchmarking is defined as 'The practice of being humble enough to admit that someone else is better at something and being wise enough to try to learn how to match and even surpass them at it' (Ellis, 1995: 25). Benchmarking encourages searching for examples of best practice from others engaged in similar practice.

Lean

In recent years, the NHS has adopted service improvement techniques that were developed in manufacturing, such as the Japanese car manufacturer Toyota. Lean is a management system that aims to maximise value through improving flow in the patient journey and eliminating all forms of waste. Waste can relate to anything that does not add value to a process. For example, 'waiting' could be for referrals, test results, TTOs, a ward round and so on. Another example of waste is transportation; this could include the moving of patients to other care areas for non-care reasons. A further key principle of Lean is the involvement of people in change and the redesign process.

Releasing Time to Care: Productive Ward

Within healthcare, comments often made by staff include 'there's not enough time' or 'we're short of staff'. A survey conducted by UNISON (2012) into staff/patient ratios on wards identified that 73 per cent of respondents did not feel that there were adequate staff numbers to deliver safe, dignified, compassionate care. There are a number of factors that impact on nurse staffing and subsequent outcomes for patients, these include: patient dependency, staffing numbers, registered to non-registered ratios, vacancies, sickness, use of bank and agency staff, and unfilled shifts. Ward staffing the *Releasing Time to Care: Productive Ward* programme is one of a series of productive programmes from the NHS III that uses improvement techniques, such as those already discussed, that have been tailor-made to enable nurses to improve upon key ward processes, with a resultant freeing-up of time that can be redirected into focusing on patient care delivery.

This approach to service improvement is based at grass-roots level and facilitates and empowers the care team to have ownership and take the lead. The Productive Ward programme also requires the commitment of the Trust Board to provide support to the care area throughout their quality improvement journey. The programme comprises a number of modules that include how to assess the readiness of the organisation to engage in this initiative, to preparing the ward, developing ward-based measures and the provision of information. Modules that focus on key processes for the practice setting to implement include drug administration, shift handovers and patient observations. Other areas included in the productive series include: Productive general practice, Productive leader, Productive mental health ward, Productive community hospital, Productive community services, and the Productive operating theatre.

Care bundles

The Institute for Health Improvement (2012) defines a care bundle as 'a structured way of improving the processes of care and patient outcomes: a small, straightforward set of evidence-based practices – generally three to five – that, when performed collectively and reliably, have been proven to improve patient outcomes'. Examples of care bundles featured in the IHI website include: central line bundle, ventilator bundle, sepsis management bundle, and induction and augmentation bundles.

'Root cause analysis' and the 'incident decision tree'

When incidents occur, it is important that lessons are learned both in the individual organisation and more widely across the NHS to prevent the same incident occurring elsewhere. Root cause analysis investigation is a well-recognised way of doing this. Root cause analysis is undertaken retrospectively and provides a methodology for the identification of causes of patient safety incidents, thereby enabling organisations to take action to prevent future occurrences. The National Patient Safety Agency (NPSA) developed a modular e-learning training programme that can be accessed on the NPSA website (www.npsa.nhs.uk).

The 'incident decision tree' has been designed by the NPSA for use following a patient safety incident. The decision tree is also available on the NPSA website. It takes the form of a flow chart that uses structured questions, and can be completed online within about 30 minutes.

Clinical audit

A clinical audit comprises a systematic assessment or estimation of the process or outcome of a care activity to determine whether it is:

- *Effective:* making progress towards particular goals.
- *Efficient:* achieving a particular target with the least effort.
- *Economic:* achieving a successful outcome with the minimum cost.

The audit measures what healthcare practitioners are doing against what they should be doing. It involves systematically looking at the procedures used for diagnosis, care and treatment, examining how associated resources are used, and investigates the effect care has on the outcome and quality of life for the patient (DH, 1993). Conversely, *research* is concerned with the identification of best practice, whereas *audit* establishes whether agreed best practice is being followed, and according to Smith (1992) 'Research is concerned with discovering the right thing to do; audit with ensuring that it is done right'. There are two types of audit:

- *Retrospective:* examines what happened after the episode of care has been completed.
- *Concurrent:* examines what is happening at the time it is taking place.

An example of a retrospective audit is the examination of case notes to establish compliance with standards of record keeping. An example of a concurrent audit is hand washing, where the auditor monitors the use of hand gel and hand washing at the point of care delivery.

A range of methods used to collect evidence about the quality of care in concurrent and retrospective audit is provided in Table 5.1.

Table 5.1 Audit data collection methods

Method	Concurrent	Retrospective
Observation	✓	—
Checklist	✓	✓
Documentation audit	✓	✓
Questionnaire	✓	✓
Interview	✓	✓
Case review	✓	✓

Risk management

Risk is part of everyday life and is similarly part and parcel of clinical practice. Throughout our daily lives we make a number of decisions that have an element of risk associated with them, such as crossing the road and driving our cars. Clinical risk management is a proactive approach that involves:

- risk identification;
- risk assessment;
- taking action to reduce the likelihood of the risk occurring; and
- monitoring the outcomes and reassessing the level of risk as appropriate.

A number of variables have been identified that have been included in risk assessment tools developed to assess risk of a particular issue happening. Examples include the assessed risk of developing pressure ulcers, developing a deep-vein thrombosis or sustaining a fall. The risk of a patient having a fall, for example, can be reduced by completing a validated risk assessment to establish the level of risk, together with an intervention plan commensurate with the level of risk identified. Interventions can include addressing both intrinsic and extrinsic factors. Intrinsic factors in this example can include co-morbidities, the presence of a cognitive impairment and polypharmacy, and extrinsic factors can include environmental factors such as wet floors and poor lighting.

Incident reporting is used as in integral part of quality assurance frameworks as a mechanism to monitor adverse events and near misses, to identify trends and to ensure that the organisation learns from the incidents that occur and is responsive to implement actions for risk reduction. The DCM has a responsibility to ensure that team members complete risk assessments as required and that any adverse incidents or near misses are reported in accordance with the policy of the employing organisation.

Sometimes care staff can consider incident reporting as bureaucratic and creating more paperwork. It is important that staff do not become complacent and that incidents are always reported, as this provides the opportunity for lessons to be learnt and actions taken to prevent reoccurrence. When completing an incident form it is important to record the impact on patient outcomes and care delivery, and also to get feedback on the outcome of the investigation in order to identify lessons learned and to strengthen practice.

Action point 5.2   Measuring quality of care

- Consider reasons why the quality of care provided within your practice setting needs to be measured.
- What methods are used to measure the quality of care delivered in your practice setting?

Monitoring Quality in Healthcare

Health and social care services are externally monitored to ensure that standards are achieved and outcomes are met. This monitoring function is provided in a number of ways, such as by Local Authorities (LAs), Clinical Commissioning Groups (CCGs), NHS England, the Care Quality Commission (CQC), and Monitor.

Care Quality Commission

The CQC is the independent regulator of health and social care services in England. Its role is to ensure that national standards of quality and safety are met by care providers, including hospitals, ambulances, GPs and other primary care services, mental health services, care homes and services provided in people's own homes.

CQC carry out unannounced inspections of services, which are undertaken on a routine basis and also in response to concerns. CQC has powers to enforce standards where it is identified that a provider is not meeting required standards. Enforcement action can range from issuing a warning notice requiring improvements, to suspending/cancelling the service's registration, or even prosecution. *The State of Health Care and Adult Social Care in England* (CQC, 2012), reported on CQC's findings regarding standards of care delivery in health and social care services in 2011/12.

Learning from the Inquiry into Failings at Mid Staffordshire NHS Foundation Trust

A Public Inquiry into the failings at the Mid Staffordshire NHS Foundation Trust (Francis, 2013) was commissioned in June 2010 by the then Secretary of State for

Health. The terms of reference were to

> examine the operation of the commissioning, supervisory and regulatory organisations and other agencies, including the culture and systems of those organisations in relation to their monitoring role at Mid Staffordshire NHS Foundation Trust between January 2005 and March 2009 and to examine why problems at the Trust were not identified sooner, and appropriate action taken.

The inquiry report builds on the findings of the first inquiry into the appalling standards of care and suffering of many patients at the Trust. The report identified a number of warning signs which, Francis stated, if considered cumulatively, or in some cases singly, could and should have alerted the system to the problems developing at the Trust. The causes Francis identified for this not having happened were due to:

- A culture focused on doing the system's business – not that of the patients;
- An institutional culture which ascribed more weight to positive information about the service than to information capable of implying cause for concern;
- Standards and methods of measuring compliance which did not focus on the effect of a service on patients;
- Too great a degree of tolerance of poor standards and of risk to patients;
- A failure of communication between the many agencies to share their knowledge of concerns;
- Assumptions that monitoring, performance management or intervention was the responsibility of someone else;
- A failure to tackle challenges to the building up of a positive culture, in nursing in particular but also within the medical profession; and
- A failure to appreciate until recently the risk of disruptive loss of corporate memory and focus resulting from repeated, multi-level reorganisation.

Francis concluded that there is need for a fundamental change in culture and made 290 recommendations centred on a number of themes:

1. Fostering a common culture shared by all in the service of putting the patient first;
2. Developing a set of fundamental standards, easily understood and accepted by patients, the public and healthcare staff, the breach of which should not be tolerated;
3. Providing professionally endorsed and evidence-based means of compliance with these fundamental standards which can be understood and adopted by the staff who have to provide the service;
4. Ensuring openness, transparency and candour throughout the system about matters of concern;
5. Ensuring that the relentless focus of the healthcare regulator is on policing compliance with these standards; and
6. Making all those who provide care for patients – individuals and organisations – properly accountable for what they do and to ensure that the public is protected from those not fit to provide such a service.

Creating a culture of quality

Organisational culture relates to the way in which the collective group of people who belong to the organisation go about their work. This includes the shared values, norms, beliefs, and assumptions; organisational culture is often referred to as 'the way we do things around here'. The literature on organisational culture also makes reference to the presence of subcultures that can exist both within organisations and occupational groups. An example of which could be differences between the shared values and beliefs of nursing staff compared to therapists, and also those that may exist between different clinical areas or departments. Davies and Mannion (2013) contend that healthcare organisational cultures are 'manifold, complex and dynamic' and suggest a degree of caution in respect of the concept of 'cultural uniformity' and the 'cultural prescription' recommended by Francis. They assert that this cultural diagnosis needs to reflect the array and depth of cultural diversity.

A starting point in creating a culture of quality is to review and understand the culture that is already in existence. A review of quantitative instruments to measure culture and cultural change (Scott et al., 2003), identified that singular attempts to define and measure organisational culture are inappropriate and the authors therefore advocate the use of a multi-methodology and tools. The 'Cultural Barometer' is a tool that has been designed to test the culture of care. The tool is intended to be used as a 'reflective developmental tool' that also supports cross-organisational benchmarking (National Nursing Research Unit, 2013). The design is intended to be non-bureaucratic and simplistic, and is underpinned by four themes that have been linked to staff commitment, engagement and productivity, namely:

- The resources to deliver quality care;
- The support needed to do a good job;
- A worthwhile job that offers the chance to develop; and
- The opportunity to improve team working.

Action Point 5.3   Organisational culture

Think about the culture of care in your organisation; write down a brief description of how you would describe to a friend the culture of:

1. Your organisation as a whole;
2. Your team/department ;and
3. Another team/department within your organisation with which you are familiar.

(Continued)

(Continued)

Consider any similarities and differences between your three descriptions, together with any trends, and analyse the possible reasons for these. You may find it helpful to look at your department, team and organisation from somewhat 'fresh eyes'. You could do this by observing some or all of the following:

- Interactions between colleagues and patients;
- The type and tone of communications e.g. e-mail, team briefings, staff meetings, etc.;
- Interactions between the manager and team members.

Do you consider the culture to be patient-focused? Now think about what you might like to change and how you can influence and implement positive change. You may find it helpful to refer to Chapters 3 and 6.

Patient safety

Patient safety represents an important element in the quality equation; patients who access healthcare services want to be protected from coming to any harm. Healthcare associated infections present healthcare providers with a major challenge. Minimising the incidence of infections such as MRSA and Clostridium difficile (C. diff), for example, require commitment from Board level and beyond. The DCM has a responsibility to ensure that staff and visitors to the care area adhere to policies, procedures and protocols related to the prevention of cross-infection.

The Annual Report 2005 of the Chief Medical Officer (DH, 2006b) made parallels between aviation and healthcare in relation to safety. The report highlighted how 2004 was the safest year for air travel, with the number of worldwide fatalities mirroring those of 1945. The improvement to safety relates to the rise in the number of passengers from 9 million to 1.8 billion per annum respectively. Conclusions drawn by the Chief Medical Officer from the comparative analysis of aviation and healthcare approaches to safety identified a number of key elements to the success of aviation, namely:

- clear goal setting;
- the collection of data that are useful and used to enable everyone to understand what is being looked for and the changes that are necessary;
- comprehensive and multifaceted approaches to risk management that focus upon the important issues;
- building a safety culture that is owned by everyone in the organisation; and
- oversight, monitoring and clear accountabilities for action.

A pilot study into adverse events in hospitalised patients in the United Kingdom identified the proportion of in-patient episodes leading to harmful adverse events to be 10 per cent, of which it was estimated that half were preventable (Vincent, 2000).

National Health Service Litigation Authority

The National Health Service Litigation Authority (NHSLA) was established in 1995 as a Special Health Authority and is the NHS body that has responsibility for handling negligence claims made against the NHS. In 2011/12, the NHSLA received 9,143 claims (including potential claims) under its clinical negligence schemes and 4,618 claims (including potential claims) in respect of its non-clinical schemes (NHSLA, 2012a). The functions of the NHSLA (2012b) are to:

- ensure claims are dealt with consistently and with due regard to the proper interests of the NHS and its patients;
- manage the financial consequences of such claims and to advise the Department of Health of the likely future costs;
- advise the Department of Health on both specific and general issues arising out of claims against the NHS;
- manage and raise the standards of risk management throughout the NHS;
- assist NHS bodies to comply with the Human Rights Act by providing a central source of information on relevant case-law development;
- provide mechanisms for the proper, prompt and cost-effective resolution of disputes between NHS primary care organisations and those providing, or seeking to provide, services for patients; and
- provide advice about, and assistance with, litigation concerning equal pay and age discrimination claims involving NHS bodies in England.

The Patient Experience

As mentioned earlier, patients have rising expectations of healthcare which relate to their overall experiences as well as to the clinical outcome of their care. There is a need to focus on continuously improving the patient experience and to understand what is important to patients. Sizmur and Redding (2009) identified the following eight domains of patient-centred healthcare that are of highest value to patients. The domains are derived from accumulated research, experience and analysis in North America and Europe, and which the authors assert apply across various care settings. The domains are:

1 Fast access to reliable health advice.
2 Effective treatment delivered by trusted professionals.
3 Involvement in decisions and respect for preferences.
4 Clear, comprehensible information and support for self-care.
5 Attention to physical and environmental needs.
6 Emotional support, empathy and respect.
7 Involvement of, and support for, family and carers.
8 Continuity of care and smooth transitions.

NICE (2012) has developed a quality standard that aims to provide the NHS with clear commissioning guidance on the components of a good patient experience. The quality standard includes evidence-based statements for commissioners that set out a foundation for what NICE describe as an 'NHS cultural shift' towards a truly patient-centred service. The quality standard includes 14 quality statements together with associated outcome measures and implementation tools.

An important part of the patient experience is treating patients with dignity and respect. Figure 5.7 sets out the dignity model developed by Galloway (2011) and is based on principles that support the delivery of dignified care.

The patient experience is a key component of the quality equation and patient involvement, participation and partnership is a central part of this. This will be addressed further in Chapter 9.

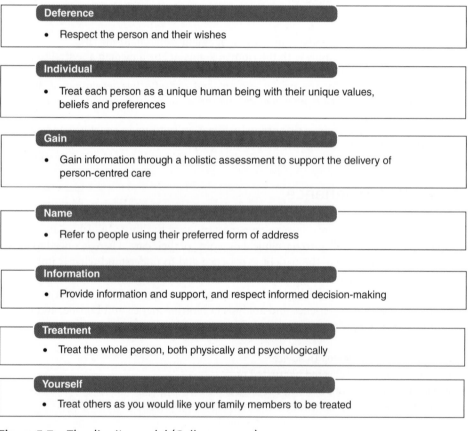

Deference
- Respect the person and their wishes

Individual
- Treat each person as a unique human being with their unique values, beliefs and preferences

Gain
- Gain information through a holistic assessment to support the delivery of person-centred care

Name
- Refer to people using their preferred form of address

Information
- Provide information and support, and respect informed decision-making

Treatment
- Treat the whole person, both physically and psychologically

Yourself
- Treat others as you would like your family members to be treated

Figure 5.7   The dignity model (Galloway, 2011)

Patient satisfaction surveys

The CQC co-ordinates the completion of a number of national surveys to collect feedback on the experiences of people using a range of healthcare services provided by the NHS. CQC use the results in a variety of ways, including the assessment of

NHS performance together with regulatory activities such as registration and compliance monitoring. Survey results are accessible on the CQC website and provide a useful opportunity for providers to access benchmarked results about their organisation and similarly provide helpful information for patients, care providers and commissioners. The surveys provide a useful snapshot at a moment in time, but do not provide 'real time' data as results are not usually published for a number of months following the actual delivery of care.

The CQC surveys include adult in-patients, community mental health, A&E, maternity services and outpatients. The 2012 A&E survey (CQC, 2012), for example, highlighted that 33 per cent of respondents spent more than four hours in A&E – up from 27 per cent in 2008 and 23 per cent in 2004. The survey also identified that the majority of respondents said they had confidence and trust in the doctors and nurses working in A&E departments.

Action point 5.4   Organisational and practice setting performance

How aware are you regarding how your organisation fares in relation to performance and quality outcomes?

- Log on to the CQC website (www.cqc.org.uk) and access the results from the CQCs latest check on your organisation.
- Now look at the results of any surveys undertaken by the CQC that relate to your organisation, e.g. in-patient survey. Consider overall how well your organisation has performed together with how it compares nationally.

Now consider your practice setting, and the information that you routinely receive to keep you appraised of how your team is performing. Look at the following list of sources of information; if you do not already have access to this information then ask your manager, who should be able to make it available to you:

- Complaints data and individual letters of complaint.
- Number of 'thank you' letters and commendations.
- Number of incidents reported.
- Performance data, e.g. waiting times, length of stay, finance.
- Quality outcomes, e.g. healthcare associated infection incidence, results of quality audits, local patient satisfaction survey results, and 'Friends and Family Test' results.

Once you have located the information, have a look through and compare it to other practice settings within your organisation to deduce how well your practice setting performed. From studying the results, can you identify any recurring themes or key areas where you consider your practice setting can improve? If so, think about the actions that you and your colleagues can take to make a positive difference. Is this type of information routinely discussed at team briefings and departmental meetings? If not, you may want to discuss the benefits of doing so with your manager.

Improving patient experiences of their care

In addition to patient satisfaction surveys, another consideration of the patient experience of health and social care is to identify ways in which care practitioners can improve patient experiences of their care.

Action point 5.5   Patient priorities

Consider if you were a patient what your top 10 priorities would be? Once you have identified your priority areas, reflect upon how your practice setting or service measures up in matching your priorities. Ask yourself the Friends and Family Test Question: Would you recommend your service to a friend or family member? If not, why not?

Do you consider there to be any scope for improvement/further improvement? If so, think about the management and leadership principles and models that have been discussed in Chapters 2 and 3, and how you can use these within your role as DCM to improve and monitor the patient experience within your practice setting.

Complaints

Complaints provide a further means for health and social care services to receive feedback from their patients regarding the quality of services that they receive. Complaints arise where the standard of service received by a patient or their relatives/carer falls below the standard expected. Arguably, every patient has the right to expect a good service from both care practitioners and the services from which they receive their care.Complainants often state that they want other people to benefit from their experiences by ensuring that the same mistakes do not happen again. Services need to learn from the experiences of complainants and take steps to ensure that root causes are addressed and remedied. In some instances the area requiring focus may be restricted to an individual service, whereas in others organisation-wide changes may need to be made to policies, processes and systems.

A framework of principles has been developed by the Parliamentary and Health Service Ombudsman (2012a) with the aim of providing statements of what public bodies should achieve to ensure good administration and customer focus. The principles identified include:

- Getting it right
- Being customer focused
- Being open and accountable
- Acting fairly and proportionately
- Putting things right
- Seeking continuous improvement.

The Local Authority Social Services and National Health Service Complaints (England) Regulations 2009 provide the statutory basis for the approach to complaints handling in health and social care. This is supported by the publication of guidance entitled *Listening, Responding, Improving: A Guide to Better Customer Care* (DH, 2009), which emphasises how complaints handling is part of a broader initiative to improve patient care in health and social care organisations.

Action point 5.6   Responding to a complaint

Ask your manager for a copy of a letter of complaint, together with a copy of the response that was forwarded to the complainant. Read the complaint and make a note of the issues raised. Think about the issues and identify any emerging themes, for example 'communication', within which to categorise the key areas raised.

Now read the letter of response to the complainant. What lessons can be learnt from the complaint? What actions can be implemented within the care area to ensure that the key issues are addressed? What actions could be implemented organisation-wide to address the issues identified?

Whistle-blowing

The DCM as a health or social care practitioner has a duty of care to his/her patients, and needs to work within the code of conduct governed by their respective professional body. The NHS Constitution (DH, 2012d) also places a responsibility on NHS staff to raise concerns at the earliest reasonable opportunity about a risk, malpractice or wrongdoing at work (such as a risk to patient safety, fraud or breaches of patient confidentiality), which could affect patients, the public, other staff or the organisation itself.

There are a number of mechanisms available to the DCM to raise any concerns that they may have about patient safety and standards and quality of care. These can include raising issues at team meetings, discussing concerns with their line manager, completing clinical incident reports and so on. Whistle-blowing provides a further avenue to raise issues of concern; however, other avenues should be used first as appropriate. You may want to contact your trade union organisation to ask for advice, or alternatively, confidential advice, guidance and signposting can be accessed from http://wbhelpline.org.uk.

The Public Interest Disclosure Act (1998) provides statutory protection for employees who disclose information in the public interest and are victimised because of this. The Health Service Circular 1999/198 (DH, 1999a) places a responsibility on Trusts to have in place local policies and procedures that comply with the Public Interest Disclosure Act (1998). This includes the identification of a designated senior manager with responsibility to address concerns that are raised in confidence, together with a commitment that concerns raised will be investigated and taken seriously.

Procedures, Protocols and Clinical Guidelines for Quality Care

Procedures, protocols and clinical guidelines are examples of quality and service improvement tools that can be used to support the delivery of high quality healthcare based on the best available evidence. Confusion can exist regarding the differences between the three approaches and the terminology is sometimes used interchangeably.

Procedures

The term 'procedure' refers to care interventions that are constituted as step-by-step actions to be followed when performing a particular care activity. Examples of procedures include:

- Hand washing
- Intra muscular injection
- Taking physiological measurements such as blood pressure
- Mouth care/oral hygiene.

In health and social care, procedures provide a mechanism to standardise practice and also allow staff to take an individualised, holistic and evidence-based approach to care. Procedures can cover a range of skills that can be performed from novice to competent, and to expert practice levels. Some are expanded role activities that involve specialist training, assessment, supervised practice and competency based assessment.

Protocols

Protocols outline the steps to be taken in a given situation, or how to care for and treat patients with a defined clinical condition or health need. The latter are sometimes referred to as 'integrated care pathways' and can be locally designed to implement national standards or, in the absence of national standards, determine care provision based on the best available evidence (NHS III, 2008b).

Protocols provide a framework for multi-disciplinary teamwork and support reduction in variation in patient care and subsequent improvement in care quality by standardising practice. Map of Medicine can be used to support care pathway development at local level; providing a collection of evidence-based care maps which amalgamate knowledge and services regarding clinical conditions (Map of Medicine, 2012). Examples of protocols include confidentiality and information sharing, and the Liverpool Care Pathway (Marie Curie Palliative Care Institute, 2012) is an example of an integrated care pathway.

Clinical guidelines

Clinical guidelines comprise recommendations for care and treatment based on a systematic appraisal of the best available evidence. Guidelines support healthcare professionals in their decision-making, but they do not replace their knowledge, skills and expertise. Examples of clinical guidelines for healthcare professionals at local organisational level can include:

- Defibrillation
- Suturing
- Drug administration
- Radiological requests by non-medical healthcare practitioners
- Wound management.

When developing a clinical guideline, the healthcare practitioner should ensure that they address the following:

- A lead clinician is identified for the clinical guideline.
- A clearly identified rationale is recorded.
- The guideline is evidence-based.
- The development process includes input from the various groups of staff that will be required to use the guideline.
- The guideline is ratified in accordance with the ratification process of the respective organisation.
- The guideline supports person-centred care.
- The guideline includes mechanisms for monitoring, e.g. audit.
- A review date is agreed, together with the opportunity to amend prior to the review date if necessary.

Clinical guidelines can be presented as algorithms, which are informative and concise, but might not include enough breadth and depth of information. Therefore a descriptive format might be used with summary points and concluding statements. They are usually constituted through a bottom-up approach in that they are initiated and devised by specialists in the particular care area. NICE develop evidence-based guidelines that aim to provide the most effective ways to diagnose, treat and prevent disease and ill health, and support healthcare professionals and others to provide both quality and value for money.

NICE provides a range of services and products including interventional procedures, technology appraisals, clinical guidelines and public health guidance. Nice also provide NHS Evidence, an online portal which provides access to a range of information and best practice.

The NHS Executive (1996) identified criteria that can be used to appraise clinical guidelines:

- Valid
- Reproducible
- Reliable
- Cost-effective
- Representative
- Clinical applicability

- Flexible
- Clear
- Reviewable
- Amenable to clinical audit.

Procedures, protocols and clinical guidelines are essential resources at the disposal of the DCM to support the delivery of care of a high standard, but they need to be regularly appraised for their evidence base.

Safeguarding

Safeguarding is everyone's responsibility and is fundamental to the achievement of high quality health and social care. 'Safeguarding means protecting people's health, wellbeing and human rights, and enabling them to live free from harm, abuse and neglect' (CQC, 2013). Health and social care organisations, together with individual health and social care professionals, have a responsibility to ensure that people in vulnerable circumstances are not only safe, but also receive the highest possible standards of care. There are statutory requirements to safeguard children; the same key principles of which apply to safeguarding adults. Individual health and social care practitioners need to ensure that they attend mandatory training and access other training pertinent to meeting their safeguarding responsibilities and individual learning needs. They also need to meet their responsibilities as outlined within the policies and procedures within their respective organisations. Managers must additionally ensure that staff are aware of and able to access policies; staff undertake the required mandatory training; and that safeguarding policies are implemented and monitored within their line of responsibility and accountability.

Safeguarding Children

High profile examples of child abuse include the murder of Victoria Climbié by her guardians in 2000; the death of 17-month-old Peter Connolly ('Baby P') in 2007; and more recently the alleged sexual abuse, predominantly the abuse of children, by Jimmy Savile, the British media personality who died in 2011. Analysis of independent reviews into such cases, together with root causes identified within Serious Case Reviews and Multi Agency Case File Audits, etc. provide valuable opportunities for learning which can be used to inform and strengthen government policy, together with local policies, procedures and inter-agency working practices.

What is the difference between 'safeguarding' and 'child protection'?

According to the Department for Education (2013), safeguarding and promoting the welfare of children is defined as:

- protecting children from maltreatment
- preventing impairment of children's health or development
- ensuring children are growing up in circumstances consistent with the provision of safe and effective care.

Child protection as defined by the Department of Education (2013) relates to the activity that is undertaken to protect specific children who are suffering, or are likely to suffer, significant harm and is therefore a part of safeguarding and promoting welfare.

Working Together to Safeguard Children: A Guide to Inter-agency Working to Safeguard and Promote the Welfare of Children (HM Government, 2013) sets out how organisations and individuals should work together to safeguard and promote the welfare of children. The statutory guidance provides clarification on core legal requirements, and aims to set out more clearly what individuals and organisations should do to keep children safe and promote their welfare. The guidance is designed to provide a national framework within which agencies and professionals at local level, both individually and collectively, can use as a point of reference to inform the development and implementation of more locally agreed ways of working together to safeguard and promote the welfare of children.

Safeguarding Adults

High profile examples of the abuse of adults at risk include the institutional abuse of patients at Budock Hospital in Cornwall between 2000 and 2005; and more recently the physical and psychological abuse suffered by people with learning disabilities at Winterbourne View Private Hospital which was broadcast by Panorama in 2011. 'Adult at risk' relates to adults who need community care services because of mental or other disability, age or illness and who are, or may be, unable to take care of themselves against significant harm or exploitation (SCIE, 2011). According to SCIE (2013),

> those who need safeguarding help are often elderly and frail, living on their own in the community, or without much family support in care homes. They are often people with physical or learning disabilities and people with mental health needs at risk of suffering harm both in institutions and in the community.

Abuse is defined as 'a violation of an individual's human and civil rights by any other person or persons' (DH, 2000e). Consensus definitions of the different forms of abuse as outlined in *No Secrets* (DH, 2000e) are:

- physical abuse, including hitting, slapping, pushing, kicking, misuse of medication, restraint, or inappropriate sanctions;
- sexual abuse, including rape and sexual assault or sexual acts to which the vulnerable adult has not consented, or could not consent or was pressured into consenting;
- psychological abuse, including emotional abuse, threats of harm or abandonment, deprivation of contact, humiliation, blaming, controlling, intimidation, coercion, harassment, verbal abuse, isolation or withdrawal from services or supportive networks;

- financial or material abuse, including theft, fraud, exploitation, pressure in connection with wills, property or inheritance or financial transactions, or the misuse or misappropriation of property, possessions or benefits;
- neglect and acts of omission, including ignoring medical or physical care needs, failure to provide access to appropriate health, social care or educational services, the withholding of the necessities of life, such as medication, adequate nutrition and heating; and
- discriminatory abuse, including racist, sexist, that based on a person's disability, and other forms of harassment, slurs or similar treatment.

The Department of Health (2013b) set out six key principles of safeguarding:

- **Empowerment** – Presumption of person led decisions and informed consent.
- **Protection** – Support and representation for those in greatest need.
- **Prevention** – It is better to take action before harm occurs.
- **Proportionality** – Proportionate and least intrusive response appropriate to the risk presented.
- **Partnership** – Local solutions through services working with their communities. Communities have a part to play in preventing, detecting and reporting neglect and abuse.
- **Accountability** – Accountability and transparency in delivering safeguarding.

All staff working in health and social care organisations must acquaint themselves with their roles and responsibilities in relation to safeguarding and protection. DCMs and managers must also ensure that relevant policies are adhered to and information brought to the attention of and shared with other professionals and agencies as per agreed information sharing protocols and in the best interests of patients and service users. Good practice guidelines should also be followed in respect of 'consent' and the differences in requirements for example between making a safeguarding alert and reporting domestic abuse.

Good practice guidelines

Good practice guidelines to support the achievement of high quality care are:

- Monitor and review the quality performance of your practice setting in relation to identified quality metrics and compare performance against that of other practice settings within your organisation.
- Discuss quality and safety issues as part of team handover and meetings, and explore ways that quality can be further improved within your practice setting.
- As you go about your day-to-day activities, ask patients about their experiences and whether they have any suggestions regarding how care could be improved.
- Ensure a high standard of record keeping within your practice setting.
- Monitor team members' compliance with policies, procedures and guidelines.
- Complete risk assessments and document interventions to reduce the likelihood of risk occurring.

- Complete clinical incident reports to report clinical incidents and near misses.
- When leading a service improvement, use a service improvement method/tool and review progress regularly; reflect on your leadership and look at how you can strengthen your approach as required.

As explored within the chapter, the DCM has an important role in improving and assuring quality of care delivery and patient safety within the practice setting. Quality assurance frameworks such as clinical governance provide a framework for quality assurance within healthcare, the various component parts of which are explored throughout the chapters within the book. The DCM also has a key role in ensuring that the patient experience is a positive one and that customer care principles are applied within the practice setting.

The DCM needs to act as a champion and role model for quality and safety and to ensure that policies, procedures and guidelines are followed and standards of care are maintained and improved upon. This chapter has therefore addressed:

- quality as a concept together with the three interrelated domains of patient safety, clinical effectiveness and patient experience;
- examples of quality assurance frameworks, namely the NHS quality assurance framework, clinical governance, Maxwell's elements of quality and Donabedian's structure, process and outcome model;
- patient safety and the roles of organisations that have identified roles in relation to quality improvement, assurance and/or regulation of healthcare;
- service improvement techniques, including process mapping, metrics, 'lean', root cause analysis, plan-do-study-act cycles, and benchmarking;
- the patient experience and mechanisms to analyse and support improvements such as patient satisfaction surveys;
- the application of evidence-based practice through the use of protocols and clinical guidelines to support the delivery of high quality care; and
- a collation of good practice guidelines for the DCM to employ to support the delivery of high quality healthcare.

CHAPTER SUMMARY

Maben J, Morrow E, Ball J, Robert G, Griffiths P (2012) *High Quality Care Metrics for Nursing*. London: National Nursing Research Unit, King's College London.

RECOMMENDED FURTHER READING

6

MANAGING CHANGE AND INNOVATION IN PRACTICE SETTINGS

Change is a necessary feature of all forward-looking organisations. Health and social care organisations in particular are subject to ongoing change as an inevitable necessity, and for a number of unavoidable reasons, change is also ubiquitous. This chapter explores why change occurs in the work settings of care organisations and the DCM's role in managing change, including initiating, participating in and influencing change, and also evaluating its impact and sustaining the change.

Chapter objectives

On completion of this chapter you will be able to:

- identify various changes that impact on commissioning, delivery and outcomes of care;
- ascertain the reasons for change in health and social care, their impact in care settings and the significance of the management of change;
- explain in detail how to manage change systematically using a well-informed change management framework; and
- demonstrate how you have developed your skills in the management of change.

Changes in Treatment and Care

Changes in health and social care professionals' care interventions are often initiated by new evidence and are usually related to assuring or enhancing quality of care provision and delivery, as discussed in Chapter 5, or the need to ensure value for money and increase productivity. It is frequently also driven by specified outcomes for the NHS set by government reforms and directives, and local policies determined by care commissioners and care providers. Other reasons for change include new and more effective technology, research and rising consumer expectations.

Action point 6.1   Changes in the way health and social care is practised

Reflect on how care is currently delivered to patients and service users in your workplace, and identify aspects of care delivery that have changed recently, that is, over the last few weeks, a month, or even year.

Next, identify an aspect of practice in your work setting that you consider would benefit from change. This may be in relation to a research article that you have read recently or discussion with colleagues regarding perhaps a new way of resolving an issue, or an innovation that you came across at a study day or conference.

You should have been able to identify a few examples of changes or developments in the ways in which health or social care is provided or delivered in your practice setting. A number of examples of such changes are identified in Box 6.1.

Box 6.1   Examples of changes affecting care delivery

- Early warning score (EWS) systems for deteriorating patients
- Meals served on a colour-coded tray to identify patients who require support at meal times
- Cardio-pulmonary resuscitation (CPR) techniques
- Cognitive behaviour therapy for depressive illnesses and psychological problems
- Non-medical prescribing, e.g. nurse prescribing
- Increased health education by practice nurses to empower patients and enhance self-care
- Treatment of leg ulcers – using Doppler technique
- Health MOTs for people over 75
- Non-medical practitioners ordering X-rays and other diagnostic tests
- Needle-safe devices
- Zero tolerance of violent or aggressive behaviour by patients or their visitors

---

There are specific adaptations of 'early warning score'(EWS) mentioned in Box 6.1, and is at times referred to as 'modified early warning score' (MEWS). With regard to another two items in Box 6.1, for instance, the latest cardio-pulmonary resuscitation (CPR) guidelines published by the Resuscitation Council (2010) changed adult basic life support resuscitation from the previous protocol to continuous chest compressions, or 30 chest compressions to two rescue breaths. For needle safe devices, this is also a relatively recent development that is deliberately designed to sample blood safely, avoid needle stick injuries, prevent cross-infection and also provide extra comfort for both patients and professionals (Morton Medical Limited, 2004). Examples of recent changes in the organisation or management of care include:

- Assistive technology in health and social care.
- Single assessment process (SAP) and common assessment process (CAP).
- Virtual wards.
- Electronic records.
- Team midwifery and the development of the CSW role in midwifery.
- NHS Safety Thermometer.
- Introducing new shift patterns.
- Integrated care pathways (ICP).
- Care bundles.
- Outreach work.
- Quality assurance programmes, such as electronic patient satisfaction monitoring.
- Allowing parents to be present in the anaesthetic room.
- Intermediate care services.
- Walk-in centres.
- The modern matron role.
- Same-sex accommodation in in-patient settings.

With the use of assistive technology, for example, people with increasingly complex health and social care needs can be supported to have their needs met in their own home, where previously they may have required monitoring in an in-patient setting or to experience 24-hour care. Similarly, prior to the SAP, care practitioners in acute, community and social care sectors would individually conduct assessments to identify health or social needs of older people, rather than one care professional undertaking a generic assessment that can be used as a foundation assessment by all. This supports subsequent care planning so that it is more effective, efficient, co-ordinated, thorough and accurate, but without procedures being needlessly duplicated by different agencies.

Changes usually occur in response to a number of drivers or catalysts, which in addition to the reasons mentioned earlier in this chapter include evaluation of services, complaints and suggestions, local systematically implemented initiatives (e.g. those by NHS III 2008a, 2008b), and rising public expectations based on information from peers and the media or the Internet. At times, changes occur naturally in practice settings. However, implementers of change also need to consider when the time is right for the change to be introduced, taking into account other initiatives, other changes that are already being implemented, and additional staff members if and as required. Changes can be implemented at organisational level, or team or individual level in the care setting.

Change can also be differentiated from innovation in that a change occurs to something that is already established, and can mean developing the care activity by adding extra dimensions, substituting aspects of the activity, or even reverting to an older (but effective) mode of practice. 'Innovation' refers to the introduction of a new method of care delivery, or area of care provision that is relatively unprecedented.

Why Changes in Health and Social Care, and Why the Management of Change?

Change is essential for improvement and enhancement of health and social care services, and for the change to be successful it needs to be managed and implemented systematically (i.e. as a step-by-step plan of actions).

Why changes in health and social care?

One of the prominent reasons for the DCM requiring expertise in the management of change is that the manager's role includes change management as identified under the 'Caregiver and practice developer' role in Table 2.2, and in Mintzberg's (1990) management role theory as 'entrepreneurial roles' (also noted in Chapter 2), which in turn implies implementing tested ideas and innovating. Thus change is closely related to practice development, which is discussed shortly. Furthermore, changes in health and social care provision are firmly based on the expectations of the users of the service, as well as on prevailing socio-economic circumstances and policies.

With increasing focus on public health (i.e. the prevention of health problems and management of longer term health problems), another reason for change is the encouragement for nurses to develop as 'nurse entrepreneurs', whose venture is to initiate new care interventions that benefit specific groups of individuals in society, or patients or service users. Such enterprises are highlighted in journal articles, reports and guidelines such as by the RCN (2007) and Liefer (2005). Examples of such enterprises include offering teenage parents one-to-one support during and after pregnancy (Nursing Standard News, 2009), and encouraging reluctant communities to access diagnosis and management of longer-term conditions such as type 2 diabetes (Mooney, 2008).

Additionally, Drennan (2007) reports on a study that explored nurse, midwife and health visitor entrepreneurship in the United Kingdom, from which she devised a typology of entrepreneurs. In the first category of the typology, Drennan distinguishes between entrepreneurs and intrapreneurs, the latter focusing on innovation and change in practice pioneered by the organisation's own employees. The second category comprises 'infrastructure services' such as non-medical consultants, independent healthcare practitioners and inventors. In the third category are, for instance, primary care services such as non-medical services including complementary therapists and nurse–GP partners. Entrepreneurship is publicised and advocated in various DH documents such as *National Search for New Ideas to Improve the Lives of People with Dementia* (DH, 2011e).

Evidence-based Healthcare

One of the key triggers for changes in care delivery is evidence-based healthcare (EBHC), which is defined by one of its pioneers as an approach to decision-making in which the care practitioner uses the 'best evidence' available for making clinical decisions (Gray, 2001), and evidence-based practice (EBP). Thus without the availability of evidence, or the use of those that are available, practice risks becoming out of date, and therefore less safe, very quickly. There are five key elements of EBHC, namely:

1 Decisions are based on best evidence.
2 Nature and sources of evidence are determined by the health problem.
3 Best evidence integrates research and personal experience.
4 Evidence is translated into action so that it affects patients' or service users' health and wellbeing positively.
5 These actions are continually appraised.

There are differences between the overlapping terms EBHC, EBP and others such as evidence-based medicine (EBM). EBHC tends to refer to groups of patients and the management of longer-term conditions, for instance, whereas EBP refers to single care interventions. Other concepts such as EBM refer purely to medical practice, but are broader generic terms that have practice implications for the specific profession. Evidence-based social work, evidence-based management, evidence-based education and evidence-based assessment of competence are also well documented in the health and social care literature.

There are a number of possible sources of evidence that can support improvements in care. These include:

• Randomised controlled trials (RCT)
• Qualitative studies
• Personal experience
• Personal intuition
• Policy directives (from local sources/central/ local government legislation)

- Textbooks
- Own professional education
- Clinical guidelines
- The patient or service user/their family
- Colleagues/other professionals
- Trial and error
- Suppliers' information
- Journal articles
- Online references
- Unpublished evidence
- Overview of evidence by specific topic (i.e. critical appraisals).

The Cochrane Library and NHS Evidence, which are accessible via the Internet or library databases at the local university or NHS Trust, are usually the nearest means of accessing published sources of evidence. The evidence available can be categorised as grades or levels of evidence to identify the strength of evidence supporting the care intervention. In broad terms, five levels of evidence can be identified, namely (see Glossary for brief explanation of some of the following terminology):

- *Level 1:* very strong evidence based on a critical appraisal of several well-designed RCTs.
- *Level 2:* evidence based on at least one well-designed RCT.
- *Level 3:* evidence from several quantitative studies (e.g. experiments, action research, surveys etc.).
- *Level 4:* conclusions from one well-designed quantitative study or from qualitative studies (e.g. case studies, focus groups or individual interviews).
- *Level 5:* conclusions drawn by specialist and experts in the field and in authoritative organisations.

When applying evidence to practice, the patient or service user needs to be provided with the relevant information to enable them to make an informed choice. A systematic review of randomised controlled trials may represent the 'gold standard', but this option may not be the preferred choice for the patient.

Practice Development

Consider the developments in care provision that are currently occurring in your particular area of practice, and the changes that have been made recently, or can be made to specific care and treatments in your care setting, or by your team. Change and innovation in patient-related clinical practice is also known as 'clinical practice development'. This concept therefore refers to changing the way particular care interventions are performed, or for providing (or instituting) new healthcare services for patients. It has to do with improving and enhancing clinical practice where there is scope to do so.

The England Centre for Practice Development (2013) indicates that practice development is an internationally recognised and sustainable approach that aims to improve patient or service user experiences of care, transforming care and services so that they are person-centred, safe and effective, and ensuring that the best evidence and research informs everyday practice. Another helpful explanation of practice development is provided by Manley et al. (2008) who indicate that it is used for creating an environment that support the engagement of clinicians in evaluating and improving their practice. Later definitions of the term are less specific and refer to change in cultures and corporate strategies, which are no doubt components of effective practice development.

The focus of practice development is therefore on improving outcomes for patients and service users, and consequently has to do with changes in hands-on or direct patient or service user health or social care interventions for particular components of professional practice. Practice development is by no means a new phenomenon, as care professionals have always looked out for ways of delivering safer, less invasive and more effective care and treatment for patients and service users.

The DCM needs to take an analytical approach to the development of practice, which can be achieved in various ways. Based on an analysis of literature, focus group interviews with practice developers and individual interviews with care practitioners on practice development, Garbett and McCormack (2002) conclude that the purpose of practice development is to increase effectiveness in patient-centred care, and transform care and the culture and context within which it takes place. The attributes of practice development are that it needs to be systematic and rigorous, a continuous process, and founded on facilitation. The consequences of practice development include improved experiences of care in terms of their sensitivity to the needs of individuals and populations for users, and increased capacity for autonomous practice by professionals. The four main themes that emerged from the study were that (p. 92):

- it is a means of improving patient care;
- it transforms the contexts and cultures in which healthcare delivery takes place;
- it ensures that a systematic approach is employed to effect changes in practice; and
- various types of facilitation are required for change to take place.

Identifying the purposes, attributes and consequences of practice development constitutes an exercise that ensures a cautious and planned approach to change. Concluding from a four-year action research study related to a task-centred service to a patient-centred service, Titchen (2003) identified three generic principles of practice development which she suggested comprise a conceptual framework. These principles are:

- Changing the practice philosophy.
- Putting the process of change into practice.
- Investing in practice development.

McCormack et al. (2006) reported on a study that indicates that practice development comprises six crucial components, namely: policy and strategy, methodology and methods, roles and relationships, learning strategies, funding and evaluating effectiveness. How the DCM achieves such change will be discussed later in the chapter under 'How to manage change'. Furthermore, practice development can be undertaken at individual level, particularly by those who have autonomy in their day-to-day work; at unit or team level; or at organisational or supra-organisational levels. The Donabedian (1988) model of evaluation, which comprises considering and identifying the standard to be achieved, along with structure, process and outcome, is a systematic approach that can be adopted to monitor the effectiveness of the development.

In the Donabedian model, 'structure' refers to the equipment, staff and materials required for performing the care intervention; 'process' refers to the procedure or protocol that has been specifically established for particular care interventions, the training, and ongoing evaluation of the activity; and 'outcome' refers to the exact final product. The model was discussed in the context of quality assurance in Chapter 5.

In the context of practice development, 'structure' also refers to identifying the practice development function of care professionals, and may have been identified as part of annual IDPR. As to process or deployment, for some staff such as practice development nurses, this comprises the main focus of their role. However, each team member can be a practice developer, and this is documented in the *NHS KSF* (DH, 2004a) under the 'service improvement' domain (i.e. dimension).

There are several key publications on practice development and innovations from the RCN, DH and other organisations, including the RCN (2005b) *Maxi Nurses: Nurses Working in Advanced and Extended Roles Promoting and Developing Patient-centred Healthcare*, and the DH (2011f) *Implementing Innovation*.

Why 'Manage' Change?

Change is essential within health and social care to ensure that care is based on the best available evidence, that new technology is instituted and that use of the available resources are maximised. The components of care provision or delivery that needs to be changed can be implemented in any of the following ways:

- imposed;
- introduced after brief discussions;
- evolve gradually over time;

- self-directed, such as in lifestyle or behaviour change; or
- managed.

Wherever groups of individuals such as care professionals are affected by change, the change needs to be 'managed' if it is to be effectively implemented and is sustained.

Action point 6.2   Ways of making changes

Consider a recent change in your practice setting and think about the way the change was made, taking into account the five categories of change implementation identified above.

Change can have different effects on the different individuals the change will affect, such as:

- involvement and ownership;
- excitement;
- stress;
- increased individual responsibility; and
- improved patient care.

How to 'Manage' Change

The management of change involves taking a planned and systematic approach. The '7-step RAPSIES model for effective change management' (see Figure 6.1) is one such approach. This model is derived from the extensive literature on the topic and on our own experience as healthcare practitioners. The 7-step model comprises the essential components of the management of change, which are:

1 *Recognition* of the need for change, to solve a problem for instance, or to improve an element of practice.
2 *Analysis* of the available options related to the contemplated change, the environment or setting where change will be implemented, and the users of the change.
3 *Preparation* for the change, such as identifying an appropriately skilled change agent to lead the implementation of the change, education of the users of the change, defining intended outcomes and involving relevant colleagues.
4 *Strategies* for implementing the change (explained later in this chapter).

5   *Implementation* of the change, including piloting the change and timing of implementation.
6   *Evaluation* of the impact of the change against the intended outcomes.
7   *Sustaining* the change, i.e. ways of ensuring that the change endures and is mainstreamed.

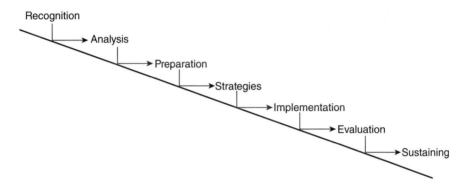

Figure 6.1   The 7-step RAPSIES model for effective change management

Recognising the need for change

Staff dissatisfaction with the way care is delivered, complaints received from patients or their relatives, and new research findings on how to improve care are some of the conduits that indicate the need for change. Several other reasons were identified earlier in this chapter under 'Why changes in health and social care?' One of the most significant attributes of a change is that it must improve or enhance the care provision experiences and outcomes for the benefit of patients or service users, and/or the organisation. More specifically, for instance, if changing to using a new research-tested care package, this should result in better care for the patient or service user (i.e. outcomes), and thereby benefit the organisation as well.

The change must also be compatible with the team's existing beliefs and values about health and social care delivery, that is, at a philosophical level, as well as pragmatic. How easily the change can be understood by patients and stakeholders must also be considered. The simplicity or the ease of using the change or innovation, and its 'trialability' (i.e. the possibility of piloting the innovation) must also be considered, as well as 'observability' (i.e. the change and its results must be explicit and tangible).

Analysis of the change

After identifying that a change is needed, the care practitioner must explore all options available before deciding on the best solution. For instance, in relation to the issue of ensuring that in-patients receive adequate nutrition, you may identify a number of changes to achieve this, such as:

- reducing other activities during meal times;
- implementing snack trolleys;
- staggering meal times;
- implementing volunteer feeders;
- implementing a colour-coded tray system (see Box 6.1);
- asking for feedback on the quality of meals;
- implementing protected meal times; and
- ensuring that assistance with eating is given to those who need it.

Several examples of real-life changes in health and social care delivery implemented by care professionals can be cited, such as using the most appropriate dressings on particular wounds, and implementing a redesigned sedation scoring system for critically ill patients in ICUs. More centrally advocated change includes personal budgeting for social care service users and the SAP mentioned earlier in this chapter. The DH (2006a) cites several other examples, such as peer-mentoring introduced by school nurses and the NHS 'Life Check' service. In response to Action point 6.1, you should have been able to identify a number of examples of changes in care delivery in your area of practice.

On deciding which specific change(s) is to be made, those involved need to consider the advantages and likely disadvantages of the change. This comprises an analysis of the specific change in more systematic ways, such as by force field or SWOT analyses (discussed shortly).

The users of the change

Analysis of the proposed change includes careful consideration of the users of the change. Planning includes 'selling' the change to the users, and exploring developmental needs as individuals or as a team. Based on research conducted some decades ago, Rogers and Shoemaker (1971) identified six categories of users of change, which were later also identified by Moore (2007) and which apply to most organisations at local level. These categories are:

1 *Innovators:* individuals in the team who get excited about new ideas and are keen to implement them.
2 *Early adopters:* individual team members who think about the new change over a few days and then adopt them.
3 *Early majority:* when a few team members adopt the new idea.
4 *Later majority:* when several members accept and adopt the new idea.
5 *Laggards:* individuals who tend to lag behind in adopting new ways of working.
6 *Rejecters:* individuals who are against new ideas or usually oppose them.

Action point 6.3   The users of change in my practice area

Consider your work colleagues and their response to a recent change that was implemented in your work setting. See if you can identify those who could fall into each of the categories identified by Rogers and Shoemaker. Consider various ways in which you could use the information about categories of users of change to operationalise the change management process.

With innovators, the change agent can, for instance, use their energy and allocate them responsibilities. The remaining categories of users comprise those who resist change either momentarily or longer term. Early adopters need recognition for their compliance with the change, whereas those who form the later majority as individuals who need more time to assimilate the new concept are given scope to try out before using the change. Laggards may need extra support and time to prevent disillusionment. As for rejecters, the change agent or the line manager will need to explore further to identify possible reasons for this. The employee may, for example, be privy to further knowledge, or has had previous experience in relation to the change, or be experiencing transient personal or domestic problems.

The setting or environment where the change is to be implemented

Another essential component of change management is the setting or environment where the change is to be implemented. The environment has to be 'ripe for change' for successful implementation. A practice environment that is conducive to change manifests:

- a progressive ethos where critical appraisal, creativity and openness are fostered;
- good channels of communication, i.e. two-way and effective communication that includes opportunities for feedback and evaluation;
- a cohesive team who work in partnership, with the patient or service user as the focus;
- team empowerment, i.e. the freedom to be innovative and creative within the wider organisation; and
- supportive leadership that actively promotes and supports a 'can do' approach.

From the critical analysis viewpoint, some of the factors that constitute barriers to research implementation or use also apply to implementing change, and include:

- Palfreyman et al.'s (2003) findings that nurses and physiotherapists have access to a wide variety of sources of knowledge, but both professions have problems overcoming the barrier of time.

- 'important research findings are not having the desired impact on practice' (West et al., 1999: 633);
- '... dissemination failings represent the single most significant factor in the research-practice gap' (Dickson, 1996: 5).

Other barriers to research implementation faced by care professionals can include:

- lack of critical appraisal and research knowledge and skills;
- lack of time to consider undertaking research;
- not having access to resources for conducting or appraising research;
- an organisational and managerial ethos and culture that do not value or encourage research;
- lack of power and financial control to implement new research findings;
- lack of valid research on specific components of practice; and
- lack of user-friendly reviews and guidelines.

McCaughan (2002) suggests that barriers to research implementation include:

- problems in interpreting and using research – it is seen as too complex, 'academic' and overly statistical;
- even healthcare practitioners who feel confident with research-based information experience a lack of organisational support;
- researchers and findings lack clinical credibility and fail to offer sufficient clinical direction in care delivery; and
- some care practitioners lack the skills and motivation to use research themselves.

Action point 6.4   Relevance of barriers to research implementation in your practice setting

Consider the above-mentioned barriers to research, and whether either of them apply to your practice setting. It should prove worthwhile discussing these barriers with a peer or work-setting colleague to ascertain their professional thoughts.

Preparation for Change

The change agent

The DCM's role in implementing change involves being both a change agent and a supporter of changes that are being implemented. Alternatively, the change agent could be a facilitator external to the organisation, or the team, or an employee within the organisation, the department or the work setting itself. The change agent is the person who is assigned to advocate, lead and implement the change, and might also be the initiator of the change. They need to be completely clear about the present state of readiness in the setting, and the potential future state after the change has been implemented. As Brookes (2011) reports, for example, the change agent can exercise 'appreciative leadership' and involve the entire team, so that each member feels ownership of the change that is needed.

In considering 'readiness for change', the change agent needs to consider how adequately staffed the care team is to accommodate the change or new mode of care intervention. Human resource issues therefore need to be addressed, but the change agent must also be cognisant of the components of change in the 7-step RAPSIES framework for effective change management, which of course includes sustaining the change after implementation. The change agent's key functions should include:

- 'selling' the change and promoting ownership by the care team;
- planning the change comprehensively;
- determining and deciding on relevant change strategies;
- identifying own and others' related development (or training) needs;
- monitoring and supporting change users throughout the process;
- evaluating the impact of the change;
- problem-solving to address any challenges that are experienced; and
- sustaining the change.

The characteristics of an effective change agent are also those of being an effective leader. Two leadership styles that are particularly relevant for managing change are transformational and transactional styles. The transactional style refers to the orderly breaking down of tasks, but the transformational style constitutes keeping a distance, and taking a strategic view of the whole. Table 3.1 identifies some of the main characteristics of the two styles of leadership.

The change agent's role thus incorporates dissemination of the evidence or knowledge base, on which change is being advocated and initiated, to all affected by the change. Scullion (2002) suggests that dissemination is a vital yet complex process which aims to ensure that key messages are conveyed to specific groups via a wide range of methods so that it results in measured reaction, impact or implementation. Methods of research dissemination include:

- Via professional associations
- Video/DVD/audio tape
- Written reports as feedback to respondents/research subjects
- Written executive summaries (most likely to be read if concise)
- Journal articles or editorials
- Journal clubs
- Conferences
- Poster presentation
- Newsletters
- Books, or chapters in books
- Inclusion in course curriculum
- Educational materials.

Social media can also be used; for example, internet forums, weblogs, social blogs, social networks and podcasts.

As for the users of the change, which can include your colleagues or patients, the key factors in the dissemination process include consideration of how ready they are to use the change, enabling them to become active sub-agents for the change rather than passive recipients, forming social networks, and choosing suitable strategies for that particular group of users.

Furthermore, change can evoke anxiety, and resistance to change can prevail because of:

- fear of the unknown;
- lack of confidence;
- lack of knowledge and skills to carry out the change;
- loss of influence and power; and
- resentment or perceived criticism of past practices.

For each of these components causing resistance to change, the DCM or change agent can take specific action to manage them. For 'fear of the unknown', this presents a degree of uncertainty in the user, in which case the change agent can, for instance, provide detailed and sufficient information to those who are resisting the change for them to become fully familiar with the proposed change. For lack of confidence, further information and support can be provided. For lack of knowledge and skills to carry out the change, organising workshops and study days might prove beneficial. For loss of influence and power, the key tasks can be made more explicit. For resentment or perceived criticism of past practices, the attributes of the change should be highlighted or emphasised as making progress towards further improvements in care.

In addition, people get accustomed to established practices as they feel comfortable and secure with them. They might also resist if they feel overburdened by too much change at a particular point in time, or if they feel the change is likely to reduce freedom or result in increased control of their movements. They might sense increase in workload while level of pay is unchanged, or feel more secure in using well-established ways and wish to retain the existing ways of practice. Therefore, the need for change should emerge through users' feeling that a bottom-up approach is being taken, including their active involvement in planning, implementation and evaluation of the process.

Strategies for implementing change

The discussion so far indicates that change needs to be managed, it needs to be planned thoroughly, and it needs to be participative to promote ownership. Various strategies are documented in the management literature that can be selected from according to their suitability for a particular change item. Strategies for effective organisational change can include:

- Plan-do-study-act (PDSA)
- Lewin's three-stage process

- Empirical-rational
- Power-coercive
- Normative-re-educative.

Plan-do-study-act

The PDSA cycle (NHS III, 2008a) (as illustrated in Figure 6.5) comprises a strategy for testing the impact of an identified change within the work setting. It allows testing to be undertaken on a small scale with the opportunity to refine it prior to making the change fully operational and subsequent wider application. The PDSA strategy involves a range of colleagues in trying out the change, and thereby also reduces the barriers to change and increases ownership of the change.

Action point 6.5   Implementing change

Think about a change that you would like to implement within your clinical practice. In order to support you to test the change, develop a PDSA cycle that addresses the following areas that have been adapted from the NHS III model:

Plan

- What you are hoping to achieve.
- What you think the outcome of the change will be.
- The support you consider you will need to be able to implement the change.
- The mechanisms you intend to use to test the impact of the change.

Do

- Implement the change in the identified area.
- Observe the change and document any problems that are encountered.
- Commence analysis of the data that you have collected.

Study

- Complete the data analysis.
- Compare the results achieved with those that you predicted in the planning phase.
- Summarise and reflect upon what you have learnt.

Act

- Using what you have learnt from the test, identify any modifications that you need to make.
- Prepare your plan of action for the next evaluation point.

Lewin's three-stage process of change

A programme of planned change and improved performance developed some years ago by K. Lewin (1951), but remains fully relevant today, involves a three-stage process entailing unfreezing, movement and refreezing.

- *Unfreezing:* reducing those forces that maintain behaviour in its present form, and recognition of the need for change and improvement to occur.
- *Movement:* the development of new attitudes or behaviours, and the implementation of the change.
- *Refreezing:* stabilising the change at a new level, and reinforcement through supporting mechanisms such as policies, resources and norms.

Systematic ways of unfreezing a set of circumstances include the well-known SWOT analysis, and also force field analysis, which entails the group together identifying the factors that are driving the change and those that are causing resistance. An example of a SWOT analysis for introducing flexible family friendly shifts in a care setting is presented in Figure 6.2.

Strengths and weaknesses are internal factors, while opportunities and threats are usually external to the individual or team. A SWOT analysis can be very subjective and therefore needs to be performed as a team whenever possible. Alternatively,

STRENGTHS	WEAKNESSES
<ul><li>Happier staff</li><li>Better staff retention</li><li>Encourage recruitment</li><li>Staff morale</li><li>Maximum use of staff time</li><li>Gives individual staff more time at home</li><li>Not working too many shifts for long stretches</li><li>Less stress of travelling</li></ul>	<ul><li>Difficult to accommodate everyone's requirements</li><li>Staff without school-age children might get less annual leave in summer</li><li>Lack of communication as they may not be present at handovers</li><li>Not feeling part of the team</li><li>Poor long-term continuity</li><li>Difficulty covering annual leave, sickness</li></ul>
OPPORTUNITIES	**THREATS**
<ul><li>Extra day at home for study/education</li><li>Spend more time with family</li><li>Individual can pursue other interests</li><li>The organisation complies with *Improving Working Lives Standard* (DH, 2000d)</li></ul>	<ul><li>Staff with no family might feel disadvantaged</li><li>Whether this can be legitimately explored at recruitment interviews</li><li>Tiredness, which can lead to unsafe patient care</li><li>Sickness rate can go up</li><li>Long-term staff might be against the changes</li><li>Fitting in with practical routine</li></ul>

Figure 6.2   SWOT analysis: Introducing flexible family friendly shifts

the change agent could facilitate the force field analysis, an example of which in relation to implementing an ICP is presented in Box 6.2.

Box 6.2 Force field analysis for introducing an integrated care pathway

Driving forces	Resisting forces
• Continuity of care needed	• Staff not knowledgeable about how ICPs work
• Consistent with government policy related to patient journeys	• Perceived criticism of current method of care delivery
• Greater patient satisfaction	• Extra paperwork
• More opportunity for health promotion	• Extra staff time required, and therefore costs
• More collaboration within MDT	• Social care and healthcare funding disjunction
• Enhances patient care	• More resources required in terms of staff time
• Increases cost-effectiveness through patient compliance	• Too many people disseminating information
• Learners get fuller picture of broader influences on personal health	• Funding
	• Patient information overload

The force field analysis in Box 6.2 has shown that many forces may be involved in driving or resisting change. According to Lewin's (1951) force field analysis theory, behaviour in any institutional setting is not static in nature, and instead comprises a dynamic balance of socio-psychological forces working in opposite directions within the institution. The force field analysis exercise can be undertaken by a team of staff or individually to identify the factors (i.e. people, resources and systems) that might facilitate or hinder change, as doing so 'unfreezes' the forces that maintain behaviour in its present form.

In attempting to change a situation to a new level, after unfreezing, three enabling actions are possible: (1) increase the driving forces by adding new ones or strengthening existing ones; (2) reduce or remove the resisting forces; or (3) translate one or more resisting forces into driving ones. If a change agent uses say only the first of these three actions, then change may occur, but it is often unstable and quickly reverts to the original condition. A combination of all three strategies is the most effectual.

Empirical-rational

The strategy referred to as 'empirical-rational' is based on the belief that people are guided by reason, that they are essentially rational, and that if they can be helped to understand the nature and reasons for the proposed change, then they are more likely to accept it. Thus, this strategy is based on empowerment through giving knowledge. Government health warnings are at times based on this strategy.

Power-coercive

The power-coercive strategy emphasises a different approach in that it is based on threats of sanctions by seniors, economic or status-wise, if the desired changes are not adopted, and where necessary the use of moral power, playing on feelings of guilt and shame are used.

The assumption is that those in control of the organisation will identify the need for change, and people with less power will always comply with their plans. If an empirical-rational approach does not prove as productive, then the power-coercive strategy might be used. It can include application of legitimate power to influence and secure compliance, and can incorporate legal considerations.

Normative-re-educative

Individuals, groups and organisations are seen as inherently active in ascertaining how similar they are in their practices and norms to other entities. This strategy includes suggesting that the proposed change is a normal practice in other similar settings, making reference to local socio-cultural value systems, norms and attitudes, and educating users in the value and benefits of the change. It incorporates the facility for personal growth and self-actualisation.

Combined strategies

Each of the latter three strategies is based on different assumptions about what makes people accept a component of change, or alter their behaviour and result in achievement of different degrees of success. The strategy used is chosen according to different situations, and requires that the individual or the group are capable of, and willing to change. It also takes into account the social, political and economic factors that influence the role of the health or social care practitioner.

However, a combined strategy can be used that harnesses and co-ordinates elements of the three above strategies, but to be effective it must encompass:

- rational (or validated) information;
- two-way communication and expertise in group processes;
- consensus on new norms and sanctions associated with a proposed change; and
- legitimate authority of the change agent, and the power to carry it through.

The combination could be staged in that one of the three strategies might be more appropriate at the very early stages of implementation of a particular change, and another at different stage.

Implementing the change

> ## Action point 6.6   Implementing the change
>
> Consider a change that you feel would be beneficial to implement in your work-place. Identify a comprehensive set of activities that would ensure that the change is successfully implemented and maintained. This can take the form of a detailed step-by-step plan.

The activities you have identified for successful implementation of change might include:

- plan the change thoroughly;
- attempt to create an environment conducive to change by encouraging a culture that encourages questioning, using initiative and a reflective-evaluative approach to care interventions;
- provide means for the acquisition of knowledge and skills, feedback and support;
- identify problems, e.g. resistance and barriers, and build ways to overcome them into your plan;
- provide a medium for staff to share experiences;
- provide supportive leadership by being involved throughout;
- provision for evaluation and feedback so that successes and difficulties can be shared and learned from;
- encourage active participation;
- ensure that there are good channels of communication; and
- ascertain opportunities for refinement based on evaluation.

Timing of implementation

The change agent also needs to identify the most suitable implementation date for the change. This ideally needs to be the time when the users are ready and the setting is 'ripe for change'. Times to avoid include periods when several staff are on annual leave, when there are staff vacancies or long-term sickness, or when other major managerial changes are imminent, or if there is organisational resistance to the change. Timing of implementation includes the point in the team's dynamics when there is openness and trust amongst staff, and morale is good.

Evaluating the change

After the change has been implemented its impact needs to be monitored both informally and in more structured ways. Informally, evaluation information can be obtained by general impressions and casual questioning. More structured ways of evaluation can involve the use of a framework, or model, of evaluation. It can be done formatively (i.e. at interim intervals rather than end stages), but summative evaluation also needs to be conducted at specific pre-determined points when the full impact of the change can be gauged.

Evaluation of the change can involve comparing outcomes to those anticipated before implementation of the change, with specific indicators such as length of hospital stay, reduction in costs and improved patient satisfaction.

Sustaining the change

After implementation, the change needs to be sustained through explicit recognition from more senior managers, and supported by the necessary resources, human and non-human. The PDSA (NHS III, 2008a) method can be used to test out progress on a small scale. The users of the change should be able to sense the benefits of the change after implementation.

A strategy for sustaining change should have been established at the very beginning of the implementation of the change. The term 'sustaining' is used to signify keeping the change in good health, that is, functioning, but more importantly, developing. This requires various forms of resources, the categories of which are discussed in Chapter 7 and include:

- appropriate human resources;
- appropriate financial resources;
- monitoring mechanisms, such as regular concurrent and retrospective audits (built-in evaluation/research);
- planned evaluation of the effects or impact of the change;
- continuing skill development in the context of new equipment and devices becoming available;
- disseminating the change to obtain external views;
- users retaining ownership of the change (active user participation);
- maintaining team spirit (as discussed in Chapter 10);
- leadership of senior staff in using the change; and
- effective communication.

At times, organisational resistance to implementing or sustaining change can be experienced, which is also referred to as 'barriers to change'. Some of the organisational barriers to change are:

- deficiency in more senior colleagues' understanding of the details of the change required in role, practices and relationships;
- lack of the knowledge and skills necessary to use the new practice;
- shortage of staff;
- lack of time;
- lack of support within the management hierarchy;

- failure of the leader to identify problems;
- lack of materials/equipment to practice the new method; and
- failure of the leader to adequately plan the management of the change.

Such resistance is less apparent in organisations that reflect the characteristics of an 'effective organisation' which Beckhard and Harris (1987) identified as including:

- having a strategic view;
- energising others lower in the system;
- having relatively open communication;
- rewarding collaboration;
- managing conflict, not suppressing it;
- valuing difference; and
- actively learning, through feedback.

The characteristics of an effective organisation should actively support change management. A change endeavour can succeed or fail depending on the various factors discussed above. However, if the components of the RAPSIES framework discussed in this chapter are fully considered, then the change should be achieved as desired.

An alternative to the RAPSIES framework for the management of change is the model of change proposed for the NHS (NHS Change Model website, 2013), which comprise seven elements:

1 Leadership for change
2 Spread of innovation
3 Improvement methodology
4 Rigorous delivery
5 Transparent measurement
6 System drivers
7 Engagement to mobilise.

See 'Further recommended reading' at the end of this chapter for more details on access to the NHS change model.

Guidelines for effective change management

The essential activities required for successful change management are:

- Ensure compatibility with existing values and practices.
- Ensure that users see advantages in the innovation over existing practices.
- Have detailed knowledge of various change strategies.
- Plan well in advance, and in detail.
- Analyse existing and proposed new structures.
- Examine adaptability to the innovation.
- Assess the readiness to change.
- Ensure effective communication at all stages.
- Institute education and training at key stages.

- Recognise early adopters' efforts explicitly.
- Assess your own knowledge continuously, and update and upskill as appropriate.
- Exercise leadership skills.
- Support the change during all stages of the process.
- Encourage active participation by intended users of the change.
- Build in evaluation/research.

CHAPTER SUMMARY

This chapter has focused broadly on the what, why, when and how to manage change, and on the DCM's role in the management of change and innovation in the practice setting, and having completed this chapter you will have explored:

- actual and potential instances of changes made in patient or service user care interventions, and in the management or organisation of care;
- why changes are necessary in health and social care and the importance of effective management of change;
- how to manage change, using the RAPSIES model for effective change management, which comprises recognising the need for the change, analysis of the available options, preparation for the change, identifying strategies for implementing the change, implementation of the change, evaluating its impact and sustaining the change; and
- analysis of issues related to the management of change in care settings, concluding with guidelines for effective change management.

RECOMMENDED FURTHER READING

- For details of hierarchy or levels of evidence in EBP, access and view the content of the following website for the Joanna Briggs Institute:

Joanna Briggs Institute (2012) *Welcome to the Joanna Briggs Institute*. Available from: www.joannabriggs.edu.au/.

- For details of the NHS's current perspective on a structured model of change, see:

Medical Directors' Bulletin (2012) *NHS Change Model Introductory Online Seminars*. Available from: www.changemodel.nhs.uk/pg/groups/29463/Online+seminars. (Accessed 3 April 2013).

- For a detailed account of leadership in successful management of change in a hospital ward, see article:

Brookes J (2011) 'Engaging staff in the change process'. *Nursing Management*, 18 (5): 16–19.

- For a discussion on change management see:

Kerridge J (2012) 'Leading change'. *Nursing Times*, 108 (4): 12–15; 108 (5): 23–25; and 108 (6): 23–25.

7

MANAGING CARE RESOURCES

The importance of effective and efficient resource management in health and social care cannot be overestimated, as without resources there would be no health or social services, but conversely, only a certain proportion of national income can be allocated to these services, the remainder being required for several other social provisions. A wide range of resources are required for effective care delivery, and DCMs have their part to play in ensuring that the available resources are used responsibly and efficiently.

Chapter objectives

On completion of this chapter you will be able to:

- ascertain the specific resources required for effective care delivery, and how available human and non-human resources can be used efficiently;
- analyse how various components of human resources can be managed, and the care professional's accountability and responsibility in doing so;
- explore budget management, taking into account what budgeting is, and why and how to budget at the care setting level in order to maximise the use of these resources; and
- ascertain the management of a range of other non-human resources such as equipment and consumables that are required for effective care delivery.

Resources required for Effective Health and Social Care

An extensive range of resources are required to deliver health and social care services. The NHS delivers healthcare to a total population of over 62 million people within the United Kingdom. For the year 2011/12 the total expenditure on health in the United Kingdom was £106 billion, and for 2012/13 it will be £108.4 billion (DH, 2010a) out of a total public expenditure of approximately £700 billion for the United Kingdom. This expenditure on healthcare represents 16 per cent of the total annual expenditure for the United Kingdom; that is a spending of approximately £1,750 on healthcare per person each year. With 1.7 million employees, the NHS is also one of the biggest employers in Europe.

For personal social services, the government is almost exclusively the sole source of funding for social care, the overall management of which is based in local authorities, the budget for which for 2011/12 was £32 billion, with local structures for social care provision. Local authorities have the responsibility for managing the allocated funds efficiently, including personal budgets in social care.

As noted in Chapter 1, the underpinning core values and aims of the NHS are enshrined in the NHS Constitution (DH, 2012d), which is that healthcare is free at the point of delivery for all British citizens who are residents of the UK. Although the NHS is a UK-wide provision, there are a few differences in the ways financial resources are used at the point of care and treatment in NHS England, NHS Scotland, NHS Wales and Health & Social Care in Northern Ireland.

As indentified in the structure of the NHS in Figure 1.2 Chapter 1, the NHS England and Clinical Commissioning Groups (CCG) replaced the previous 10 Strategic Health Authorities (SHAs) in England and over 150 Primary Care Trusts (PCT). NHS England's role is to provide leadership to CCGs and to apportion the financial resources that are available for care and treatment and improvement of local healthcare, based on the annual budget required for commissioning care by each of the over-200 CCGs in England. The money is then passed on to service providers (e.g. Foundation Trusts) for spending on healthcare professionals' salaries, equipment, medication and other materials that are required for care and treatment.

Thus CCGs are at the centre of the NHS in that their role is to make sure that all other health services are provided, including hospitals, dentists, opticians, mental health services, NHS walk-in centres, NHS Direct, patient transport (including A&E), population screening and pharmacies. They are responsible for commissioning services for the population of an identified geographical area, or the population of a group of GP practices.

The health of the nation and healthcare has featured prominently in the priorities for the various governments who have been in office. Numerous short- and long-term strategies for specific aspects of healthcare are issued periodically by the DH such as the *Health and Social Care Act* (DH, 2012a), which was discussed in detail in Chapter 1.

A major shift in care provision is the government's decision for healthcare trusts to become NHS Foundation Trusts (DH, 2012a, 2012f). The basis for NHS Foundation

Trusts is that the management of the trust has much more autonomy in decision-making related to care delivery and management of resources from central government, although they will still be answerable to Monitor, the economic regulator, and to CQC the care regulator.

Each healthcare trust is a separate organisation, which is ultimately managed by a chairman and their Board, with a Chief Executive appointed for general management. The Chief Executive's remit is to ensure that appropriate structures are instituted so that operational activities achieve the aims of the trust. These aims, along with their trust's mission statement and objectives, are stated in the operational (usually annual) plan, and strategic longer-term (usually five to ten years) plan. These documents state the vision for the future for the organisation. Subsequently, business plans are also determined with further specific details, including the resources required for meeting particular strategic aims.

Operational and strategic planning is performed in NHS trusts as well as care providers in the independent sector, such as in care homes, by domiciliary care providers, GP practices, and by social care teams. Decisions made at healthcare trusts' Board meetings impact directly on DCMs' roles in delivering the services that are scheduled for their care setting, and the required human and material resources are made available for them. Regular budget statements are issued to indicate areas of underspend and overspend to enable budget holders to monitor their expenditure. The next section considers all of the resources that are required for providing and delivering care in care settings.

Resources at Ward/Unit/Department/Organisation Level

As noted earlier, various resources are required for an organisation to function effectively in providing care and treatment for the local population.

Action point 7.1   Resources for care organisations

Think of your own care setting, and list all of the resources that DCMs require for care delivery in the day-to-day management of care in your work area. 'All resources' include several different healthcare professions, and a range of ancillary staff, as well as equipment and materials.

As the word 'resource' signifies, it constitutes items and means that enable the achievement of organisation goals. In response to the above action point you might have mentioned that the resources required for most care areas include staff, and money for staff salaries and for purchasing equipment, maintaining and repairing them and so on. Organisations generally differentiate between human resources (or pay expenses) and non-human resources (or non-pay expenses or consumables). Another classification comprises grouping resources under human and hardware resources, namely human resources (e.g. staff clinical knowledge, skills and time) and hardware resources (e.g. accommodation, medications, equipment).

A wide range of human and non-human resources need to be available for the management of care delivery. They can be grouped under the acronym BEICHMM (though the order is not significant) to ensure that every resource is considered and readily available, and which stands for:

- Buildings
- Equipments
- Information technology
- Consumables
- Human resources
- Methods
- Money.

BEICHMM therefore comprises a checklist of headings under which all of the resources required by the organisation or by the care setting to fulfil its obligations can be identified. The need for one main building or a number of *buildings* is obviously a requirement to accommodate the designated care delivery facilities. *Equipment* as variety of resources includes X-ray machines, telephones, manual handling aids, patient-attached equipment such as cardiac monitors or syringe drivers, specialist equipment that is pertinent to the area such as a minibus for use by patients within a rehabilitation service. *Information technology* is of course now all pervasive as a resource, which in healthcare often enables instant communication of patient or service user information between health and social care professionals and departments. For *consumables*, the resources comprise disposable single-use items such as medication, dressings and so on.

Human resources, or workforce, refers to all categories of staff (e.g. nursing, AHPs, medical staff, social care professionals, CSWs, ancillary staff, managers and administrators etc.), and therefore include the correct skill mix of staff (proportion of qualified and unqualified staff, specialists etc.), communications, recruitment and retention. It includes consideration of pending maternity leave and retirement, which creates temporary or longer-term vacancies. It also includes having to make a case for more staff, contingency requirements (e.g. if there is an increase in the number of influenza sufferers during winter months). Human resources also include the initial and continuing training and education of staff, their motivation and morale.

Methods as resources include procedures, policies, protocols and clinical guidelines, together with the training and assessment of competence to be able to use them. It includes ways of meeting professional updating requirements for structuring of care by ICPs, for instance, and for making referrals to medical staff, specialist nurses and therapists. For *money*, the resources include the cost of maintaining the building(s), purchasing equipment, employing staff and so on; in fact, for all other resources just mentioned.

The resources allocated for care and treatment need to be used efficiently. 'Efficiency' refers to the achievement of expected outcomes at minimum financial cost, in the minimum amount of time, but to the required standard. It refers to achieving maximum effect from available resources. The associated term 'effectiveness' refers to the appropriateness and extent of what is being achieved, and should be measurable in terms of patient outcomes.

Managers are accountable for the efficient use of the money allocated to their part of the organisation, and they have to manage all their resources responsibly. Resourcing care and treatment in hospitals and primary care settings is challenging as novel treatment methods and new medications for conditions that have thus far proved difficult to manage appear and compete for a proportion of the NHS budget.

It is important to note, therefore, that the health and social services provided are cash-limited services which are allocated a set amount of money by the government each year, and therefore the decisions made regarding the allocation of resources are critical. There can also be challenges faced in the management of these resources, such as delays experienced in the appointment of staff, or receiving required equipment, or servicing those already in use, together with depreciation and replacement costs.

Why 'Manage' Resources?

There are several reasons why DCMs need to be knowledgeable about the way in which resources are managed. Cash limitation of financial resources allocated for care provision is one such issue. Additionally, the source of NHS funding is predominantly taxpayers' money, and therefore needs to be managed responsibly and intelligently. Hence it is also important to consider economy, effectiveness and efficiency in the use of these resources, and the accountability and responsibility of resource managers that goes with this activity. It has been argued by some that personnel who spend such money have a moral duty to ensure that it is spent responsibly.

Managing resources also signifies identifying the cost of new or extra resources that may be required, either in the short term (e.g. use of 'bank' staff) or longer-term (e.g. appointment of a specialist nurse, or purchase a better diagnostic machine or equipment). The use of extra resources needs to be carefully evaluated to ascertain their effectiveness, and the need for their continuing use.

How resources are used, however, needs careful planning, which means deciding in advance, strategically and locally, how they will be used, the activities that the trust plans to engage in, how they will be achieved and which personnel will ensure that they are.

The remainder of this chapter discusses the management of care resources in two major parts: (1) human resources, which include skill mix, recruitment and retention of staff, and expectations of both the organisation and its staff; and (2) non-human resources, namely money, equipment, information technology, consumables as well as protocols and guidelines for care delivery.

Managing human resources

With his notion of 'upside-down thinking', Handy (1984) is well-known for suggesting that employees should be treated as assets rather than costs, and hence be invested in. Armstrong (2012) suggests that employees should be perceived as 'human capital', which also implies that they should be treated as assets that the organisation values. If this logic is followed, then in health and social services, employees should be treated as their most valuable resources that should be managed in appropriate ways to enable them to fulfil their roles in a way that is mutually beneficial for employees, employers and patients or service users.

The concept of human resource management (HRM) has evolved over the last few decades from referring to the employees of the organisation as workers who cost money in terms of wages that are paid to them, to recognising them as individuals who contribute to the success of the organisation. HRM is defined by Armstrong (2012: 3) as 'a strategic and coherent approach to the management of an organisation's most valued assets – the people working there who individually and collectively contribute to the achievement of the objectives of the business.'

Mullins (2010: 494) cites the Chartered Institute of Personnel and Development's definition of HRM as the 'design, implementation and maintenance of strategies to manage people for optimum business performance including the development of policies and processes to support these strategies and the evaluation of the contribution of people to the business.' HRM, therefore, aims to improve the productive contribution of individual employees whilst simultaneously attempting to attain the employer's, society's and individual employee's objectives.

In health and social care, HRM largely refers to ensuring that appropriate individuals are employed with the right skills and in the right numbers at the right time to ensure that the care organisation's goals are achieved (see discussion on organisations in Chapter 2).

> ## Action point 7.2   Specific human resources in healthcare
>
> Identify as many different categories of staff as you can who contribute to health and/or social care delivery in your care organisation. Then, identify precisely how many of each type of care practitioner have input into care provision in your actual care setting/workplace, including support workers. Which of these care practitioners are full–time, and what are the WTE of those who are employed on part-time contracts?

A wide range of skills and knowledge are required to ensure the safe and effective delivery of care so that the organisation's annual and long-term aims and objectives are achieved. This also signifies that a variety of specialist and non-specialist personnel need to be appointed, ensuring that they remain competent, and possibly see their job as a career. Grouped under 'human resources', they include:

- Managers at top, middle and first line levels
- Administrative staff
- Estates department employees (site and building maintenance staff, e.g. electricians, plumbers gardeners, etc.)
- Medical practitioners (including consultants and junior doctors, possibly professors)
- Nurses, midwives and CSWs
- AHPs (including social workers)
- Ancillary staff (e.g. porters, domestic staff)
- Catering staff
- Pathology staff and laboratory technicians
- Chaplains/faith representatives
- Housekeepers.

From another angle, the health and social care workforce in the twenty-first century (i.e. the people that DCMs manage) has been changing for some time in the broader context of employment and changes in society. This includes:

- an increase in the number of CSWs as part of workforce redesign;
- increasing specialisation and advancing practice;
- changes in shift patterns such as 12-hour shifts;
- awareness of family friendly policies;
- moves for pre-registration educational preparation for healthcare professions to be at undergraduate (degree) level.

Furthermore, some years ago Maslin-Prothero (1997: 432) explored the prevailing literature on healthcare employment in organisations, and concluded that largely the 'concept of job for life no longer exists'. This is because organisations want an adaptable workforce of individuals who adapt and change as required by the organisation, and are prepared to be lifelong learners. Various changes that impact on healthcare delivery, including technological, demographic and social attitude changes, are identified in Chapter 6 where the management of change is examined. The development of a variety of transferable skills including skills in critical thinking, problem-solving and reflective practice is seen as essential.

The DCM needs to be aware of the dynamics of employment whilst ensuring that there are appropriate numbers of staff with appropriate knowledge and skills for care delivery. New roles are also being developed, such as physician's assistants and anaesthetic practitioners, which further expands the professional groups that constitute the MDT.

Managing human resources also includes ensuring that staff comply with their codes of practice, with various regulations and legislation such as those for health and safety, as well as the need to work and learn together as inter-professional teams (see also discussion on teamwork in Chapter 10).

Skill mix

Naturally, the various personnel that you identified in response to Action point 7.2 are crucial for effective treatment and care delivery. This comprises an appropriate combination of registered health and social care professionals and non-registered staff who are trained and competent in selected skills. This combination is known as 'skill mix', which is a term that refers to the numbers and ratio, capability and experience of qualified and unqualified staff in a particular unit or team.

Ascertaining the precise ratio of registered to non-registered healthcare professionals for individual care settings is not easy. On examining the tools available for the systematic assessment of skill mix, Hurst (2006) concludes that there are some quick and easy methods as well as those that are more complex. The three main methods used are: (1) the top-down method used by workforce planners; (2) professional judgement methods based on consensus with colleagues, and (3) bottom-up methods which are workload driven, and based on patient demands at care delivery level. Hurst identifies various categories of bottom-up methods, but notes that there is no perfect method as each has strengths and weaknesses. A few years ago, the Healthcare Commission (taken over by CQC since) (2005) reported, however, that nurse staffing methods are predominantly unsystematic and irrational.

Earlier methods of gauging skill mix have tended to be criticised for being aimed at reducing the ratio of qualified to unqualified staff, and for shifting workload on to CSWs. It included so-called 'unproductive time', that is, paid meal breaks and rest periods, and discussion on subjects not related to work.

The reason for ensuring the correct skill mix in care settings is that various studies (e.g. RCN, 2006, 2010; Rafferty et al., 2007) support the argument that quality of care improves proportionately with more qualified staff available to provide care, and patient outcomes are better when nurses care for fewer patients. Such studies indicate that a poor skill mix of qualified and unqualified nurses lead to comparatively poorer patient outcomes, staff burnout, job dissatisfaction and low morale.

Action point 7.3   Skill mix in my care setting

Consider the skill mix in your care setting. How many whole time equivalent (WTE) staff are employed to work in the setting? What is the ratio of registered to non-registered staff? Overall, what is your personal opinion regarding the current skill mix in your care setting or organisation?

The RCN (2006) recommends a skill mix ratio of 65 per cent RNs to 35 per cent CSWs as a benchmark for general hospital wards. In other care settings, however, such as intensive care areas, a much higher ratio is necessary. WTE refers to the total number of staff hours expressed as a percentage of full-time positions. For example, a nurse who works full-time (37.5 hours per week) would be expressed as 1.0 WTE; one who works 30 hours per week would be expressed as 0.8 WTE and so on. Furthermore, in its response to the Francis report (Gov.uk, 2013), the Government indicates that CSWs in health and social care should undergo consistent training, and also be regulated by a registration scheme.

However, even after the publication of the Francis report, and the government's response to the report, the 'Safe Staffing Alliance', which includes the RCN, Unison, the Patients Association and a number of directors of nursing at English hospitals (BBC News, 2013), indicated that wards regularly have one registered nurse caring for eight patients, and that more nurses are needed to provide safe, more effective and compassionate care.

Recruitment and retention of staff

Identifying appropriate numbers of qualified and unqualified staff required to deliver a service is only one part of the equation in the management of human resources as team members can be mobile in that they may apply for promotion, retire or leave because they are not getting job satisfaction in their current duties. The DCM needs, therefore, to be knowledgeable with regard to the retention and recruitment of staff.

Various reports over the years have indicated that healthcare staff are highly dissatisfied with aspects of their work, and that improvements need to be made to retain staff (e.g. Meadows et al., 2000; RCN, 2012b). A staff survey is also conducted and published each year by the CQC (2011b), who in their *2010 NHS Staff Survey*, for instance, identifies healthcare trusts' review of the experiences of their staff in enabling them to provide better care to patients and service users as follows:

- 77% have had appraisals in the last 12 months (69% in 2009).
- 64% are happy with the standard of care provided by the trust (an increase from 62% in 2009).
- 68% say hot water, soap and paper towels are 'always' available when they need them (compared to 71% in 2009); and for patients this has also dropped from 63% in 2009 to 60% in 2010.
- 41% have good opportunities to develop in their work (compared with 44% in 2009).
- 28% said that they will look for a new job in the next 12 months (compared with 22% in 2009).
- 8% overall reported experiencing physical violence from patients, relatives or other members of the public, while 15% said they had been subjected to bullying, harassment and abuse.

If comparing the findings of the 2010 and 2009 surveys can be seen as a trend, then the CQC findings imply a small decline in general standards in the NHS trusts surveyed. In addition to the CQC, the National NHS Staff Survey Co-ordination Centre (2012a) also conducts annual staff surveys to ascertain NHS staff's feelings related to identified aspects of working in the NHS. The 2011 survey for 'Acute Trusts' contained the questions under the headings:

- Work–life balance – including number of hours worked by the respondent
- Training, learning and development
- The job and organisation – includes appraisals and personal development plans
- Errors, near misses and incidents
- Violence, bullying and harassment
- Occupational health and safety
- Infection control and hygiene

- Health and wellbeing
- Background details.

Optional questions are also identified with regard to pay and conditions, clinical supervision, partnership working and communication. Recruitment and retention of staff was also highlighted by the *Wanless Report* (DH, 2002), which emphasised the need for a more concerted longer-term planning for the NHS workforce.

Action point 7.4   Promoting staff retention

What is the rate of staff turnover within your care setting or your organisation? Staff turnover refers to the number of staff who leave the organisation each year, expressed as a percentage of the overall workforce. What initiatives are you aware of that have been implemented to promote staff retention? You may find it helpful to look at the Improving Working Lives (IWL) publication (DH, 2000d).

Relevant areas of IWL with regard to family friendly employment are discussed in the next chapter.

Organisations and their employees – expectations of each other

To be able to function effectively as teams and individuals, organisations and individual members of staff have certain expectations of each other. In addition to contractual commitments, the employee also has other expectations of the organisation, such as the provision of a safe working environment. In turn, the employing organisation also has certain expectations of their employees.

Action point 7.5   Employer-employee expectations

Consider the notion of expectations and compliance within your own organisation, and make notes on what you as an employee expect from the organisation that employs you, together with what the organisation expects from you.

There are likely to be a range of expectations by both parties in the employee–employer relationship. This is referred to as a 'psychological contract' that involves a process of giving and receiving by the individual and by the organisation. It covers a range of expectations, rights, privileges, duties and obligations that have a significant influence on people's behaviour but which are not in the form of a written agreement.

You may have mentioned some of the following points within your list of employee expectations:

- Provide safe and hygienic working conditions.
- Make every reasonable effort to provide job security.
- Attempt to provide challenging and satisfying jobs and reduce alienating aspects of work.
- Adopt equitable personnel policies and procedures.
- Allow staff genuine participation in decisions that affects them.
- Provide reasonable opportunities for personal development and career progression.
- Treat members of staff with respect.
- Demonstrate an understanding and considerate attitude towards personal problems of staff.

The nature and extent of individuals' expectations vary widely, as do the abilities and willingness of the organisation to meet them. Expectations also change over time, and they are part of the social responsibility of management and are in addition to any statutory requirements placed upon the organisation. IWL standards (DH, 2000d) identify some of the employee expectations that employers should endeavour to meet.

The organisation expects the employee to adhere to a number of rules and regulations that will be agreed and signed as part of the employment contract. Furthermore, the employer expects the employee to fully accept the established philosophy of the organisation; contribute to the achievement of its objectives; to be loyal to the organisation when on and off duty; and not to abuse facilities that the employee is entrusted with.

In the context of the organisation's expectations and requirements from their employees, Stewart (1993) also focuses on employees' loyalty to organisational goals. She identifies a number of ways in which an organisation can achieve this (also referred to as 'theory Z'), which are:

- long-term employment;
- a unique philosophy and clear statement of objectives;
- structured facilities for socialisation of recruits;
- staff mobility through job rotation, and therefore more generalist rather than specialist skill, although this can result in slower promotion;
- an appraisal system that emphasises individual performance and longer-term goals to gauge where the employee wishes to be some years hence;
- emphasis on work groups, but being non-directive once a task has been assigned;
- open communication encouraging contacts with other departments;
- consultative decision-making; and
- showing concern for the employee by managers spending substantial amount of their time talking to employees about what matters to them.

Managing Non-human Resources Effectively – Budgets and Budgeting

A range of non-human resources are available to the DCM to deliver care and treatment in their care settings. This section therefore provides an overview of how 'money' is spent on health and social care, and to do so explores budgeting by looking at what a budget is, why prepare budgets, the different approaches to budgeting, and the likely advantages and disadvantages of each approach in health and social care organisations. The DCM has to be aware of the costs of care and treatment, the requirement to achieve outcomes, and the amount of money being spent each month on care services in the work setting. The DCM's role in budget management is to ensure that they are managing within existing resources. So what are the sources of financial resources for care services?

Sources of NHS income and expenditure

Money for the annual NHS budget is generally drawn from:

- Tax revenues – approximately 85 per cent
- National Insurance contributions – approximately 9 per cent
- Other sources such as charges to patients, e.g. prescription charges.

At NHS trust level, resources are allocated by the government as 'revenue' and 'capital' funding. *Revenue funding* is money that is used for day-to-day running costs of the area of practice (e.g. expenditures on salaries) and consumables (e.g. medical and surgical supplies, heating, lighting and medications).

Capital funding (or *Capital expenditure*) is the money that is allocated for the purchase of: (1) items which have a life of more than one year; and (2) items of equipment which cost, either individually or as a group of related items, more than £5,000.

Any item of plant or equipment that meets either or both of these conditions may be called a capital item, tangible asset or fixed asset, and capital funding includes earmarked or ring-fenced funding. Of the £108 billion NHS budget for 2012–13, £104 billion have been identified for revenue expenditure, and £4.5 billion for capital expenditure.

Thus, more than 90 per cent of NHS income comes through the DH, and are allocated to CCGs via NHS England. The rest is either: (1) generated by the healthcare trust itself; (2) donated by outside organisations as gifts and bequests (trust funds); or (3) taken by the trust as a loan income (to self-governing trusts only).

- *Generated income:* The money that is raised by care organisations, from the level of NHS Trusts to individual wards or departments, including

  o   private patients' fees
  o   rents from land and premises

- ○ income from retail sites on hospital premises that pay a fee to the care organisation for use of their premises
  - ○ money received from the sale of buildings, land and/or capital items
  - ○ money raised from diverse things such as lease of space on the ward for advertising, hiring of a room.
- *Gifts and bequests:* These can be donations of money or equipment to a specific unit, individual or organisation. It includes legacies, gifts and appeal funds sometimes for pre-identified specific purposes, e.g. research, or continuing education for staff in the area. A potential problem with gifts and bequests is that at times they are donated as capital items but without the revenue funding to support their ongoing use.
- *Loans:* Trusts can borrow money if a monthly shortfall is predicted, especially when approaching the end of the budget year. Self-governing trusts may arrange to obtain loans, but have to pay interest on them.

Immaterial of the sources of funding, the NHS needs to spend its allocated money efficiently. An area of activity in the Health and Social Care Act is to make £20 billion of efficiency savings to be achieved through QIPP (DH, 2011b) by 2014–15. QIPP relates to improving productivity in the NHS, and it operates number of national 'work streams' designed to support the NHS to achieve the quality and productivity challenge it has been set, such as:

- How care is commissioned, for example covering long-term conditions, or ensuring patients get the right care at the right time.
- How NHS organisations are run, staffed and supported to improve staff productivity.

A potential disadvantage of such savings is that it could also impact on the allocation of resources, both staff and material.

Income and spending in the NHS are audited at various levels, and in particular Monitor is an organisation that has been instituted to ascertain specifically how NHS foundation trusts are functioning with their allocation of funds. Monitor was established in 2004 as a body that is independent of central government and directly accountable to parliament. Its principal role is to authorise and regulate NHS foundation trusts, three main strands to their work being to (Monitor, 2012):

- determine whether NHS trusts are ready to become NHS foundation trusts;
- ensure that NHS foundation trusts comply with the conditions they signed up to – that they are well-led and financially robust; and
- support NHS foundation trust development.

NHS funding has also been changing gradually since 2007/8 to 'payment by results' (DH, 2012g) as a way of funding that comprises hospitals and other providers being paid for the care activities actually undertaken rather than 'block agreements'. The amount of money paid is based on standard national tariff, although adjusted for regional variations (in wages, for instance). They are commissioned by CCGs (previously commissioned by PCTs) for the wide range of activities required to deliver healthcare services.

In 2012, a number of payment-by-results pilot sites were launched, such as for drugs and alcohol recovery treatment services and for various aspects of mental healthcare (e.g. modes of interventions and therapy for different mental health problems). Updates on progress with this mode of funding are regularly posted on the DH website.

Budgeting – what is it and why explore it?

DCMs have to be aware that there is a set budget for delivering care in their care setting. So what is a budget, and what does the DCM need to know about budgeting? A budget can be defined as a statement of revenues and costs in financial terms that are anticipated and identified in advance of a period of time for spending on specific activities that reflect the agreed policies and strategies for meeting the objectives of the organisation.

One of the reasons for exploring budgeting is that managing human and non-human resources is an essential managerial role for DCMs as identified in Chapter 2, and by Mintzberg (1990) as a 'resource allocator'. It involves deciding where, what and how resources will be deployed, and what other resources are needed.

Other reasons for preparing organisational budgets are to:

- determine income and expenditure as precisely as possible with the available information;
- identify organisational objectives and priorities, with awareness that some expectations may not be met;
- communicate plans and co-ordinate activities;
- authorise expenditure and activity; and
- measure performance against objectives.

Budgeting also needs to be examined in the context of government policy, accountability and monitoring:

1 *Policy:* A budget explains to the person responsible for controlling expenditure not only how much money has been allocated over a specific period of time, but also for what purposes that money has been allocated (i.e. the resources it is intended to purchase). The budget also indicates the relative importance given to different clinical services (in terms of the amount of money to be spent on them), and is therefore a statement of policy.
2 *Accountability:* Once a budget has been created, responsibility for managing the money and resources is delegated. There is usually a hierarchy of responsibility, but each person in that hierarchy becomes accountable for the money and resources allocated.
3 *Monitoring:* A budget breaks down expenditure month by month, and by monitoring the amount of money that is being spent it is possible to assess each month whether a care setting has spent more or less money than it has been allocated.

Budgeting at ward/local level

A monthly statement of expenditures is usually despatched to designated care managers identifying the exact amount of money spent on their ward or unit. So what are the items you would expect to see listed in the statement? Box 7.1 identifies the key items in a monthly budget statement for a care setting indicating items and activities on which money was spent in the preceding month.

Box 7.1   Key items in the monthly budget

Pay expenses	Non-pay expenses
• Nursing staff on various pay bands, and manpower equivalent hours worked • Agency staff used • Clerical staff wages • CSWs on pay bands 2 or 3	• Drugs • Dressings • Medical consumables • Equipment and medical devices

---

The monthly budget also shows the total amount spent during the month, and therefore also the amount overspent or underspent.

Budgeting is also used in long-term planning to ascertain the financial effects of, for example, the purchase and running of a large item of equipment in a care setting, or the provision of a new service. Some flexibility needs to be built into the budget in case expenditure in one area requires cutbacks in another.

Approaches to budgeting

There are three principal approaches to devising budgets for each financial year: activity-based budgeting; incremental budgeting; and zero-based budgeting. These are briefly explored forthwith.

Activity-based budgeting

Activity-based budgeting is the approach that the DCM is most likely to have some involvement in. It entails estimating the volume and nature of the planned workload, identifying the fixed costs necessary to operate the planned workload, calculating the detailed and total costs of each 'unit' of work, and setting the budget by multiplying the planned activity by the unit cost.

Applied to the care setting, activity-based budgeting can involve estimating, for instance, how many episodes of different operations will be carried out by the Day Surgery Unit during the forthcoming financial year, or how many immunisations need to be performed at a particular health centre, and the cost of the resources that will be required to perform them effectively.

The advantages of activity-based budgeting are that:

- the budget is set with a clear view of the workload expected;
- it has some flexibility built in to reflect actual workload;
- actual unit costs can be compared with planned unit costs (standard costs) to monitor the efficiency of the service; and
- it enables management to focus on efficiency (unit costs) and on controlling fixed costs within the budget rather than on workload over which they may have less control.

The disadvantages of activity-based budgeting include:

- identifying simple measures of workload is difficult, as the actual cost of each unit is rarely standard;
- unit/standard costs based on historic costs may not provide a measure of efficiency;
- variable cost elements of budgets must be recovered by additional contract income, or else there will be an overspend;
- fixed costs are often fixed only in the short term; and
- relatively sophisticated information systems are required.

Incremental budgeting

Incremental budgeting involves ascertaining the actual necessary budget for the current financial year, and increasing it by a percentage approximating the prevailing inflation rate but without non-recurring costs. Anticipated new activity or agreed changes in service need to be allowed for, and an inflation reserve in case it rises during the financial year.

Recurring items include all activities of the current financial year. Non-recurring items at trust level include, for instance, if the A&E department is being closed down at one healthcare trust because it is being moved to another.

Inflation reserve includes pay awards and price indices. Approved variations to budgets include additional contract income due to increased workload and items released from reserves. They can also be:

- changes to services agreed during the year;
- recognition of unfunded workload pressures; and
- extraordinary circumstances, e.g. costs due to fire or flood damage.

There are advantages and disadvantages in each type of budgeting. The advantages of incremental budgeting are that they are easy to operate and understand; undemanding on management and time; and can operate even with weak information systems.

The disadvantages include changes in activity/mode of delivery are not always reflected in the budget; it can perpetuate inefficient use of resources; and there can be a lack of ownership of budgets by managers responsible.

Zero-based budgeting

Zero-based budgeting involves costing every item of resource, human and non-human, ascertaining the need for each of them for the forthcoming year, and costing them anew every time. This means identifying the quantity and quality of various services required, and then building up a budget from a zero base with optimum staff numbers and paybands, consumables, equipment and accommodation.

Zero-based budgeting is used, for instance, when a new outpatient's clinic is being planned for a particular healthcare site. The advantages of zero-based budgets are that:

- they are directly linked to the quality of service required and the planned level of activity;
- they encourage efficiency and discourage incremental budgeting;
- they are usually realistic and achievable; and
- managers take ownership of them.

The disadvantages are that they can be very time consuming and expensive to constitute, there is a danger of 'reinventing the wheel', and it is usually difficult to be certain of the exact costs that will be incurred in the financial year.

Budgeting considerations

In addition to the approaches to budgeting detailed above, there are other important considerations regarding budgeting that are now examined, some of which have been mentioned in other contexts earlier on.

- *Planning:* There are two main elements of planning:

  o 'strategic planning', which refers to planning that identifies a long-term view of the objectives for services in the locality – this can be for 5, 10 or 15 years; and
  o 'operational planning', which refers to planning on a day-to-day, month-by-month basis.

- *Considering effectiveness and efficiency:* These terms were defined earlier in the chapter, and are at the very heart of accountability of the budget-holder for justifying how allocated money is spent.
- *Prioritising:* Health and social care professionals need to be aware that budgeting usually takes into account the activities that are highest priority, and they are allocated monies in preference to those classed as lower priority.

- *Budget statements:* Budget holders and budget managers generally receive a monthly statement from the finance department indicating usually in retrospect the amount spent on various items during the preceding month. It highlights areas of overspend as well as underspend (see Box 7.1).
- *Matching supply and demand for CPD:* A certain amount of money is always allocated for the CPD of qualified and unqualified care practitioners. Healthcare organisations' training budgets may be held centrally with individual care settings meeting the costs of staff replacement for members who are away on study leave. The budget needs to be spent appropriately in ensuring that they meet the costs of the course that equips or updates employees in areas of skill or knowledge that are required for meeting patient or service user care needs.
- *Problem-solving and decision-making:* Managers are normally equipped with skills and resources for attending to unanticipated eventualities that surface during day-to-day care activities. They have to be resolved as they occur, bearing all possible consequences in mind.
- *Providing leadership:* This is done by practising what one preaches.

Another consideration is that periodically top-sliced money is made available to NHS trusts for a particular activity, such as appointment of a certain number of modern matrons or consultant nurses, or implementation of preceptorship, which may be available for a fixed number of years after which the trust is expected to absorb the costs of the activity or post from its normal annual allocations of money.

Managing Non-human Resources – Equipment, Consumables and Clinical Guidelines

Of the seven groups of resources required for achieving the care organisation's goals, buildings, equipment, information technology, consumables, human resources, methods (i.e. procedures, protocols and guidelines) and money (BEICHMM), human and money resources have been discussed in detail so far in this chapter. The relevant key items were identified in Box 7.1 in the monthly budget statement. The remaining resources in this acronym are now examined.

Buildings, equipment, information technology and consumables

There are a number of reasons for the buildings of care organisations, be they hospitals or smaller units, to be adjusted with the passage of time. Often driven by government policy to deliver a more patient-centred and more efficient service, new departments and units may be built, and others closed. They, however, need to meet various legal requirements, such as health and safety and energy efficiency.

Equipment such as those for performing electrocardiographs, electro-convulsive therapy, relaxation therapy, hoists for moving and handling, beds or cots and so on are purchased to aid patients' recovery. They have to be regularly checked for safety as guided by various health and safety acts and regulations, such as the *Provision and Use of Work Equipment Regulations 1998*, and the *Approved Code of Practice and Guidance* (Health and Safety Executive, 2008). Medical devices such as glucometers, intravenous fluid administration devices and their attachments also have to be purchased and stocks replenished. Access to information technology in clinical settings has increasingly become available in the last decade to support patient or service user care and treatment, and comprises predominantly of computers, especially with access to the internet to facilitate evidence-based practice. Consumables also include single-use items such as dressings, stationery, medications, intravenous administration sets and disposable gloves and aprons.

Procedures, protocols and clinical guidelines (methods)

To ensure the care activities of the care organisation are performed to the highest standards, trusts need to have well-established clinical protocols, clinical guidelines and procedures as resources that support the processes of care delivery. Each of them needs to be reviewed by a pre-determined date, but are usually continually updated with addenda based on new evidence for changes.

The benefits of having protocols and clinical guidelines, and the potential problems with them, were discussed in the context of ensuring quality of healthcare in Chapter 5. Procedures need to be performed in the context of individualised, holistic and evidence-based approaches to care.

Guidelines for efficient and effective resource management

The characteristics of an effective organisation are dependent upon the effectiveness of all its managers, including the DCM fulfilling his/her managerial role (as detailed in Chapter 2) effectively. Guidelines for effective and efficient use of resources in health and social care are:

- Review budget statements each month to monitor expenditure.
- Where you identify areas of overspend, discuss possible ways to reduce the overspend with your manager and ask them if you can shadow them when they meet with the finance manager.
- When a vacancy arises, review the post to ensure that the replacement post meets service requirements rather than replacing like with like automatically.
- Establish the unit cost of consumable resources and raise awareness amongst the team.
- In instances of acute staff sickness, look at working within existing resources in the first instance rather than automatically requesting temporary staffing.
- Discuss productivity with your manager and team members to consider how it could be improved (see 'the productive ward' in Chapter 5).
- Ensure that you genuinely value your staff and openly recognise their input towards the success of the organisation.

This chapter has examined the resources required for effective health and social care delivery, which entailed examining:

- the human and non-human resources that are required by the health and social care organisation to achieve its goals; the question why 'manage' resources was addressed after identifying present-day actual care expenditure; how resources are managed;
- managing human resources, which incorporate skill mix, staff morale as well as recruitment and retention of staff;
- managing non-human resources, which included an examination of budgets and budgeting, the sources of NHS income, the reasons for exploring budgeting, different approaches to budgeting and budgeting at ward/local level; and
- managing other non-human resources such as equipment, medical devices and consumables, as well as clinical guidelines, protocols and procedures; guidelines for efficient and effective resource management were also presented.

- For details of the *2010 NHS Staff Survey* conducted by the CQC, see:

The Care Quality Commission (2011) *Annual Report and Accounts 2010/11*. Available from: www.cqc.org.uk/sites/default/files/media/documents/20110713_care_quality_commission_annual_report__accounts_2010–11_tagged_1.pdf.

- For further details on National NHS Staff Surveys, see: www.nhsstaffsurveys.com/cms/.
- Payment-by-results implies costing each care intervention, and there are 1,500 healthcare resource group (HRG) – clinically meaningful groups of diagnoses and interventions that consume similar levels of NHS resources – identified, to which an actual cost is identified. For further information on payment-by-results and HRGs, see:
Department of Health (2012) *Simple Guide to Payment by Results*. Available from: www.dh.gov.uk/health/2012/11/pbrguide/.
- For further details on the government's response to the Francis Report in relation to skill mix and regulation of CSWs please see: Gov.uk (2013) The Government's response to the Francis report. Available from: www.gov.uk/government/speeches/the-government-s-response-to-the-francis-report.

8

SUPPORT STRATEGIES FOR CARE PROFESSIONALS

Over the years, care professions have been identified as some of the most demanding and potentially stressful occupations (e.g. Meadows et al., 2000; Leners et al., 2006; RCN, 2012b). Provision of support mechanisms by employing organisations and the development of peer support opportunities can contribute to reduction or avoidance of stress, and enable care professionals to perform their duties with the usual energy and optimism, whilst further complementary mutual support mechanisms can make it easier for them to manage challenging situations more comfortably.

This chapter examines the availability of organisational, peer and personal support mechanisms and facilities for care professionals, and ways in which they can be used to not only prevent or deal with problematic situations, but equally importantly to perceive them as learning opportunities. This chapter addresses this aspect of the management role, and explores organisational support provision as well as peer support that can be available for care professionals for gaining external impressions and feedback on their professional competence, and for identifying further learning. Such feedback and support comprise healthy means for professional development and staff satisfaction at work.

Chapter objectives

On completion of this chapter you will be able to:

- recognise the manifestations and sources of stress in care settings, and other reasons for availability of support mechanisms as important means for enabling health and social care professionals to deal with the challenges that they encounter in their day-to-day care activities;

(Continued)

(Continued)

- analyse formal support mechanisms in health and social care, such as the role of clinical supervision, the occupational health department, and possibly social peer support networks;
- identify informal peer support mechanisms in care professions, their significance, recommended techniques for encouraging these, and their strengths and weaknesses.

Reasons for Support Mechanisms for Health and Social Care Practitioners

There are several reasons for care managers having to be cognisant of the personal and professional support mechanisms that are available to health and social care practitioners. This section examines those reasons.

Challenges in the care professions

Duty care managers, like the majority of care professionals, have continuing demands made upon them by a number of stakeholders for specific information and attention, both during a span of duty and over longer periods of time. This is in addition to their patient or service user care activities. A few specific examples of such demands on DCMs are identified in Figure 8.1.

You should be able to add to the empty circle in Figure 8.1 the elements that are specific to your care setting and specialism, such as those of consumer groups, patients waiting on trolleys for hospital beds and so on. At times an unexpected death in the care setting, or an unanticipated aggressive or violent episode by patients or relatives in the A&E Department, for instance, could prove emotionally demanding, and mechanisms for a debrief following such incidents can prove beneficial. Various sources of stress can be identified in care professions, such as:

- Work–life imbalance
- Working with temporary care practitioners (e.g. new agency nurses)
- Unavailability of resources
- Competing demands for time
- Paperwork and bureaucracy
- Staffing challenges such as sickness and vacancies
- Professional relationships
- Lack of teamwork
- Cliques
- Capacity issues
- Inefficient systems of work
- Clinical incidents

Figure 8.1   Demands on DCMs

- Changes in shift work
- Changes in off-duty roster
- New paperwork, or IT to be introduced
- Redeployment of self or team members
- Lack of job security
- Lack of career opportunities
- Financial constraints
- Restructuring
- Under-achieving pre-registration students.

For community care professionals, sources of stress can include heavy caseloads, and the knock-on effects of general practitioners being under pressure to meet government health directives. Some employers feel that workload has increased, and peer contact diminished as care delivery has shifted from secondary to primary care, and has become more high-tech. Evans (2002) explored district nurses' experiences of stress at work and found that the most stressful aspects of work for the particular group of district nurses were: work overload, climate of change, nursing patients with complex care needs, lack of teamwork with other departments, and their family–work interface. Some years before, Ballard (1994) reported on a RCN-supported study that found considerably higher levels of work-related stress and sickness/absence amongst district nurses than for nurses in general, and even higher than in the general working population. Poor managerial support and lack of availability of counselling were causes of further dissatisfaction.

Hawkins and Shohet (2012) suggest that stress is a state of fatigue, ill-health and at times depression caused by distressing, strenuous and emotionally overwhelming situations. They identify various symptoms of stress, including:

- Overtiredness
- Loss of appetite
- Insomnia
- Headaches or migraine
- Diarrhoea, indigestion
- Inability to concentrate
- Paranoid thoughts
- Avoiding friends/colleagues
- Increased alcohol intake, overeating
- Sudden mood swings.

However, over time, if experiences of stress are not recognised and positive action is not taken, then the care practitioner could experience burnout. A study by the *British Medical Journal* recently reported that 42 per cent of nurses in England stated that they felt they were experiencing burnout (Duffin, 2012). The term 'burnout', according to Hawkins and Shohet (2012), refers to a state of emotional and physical exhaustion accompanied by a lack of interest in one's job, low trust in others, a loss of caring, cynicism towards others, self-deprecation, low morale and a deep sense of failure. Such consequences could be avoided or their effects reduced if appropriate support mechanisms or structures are instituted and are functional.

Another likely source of stress or emotional demand is bullying and/or aggression in the workplace. A survey by NHS Employers (2006a) revealed high levels of bullying in NHS trusts. NHS Employers (2006b) indicate that bullying in the NHS may be characterised as offensive, intimidating, malicious or insulting behaviour, an abuse or misuse of power, with intention to undermine, humiliate, denigrate or injure the recipient. Practical steps that can be taken to combat bullying include those suggested by Randle et al. (2007) as:

- disclosing to a friend or trusted colleague;
- exploring knowledge of workplace policy, and discussing with a trade union representative;
- maintaining a written log or diary of bullying incidents; and
- being assertive and recognising yours and others' rights.

Specific guidelines on bullying at work are available from the RCN (2005c), UNISON and other trade unions. It might be difficult to act upon both stress levels and the need to follow up the above-mentioned suggestions during paid working hours, and various concerns may pre-occupy the manager long after they have gone off-duty from the care setting. Over prolonged periods of time, these may lead to the care practitioner experiencing stress and even burnout.

Action point 8.1   My own sources of support

Make a list of who you turn to for support when uncertain about (1) a professional issue, and (2) a personal issue.

The support structures that may be available to you may include work colleagues, family members and friends. These support mechanisms can be grouped under formal and informal mechanisms, and are discussed shortly.

There are several ways in which care practitioners can develop positive coping mechanisms to prevent or deal with stress. These include exercise, eating healthily and looking after your own personal health, as opposed to negative strategies such as smoking and drinking more than usual. Instead of complaining among friends and being a victim, care practitioners can take proactive actions, and explore potential ways of resolving challenging situations such as by working differently, using team meetings, reflecting on practice, supporting team members and recognising stress in them. Sickness management and treating staff fairly and equitably are approaches that DCMs can adopt towards their juniors.

Staff satisfaction at work

As noted in Chapter 7, in its annual NHS staff survey, the CQC (2011b) endeavours to identify the problematic aspects of work in care organisations. Without adequate support, staff dissatisfaction at work experienced by care practitioners may not be identified, which can result in feelings of stress and burnout. The National NHS Staff Survey Co-ordination Centre (2012b) also conducts NHS staff surveys, which includes questions related to the use of the organisation's occupational health department, for example, and detailed results of the survey are then published over the Internet.

Staff satisfaction survey mechanisms can be used periodically (usually annually) by organisations to gauge employees' morale and how far job expectations are being met. The organisation can thereby gain feedback from their workforce on various aspects of working life identified by the CQC and the national staff surveys. The

CQC survey can be adapted with open and closed questions on the following aspects of the post.

- Existence, clarity and strategies for achieving the organisation's vision.
- Extent of top-down, bottom-up and peer communication.
- Learning and development opportunities.
- Availability of IDPRs.
- Opportunities to use own initiative.
- Career opportunities.
- Health, safety and welfare in the working environment.
- Stress and availability of counselling.
- The general physical environment of the workplace.
- Harassment and bullying.
- Staff involvement in decisions.
- Feedback on performance.
- Diversity and equality.
- Management of change.

As can be seen in the above list, staff satisfaction surveys can include questions on harassment and bullying at work, for instance, and if they do exist, then there can be questions on whether they were reported, and what the outcomes of reporting were. If they are not reported, then the reasons for this can be explored.

Action point 8.2   Staff satisfaction surveys

Explore when a staff satisfaction survey was conducted by your employing organisation, which office it was initiated by, whether it was anonymous, where the results were published and what the outcomes or ensuing action plans were. Alternatively, access the CQC's (2011b) NHS Staff Surveys website and view the most recent staff survey for your organisation, and identify its findings.

Staff satisfaction surveys comprise a useful means of gaining employees' perspectives on aspects of work and the workplace and the inherent dynamics that they are happy with and those that are more problematic.

On countenancing the above-mentioned challenges, care practitioners may wish to explore their thoughts with peers or seniors with appropriate knowledge. Such a milieu or vehicle can be available through formal support mechanisms and more informal ones, some of which are well-instituted organisationally, and others are potentials in that they are at developmental stages.

Formal Support Mechanisms

The formal support mechanisms available to health and social care professionals can be at individual, organisational and supra-organisational levels. Such support can be gained from:

- line managers;
- working spans of duty that accommodate family commitments;
- the occupational health department;
- clinical supervision;
- reflection-on-action mechanisms;
- professional forums;
- peer-learning;
- mentorship; and
- buddy systems.

Line managers

An important and easily accessed source of support is often the care professional's line manager. Line managers' roles include staff support in that the DCM should provide appropriate support to those who they manage, and also expect support for themselves from their own line managers.

Accommodating other commitments

One of the most significant staff support strategies identified over a decade ago in *The NHS Plan* (DH, 2000b) was that the NHS would invest in its staff in ways that enable them to lead balanced working lives. How this could be achieved was subsequently documented in the IWL (DH, 2000d), which comprises a blueprint by which NHS employers and staff can measure the management of human resources. Organisations are given kitemark certification for their ability to demonstrate a commitment to improve the working lives of their employees.

IWL is based on the premise that improving the working lives of staff contributes directly to better patient or service user care through improved recruitment and retention. In *The NHS Plan*, the DH (2000b) also indicated that patients and service users had previously stated that they want to be treated by well-motivated, fairly rewarded staff. It also indicates that the way NHS employers treat staff will later become part of their core performance measures and linked to the financial resources they receive. Consequently, NHS employers were instructed to create well-managed, flexible working environments that support staff, promote their welfare and development, and respect their need to manage a healthy and productive balance between their work and their life outside work. How such balance can be achieved according to IWL are identified in Box 8.1.

Box 8.1   How work–life balance can be achieved according to IWL (DH, 2000d)

- HR strategy and commitment to support service objectives
- Team-based employee self-rostering
- Annual hours arrangements
- Childcare support
- Reduced hours options
- Flexi-time
- Carers support
- Career breaks
- Flexible retirement
- Building a diverse workforce that reflects the local community
- Changing the long hours culture

- Healthy workplace commitment
- Managers leading by example
- Finding out what working arrangements work for staff
- Challenging traditional working patterns
- Involving staff in the design and development of better, flexible working practices
- Conducting annual staff attitude surveys – asking relevant questions and acting on the key messages
- HR policies and processes that make a difference to individuals
- Reducing staff turnover
- Accessible training and development packages for all staff

NHS employers are expected to provide for all these components, which include high-profile activities such as childcare support and flexible working hours. IWL standards were to be achieved by NHS employers providing evidence of commitment to improving the working lives of their staff in the following components:

- recognising that modern health services require modern employment services by having a HR strategy in place for the organisation to deliver against IWL recommendations;
- understanding that staff work best for patients when they can strike a healthy balance between work and other aspects of their life outside work by demonstrating leadership from the top and Board commitment to more flexible, supportive, family friendly and culturally sensitive ways of working and training;
- accepting a joint responsibility with staff to develop a range of working arrangements that balance the needs of patients and services with the needs of staff, by finding out which working patterns staff prefer;
- Valuing and supporting staff according to the contribution they make to patient care, and meeting the needs of the service by staff across the organisation from all disciplines,

and irrespective of their role in the organisation or working patterns, demonstrating their commitment to the organisation and feeling the organisation is committed to their wellbeing;

- providing personal and professional development, and training opportunities, that are accessible and open to all staff irrespective of their working patterns by demonstrating appropriate investment in training for staff who have patterns of working that are not standard; and
- having a range of policies and practices in place that enable staff to manage a healthy balance between work and their commitments outside work and practical support in place to meet the specific needs of staff.

These IWL standards are obviously quite specific and detailed, and various guidelines on how different care professions can achieve these components of IWL and standards have been published since the initial *IWL* publication. One alternative to institutional support recommended by Hawksley (2007) for combating work-related stress and building a work–life balance is personal life coaching, but there is usually monetary cost attached to such provision.

The occupational health department

Another support mechanism available to care practitioners is the care organisation's occupational health department. The staff-support element of their remit generally includes:

- Health surveillance
- Health and safety advice
- Work station assessments
- Health education and promotion
- Counselling
- Return to work rehabilitation programmes
- Ad-hoc advice
- Sickness and absence management.

This department's provision is thus quite comprehensive, and some include other functions such as planning for retirement. It is through their 'counselling' and 'ad-hoc advice' that occupational health services provide individual personal support to care practitioners. Individuals can be referred to a staff counsellor if more specialist support is required. They can provide advice for work-related issues via telephone or on a 'drop-in' basis.

Clinical supervision

One of the most widely advocated specific forms of organised individual and peer support is clinical supervision. This section explores what clinical supervision is, the aims and benefits of clinical supervision, how clinical supervision is implemented and used, and also the likely problems that need to be addressed beforehand.

Earlier on, the NHS Management Executive (1993) indicated that clinical supervision is a formal process of professional support and learning that enables individual practitioners to develop knowledge and competence, assume responsibility for their own practice and enhance consumer protection and safety of care in complex situations. Two decades later, McColgan and Rice (2012: 36) provide a more current definition of clinical supervision, which they state is 'a process of professional support and learning that enables practitioners to develop knowledge and competence to improve care'. Both definitions indicate that clinical supervision is about 'professional support' for the care professional, which incorporates a form of professional development, with the eventual beneficiary being the patient or service user. On the other hand, Shanley and Stevenson (2006: 586) suggest that clinical supervision is a 'multi-meaninged phenomenon defined through the context of its use'.

Thus, clinical supervision allows a registrant to receive formal professional support in the workplace by an appropriately skilled clinical supervisor. Regular pre-arranged meetings are held which enable the supervisee to discuss areas of professional development for both self-improvement and enhancement of patient care. The learning associated with advancement of knowledge and skills through professional development can also be used to meet revalidation requirements – previously referred to as post-registration education and practice (PREP) (continuing professional development) standard (NMC, 2011a). The NMC (2012b) also sees clinical supervision as an important part of the care setting's quality assurance mechanism.

Similar arrangements for clinical supervision are recommended for registrants in allied health and social care professions, and should be available throughout their careers so that they can constantly evaluate and advance their professional knowledge and skills as accountable practitioners.

The anticipated benefits of clinical supervision are that it should lead to improved job satisfaction through greater empowerment, and improvement in the quality of care provided. However, 'supervision' itself is a concept that prevails in various arenas, within and outside care professions with similar meaning to clinical supervision, but with specified functions. Midwives, for example, have a system of statutory supervision through Local Supervising Authorities, as detailed in the *Midwives Rules and Standards* (NMC, 2010c). It is used beneficially in varied fields such as social work, counselling, education, probation, police and even for refugees and asylums seekers, that is, in most 'people professions' (Hawkins and Shohet, 2012).

However, the term 'clinical supervision' itself can be interpreted in different ways, and some suggest that perhaps 'clinical support' or 'peer-supervision' might be more appropriate. Another possible weakness of clinical supervision is that some care practitioners are apprehensive about it, fearing that it could be associated with some type of inspection of individuals' weaknesses as a management-led function that is designed to control rather than facilitate.

Furthermore, Gilmore (2001) and others note that some care managers are unable to gauge and account for the time and resources required for clinical supervision. Also, some care practitioners fear that managers could link clinical supervision with

IDPR, although this notion is firmly discarded by the advocates of clinical supervision in nursing. This is because it may be felt by employees that if objectives set in IDPRs are not achieved for whatever reason, then the reviewee may be deemed incompetent, with the associated risk of disciplinary procedures being invoked. The intention of clinical supervision is to use supportive, clinically legitimate and confidential ways of aiding care practitioners to identify professional development needs and means of achieving them. It is thus also a constructive medium for assisting individuals with practice deficits to improve their practice voluntarily, and in a collegial and mutually supported environment.

Other barriers to clinical supervision include:

- pressure on time that can be used on direct patient or service user care;
- too few adequately trained supervisors;
- cost in terms of time allocated;
- exercise of 'position power' if the supervisor is of a more senior status; and
- availability and accessibility of supervision.

If the supervisor–supervisee relationship breaks down, this can be problematic as well. Furthermore, with regard to confidentiality as governed by the NMC (2010b) *The Code – Standards of Conduct, Performance and Ethics for Nurses and Midwives*, nothing that happens during supervision should be revealed to others without the explicit consent of the supervisee. If a record of supervision is maintained, it should be the property of the supervisee, and likely to be retained in their own portfolio. However, as in other situations, if during supervision a practitioner discloses a breach of the code, then confidentiality cannot be assured. On the other hand, when appropriate, the NMC (2012b) also allows registrants who have been reported to them for suspected misconduct to continue practising based on the condition that he/she receives structured clinical supervision from a clinical supervisor nominated by the employer.

Clinical supervision can be conducted at individual or one-to-one level with a more experienced care practitioner supervising someone less experienced. Alternatively, it can be provided through peer supervision, which is peer-led, group or team supervision. Group supervision, however, can vary to some extent from one group to another. Sloan and Watson (2002) note that in group supervision the clinical supervisor facilitates a group of four to six supervisees.

Facilitation and helping skills are prerequisites which can be acquired through appropriate training, even in pre-registration nursing courses, as reported by Carver et al. (2006), for instance. The facilitation of clinical supervision needs to be systematic through the use of a framework or model of clinical supervision. Two popular models of clinical supervision are Proctor's (2001) three-function interactive approach and Heron's (1989) six-category intervention analysis framework. Proctor's (2001) model entails three main functions of clinical supervision:

- *Normative:* Addresses the quality control aspects of practice as well as managerial aspect related to policies and procedures, developing standards and clinical audit.

- *Formative:* Refers to the educational process of skill development, including EBP.
- *Restorative:* Providing supportive help for those working with regard to stressful situations, with the aim of enabling the professional to understand and manage these situations during professional practice.

This model constitutes a framework that enables both parties to focus on the purpose of the activity. Sloan and Watson (2002) argue that Proctor's model is not too prescriptive and therefore allows leeway, but at the same time gives insufficient guidance to supervisors, especially in the restorative component. Heron's (1989) six-category intervention analysis model provides another suitable framework, as identified in Chapter 2.

The supervisor–supervisee relationship, however, needs to be non-competitive, clear and with well-focused objectives. Use of models of clinical supervision needs to be supported by the conditions for a therapeutic relationship, which according to Rogers and Freiberg (1994) include 'acceptance' of the supervisee for who they are and the situation that they find themselves in; genuineness (i.e. being honest about oneself as a person); and empathy. These are essential components of 'helping' (a term often used interchangeably with counselling), and counsellors and psychotherapists value supervision from peers. However, counselling is a deeper and much more complex process than supervision, and therefore supervision sessions must not be interpreted as counselling.

Various research studies have highlighted the benefits of clinical supervision. Hyrkas et al. (2005), for example, found that clinical supervision has long-term positive effects on an individual's clinical practice and self-development. However, Jones (2006) and Gilmore (2001), amongst others, highlighted issues with clinical supervision in nursing, in that Jones (2006), for instance, notes that the implementation and use of clinical supervision is haphazard, and the processes are not generally well understood.

However, Leners et al. (2006) extend the clinical supervision concept further, and suggest that in view of sporadic inadequate staffing and negative knock-on effect this has on desired patient outcomes and on nurses' job satisfaction, a career-long mentorship programme should be established for nurses at various stages of their professional careers. The term 'mentorship' thus extends such support beyond how it is currently experienced through episodic clinical supervision, to interactions and relationship between mentor and mentee on a more continuous basis, and thus 'empower, inspire, guide, advise and model clinical behaviours that promote quality patient care outcomes in a team-based work environment' (p. 653). Clinical supervision often involves reflective learning, which is discussed in Chapter 11.

Non-formal and Informal Support Mechanisms

Non-formal modes of personal and peer support can prevail through peer-review and peer-learning. It occurs through individuals investing time and effort to impart knowledge and skills to peers and learn from each other, a notion that is also referred to as 'social and human capital', and is discussed shortly in this chapter.

The role of peer-review and peer-learning

This section examines the role of peer-review, together with the inherent and associ-ated activities peer-learning and self-assessment of knowledge and competence within care professions, systems that constitute support and feedback.

The DH's (1999b: 30) nursing strategy document *Making a Difference* indicated that 'learning that takes place at work through experience, critical incidents, audit and reflection, supported by mentorship, and clinical supervision and peer-review can be a rich source of learning.' Thus when the care practitioner is allocated a new activity or project, they might feel that they will benefit from sounding their thoughts out informally with trusted and appropriately knowledgeable colleagues or peers. Peer-review can be used for benchmarking purposes, or for exchange of protocols and clinical guidelines between peers at different care organisations.

As to who a 'peer' could be, this may be:

- a colleague of equal status in the same care setting;
- a colleague of equal status from another care setting in the same specialism or department;
- someone of higher status in the same care setting or another practice setting in the same specialism;
- someone of equal or higher status from another organisation; or
- an individual in a very similar or identical vocation, and perhaps also from a similar social background and age group.

Access to the Internet in the work setting for literature searching and locating criti-cally appraised material can itself constitute informal peer-education. They can be available in the care setting's resource room or the staffroom for informal social learning, or in the healthcare trust's post-graduate department. Another angle on peer-learning is provided by Goldsmith et al. (2006) who report on a formal peer-learning strategy, which is through partnering first-year and third-year student nurses for clinical practice sessions. Both groups of students commended peer-learning as useful and positive learning experiences. Yuen Loke and Chow (2007) also report on positive effects from similar arrangements. Brooks and Moriarty (2009) reports on a successful structured buddying system for nursing students during clinical placements that provides improved level of professional, personal and pastoral support for those students.

Furthermore, for student nurses, practice education facilitators can arrange regu-lar 'student support meetings' within the care provider organisation, whereupon all students on placement at the particular organisation (e.g. NHS Trust) are notified, and attend. Since students have supernumerary status, there are usually no problems in releasing them to attend these sessions. It is helpful for DCMs to be aware of all these means of support for students, which should free up time for qualified health-care professionals to dedicate the time to patient or service user care.

Related to peer-learning is the concept of 'synergogy', as suggested by Mouton and Blake (1984). Synergogy comprises a deliberate plan designed to enable very small groups of learners who are on the same programme of learning, who have good rapport with each other, and who learn from each other, and not to have to learn from an educator if they see the latter as an authority figure. This concept is also based on an interpretation of synergy which suggests that significant learning takes place when two or more individuals study together than when they do so separately. The learning is supported by learning materials being managed by a learning administrator.

Action point 8.3   Synergogy and protected time for learning

The notion of protected or allocated time specifically for CPD is often advocated. With libraries and other learning facilities, including electronic databases, increasingly being instituted in care organisations, can you envisage if and how synergogy can be organised by groups of care practitioners of equal status, and used efficiently?

Another mechanism for peer learning being instituted by care organisations is 'action learning sets', as advocated by McGill and Beatty (2001) and others. Such learning sets comprise small discussion groups, with pre-agreed membership, who meet regularly to discuss innovations, issues, new policies or guidelines and so on. A range of mentoring and buddying mechanisms have also been established.

Self-assessment and peer review

Peer-learning can be based on self-assessment. The development of professional knowledge and competence by individuals as lifelong learners is usually based on self-assessment (Gopee, 2000), but self-assessment in isolation is not sufficient for learning and development, and individuals at times look to their peers for their views and judgements. Hollis (1991:47) asserted a while back that while 'self-monitoring is a useful tool, it can be unrealistic and does not overcome the problem of learners needing the intellectual stimulus of others and acquiring subtle insights from peers.'

Jarvis and Gibson (1997) observed that during one's career, as care practitioners become more skilled and autonomous, their competence is less likely to be assessed by others. For practice nurses, for example, Cairns (1998:24) indicated that because they work autonomously or in isolation, they need the mechanism of clinical super-vision for peer-feedback. The same may apply to clinical nurse specialists, whose roles also often involve autonomous decision-making. The DH (1999b) identified professional autonomy as both a privilege and a significant responsibility that has to be matched by commitment to public accountability.

Considering the likely strengths and weaknesses associated with peer-assessment, one of the strengths is that it constitutes an opportunity to the care practitioner to practice a skill in a safe environment, and to receive instant feedback on performance. Such feedback tends to have powerful impact. The likely weaknesses include the probability of individuals being overcritical, their own lack of knowledge of the skill area, the possibility of disagreement between peers, and even the lack of availability of peers, or of opportunities for peer-assessment.

There is also a risk of peer-assessment becoming an avenue for the 'blind leading the blind', whereupon unsafe practice may continue and is transferred to others. However, Welsh (2006) argues that peer-assessment comprises an essential transferable skill. Peer-assessment is part of professional regulation or self-regulation which is a requirement for all care professions (e.g. GMC, 2010).

Peer-review, on the other hand, lies at the foundation of professional accountability and autonomous practice in care delivery, and is associated with clinical supervision and various quality assurance activities. It can be initiated and implemented at one-to-one, departmental or organisational level. Peer-review is different from clinical supervision in that it specifically refers to professional care activities, while clinical supervision can extend to consider personal problematic experiences.

Malby and Manning (1998: 24) report on an inter-trust peer-review learning network whose key principles include participants being keen to 'learn and support others in an atmosphere of trust and openness'. A collaborative, non-competitive learning environment at all levels of the organisation is also seen as important. They conclude that peer-review 'can make a valuable contribution to organisational and personal development and professional practice' (p. 25).

As to what to review, some other activities that may benefit from peer-review include:

- determining evidence of professional updating – in care activities, managerial, and clinically or work-based teaching;
- post-conference reflections;
- exploring accountability towards various parties, such as the profession, the public, the employer; and
- self-assessed further developmental requirements.

The GMC (2012a) has advocated peer-review in various areas of medicine, including in relation to performance assessment of doctors when concerns have been expressed in relation to their competence.

Empirical evidence of the effectiveness of peer-review is variable. McAllister and Osborne's (1997: 40) study indicated that peer-review 'increases personal accountability and has demonstrated improved quality of care and clinician performance.' Box 8.2 presents good practice guidelines for peer-review.

Box 8.2   Good practice guidelines for peer-review

- Ascertain assessment or performance criteria prior to the event.
- Be skilled in giving constructive and supportive feedback.
- Always be sensitive to the assessee's or reviewee's responses, verbal and non-verbal, to the feedback being given. The degree to which weaknesses are pointed out straight after the performance must be balanced to prevent being overcritical.
- Be objective, as the assessee may feel that he/she is already fully aware of their weaknesses in the performance being assessed.
- Additional written feedback can also be given, for a more complete picture.
- Always encourage self-assessment prior to peer or assessor feedback.
- Strict use of Rogers and Frieberg's (1994) acceptance and warmth, empathy and genuineness, is important.
- Need to be a skilled facilitator to ensure that emotional damage is not being done to the assessee if the peer-assessment is being formally assessed.
- The facilitator role is to guide and support peers, and enable them to develop self-confidence.
- Consider recording the peer-review centrally so that action plans, improvement and progress can be recorded. This can be private or open to inspection (Pedler et al., 2007).

Peer-review is increasingly becoming a part of autonomous practice and professionalism. Garbett et al. (2007) report on a study of peer-review facilitated by the 360-degree feedback method (discussed in Chapter 3), suggesting that this facilitates collection of evidence for clinical expertise development, and also might contribute to improved working relationships. However, being a relatively novel idea in most nursing circles, initial participation in peer-review should be introduced as a highly recommended but voluntary and consensual activity.

Professional forums

Another vehicle for peer-reviews are professional forums, which comprise special interest groups that are convened based on clinical specialisms. The RCN, for example, has approximately 85 of these forums, which can provide a supportive medium for peer-consultation, including, for example, forums for critical care nurses, mental health nurses and so on.

Social and human capital as peer-learning mechanisms

Another increasingly recognised means of peer support and peer-learning involves the notion of social and human capital, which comprises the ad-hoc or informal support that individuals give to and receive from course peers, friends, colleagues and even families. 'Social capital' refers to time, patience, information and teaching that individuals 'invest' in each other in relatively closely knit social groups, and amongst peers. The influence of care colleagues, co-students and personal relations on learning is thus very significant and valuable.

In a review of the literature on human and social capital in nurse education, Royal (2012) found that with nurse education located in higher education, there has been an increase in human capital (time and effort invested by individual in their own education and skill acquisition), although appreciation of ways of benefiting from social capital remains limited.

A while back, Putnam (1993) suggested that social capital is characterised by:

- the existence of community networks;
- local identity and a sense of solidarity and equality with other community members; and
- norms of trust and reciprocal help and support.

Field (1999:12) asserts that a great deal of learning is social in nature, and connected to this is the gap in current knowledge as to the level of informal learning that occurs as and when people 'learn in corridors, over tea, in the car park, as well as through unnoticed patterns of behaviour and interaction in the classroom itself', although the amount and effects of this mode of learning is difficult to quantify. Practitioners on the same course, for instance, meet socially and e-mail each other to share articles and references related to module assignments, thus forming informal networks that instigate learning, or even use electronic networking facilities such as 'Facebook' to do so.

Social and human capital therefore entails the social investment of personal time and knowledge, which can enable the continuation of professional learning, a feature that care managers can support and further develop to enhance learning. Moreover, social capital thrives in settings that constitute learning organisations, which are inherent features of lifelong learning. The work environment in which the care practitioner delivers care tends to have considerable effect on their learning, as discussed in Chapter 11. Bahn (2001: 115) discusses this in the context of social learning theory, and notes that the social environment has considerable impact on a 'collaborative approach to learning through the use of peers and expert practitioners as role models'. Even crisis situations comprise fertile grounds for novel ideas and methods to develop. Such suggestions should be endorsed and the notion cultivated, and such conditions seem to be germinating already within networks of friends and colleagues, and need to be recognised (Gopee, 2002; Taylor, 2012).

Thus, infrastructures and facilitatory mechanisms often unbeknown to employers seem to support lifelong learning for the registrant, and the practice setting ultimately benefits from them. Social capital is also related to the concept of the 'informal organisation' which Mullins (2010) and others identify as non-formal structures that constitute a powerful force in shaping cultures in organisations.

Colleagues may encourage learning and development with an enquiring mind by bringing back appropriate literature acquired from conferences and workshops. These can be made available in the practice setting as learning materials, or colleagues who have been on CPD courses subsequently share aspects of what they have learnt perhaps by giving a talk, or facilitating a workshop, to disseminate their knowledge.

A seemingly equally important factor is the role played by non-healthcare individuals such as parents, friends and the individuals' partners or spouses in the context of the external perspectives that they might provide, and can constitute instigators or supportive mechanisms for learning. Social and human capital is also reflected in doctors influencing care practitioners' learning as they work on joint projects such as setting up specialist clinics, or on an RCT.

Furthermore, the impact of social networking websites is also widely felt as a vast number of people, including students, use them to communicate their thoughts quite extensively with peers and with others with similar interests. However, as Field (1999) notes, socially unacceptable learning can also prevail, as in learning new criminal behaviour from prison inmates, and similarly there is a risk that incorrect information can be passed on to peers in such informal, unmonitored provisions.

The NMC (2011b) has therefore published advice on the use of social networking sites on the Internet, such as Facebook and Twitter, by nurses, midwives and students. The advice primarily indicates that the NMC's (2010b) code of practice also applies to communicating through social networking sites (such as maintaining patient confidentiality), and provides practical advice for using social networking responsibly.

Moreover, more structured peer communication channels are made available through education institutions' online learning discussion forums as part of intranets. This facility is fairly widely used, and course or module leaders may either formally participate in the discussions or merely conduct ad-hoc monitoring, and take action to advise on parameters or ground rules if necessary.

Some time back, Watkins and Marsick (1992: 115) suggested that human resource development should be re-defined to endorse and incorporate 'greater inclusion of informal and incidental learning strategies' by personnel responsible for this role. Peers and managers could therefore appreciate the contribution of social and human capital and other 'informal' modes of learning, and accommodate mechanisms to facilitate this whenever they can, as ultimately patient or service user care is enhanced through better informed care. Baron et al. (2000: 38) explored the concept from various standpoints in the general literature, and suggest that in the spirit of the 'current questing age', the concept should neither be dismissed as an empty vessel, nor overblown as a concept that will address all social issues.

Guidelines for effective peer support

Some guidelines for effective peer support are:

- Encourage formal and informal peer-learning.
- Implement and sustain clinical supervision either on a one-to-one basis or as group supervision.
- Use, and encourage use of, the care organisation's support mechanisms.
- Normalise reflection-on-action.
- Ensure annual IDPRs are conducted for yourself and your team.
- Ensure that colleagues know of other management support anchors, other than the line manager.
- Maintain confidentiality.

- Encourage colleagues to be members of professional special interest groups or forums.
- Use social networking websites if you wish, but responsibly.
- Use education institutions' online discussion forums to test out your own thoughts and impressions.

This chapter has explored the key components of peer and personal support strategies available to care practitioners. This included:

- the reasons for support mechanisms being important components of care organisations, including enabling care practitioners to deal with the challenges that they encounter in their day-to-day clinical activities with positive coping mechanisms; and staff satisfaction at work;
- formal support mechanisms which include the role of occupational health departments, clinical supervision and reflective practice, and the availability and accessibility of support mechanisms; and
- non-formal and informal support mechanisms, including the role of peer-review, peer-learning and peer-assessment, the distinction between these mechanisms, their likely strengths and weaknesses, and recommended techniques for implementing them; professional forums and the concept of social and human capital, together with guidelines for effective staff support.

It is clear from the elements addressed in this chapter that one of the benefits of peer-support mechanisms is that they constitute a medium for proactive and informal learning, and for care practitioners to develop personal management plans to avert or manage stress that DCMs can draw on as and when required.

CHAPTER SUMMARY

- For full details of the DH NHS Staff Surveys, see:

National Staff Survey Co-ordination Centre (2012) *Guidance Manual for the NHS Staff Survey 2011*. Available from: http://nhsstaffsurveys.com/cms/uploads/ST11_GuidanceNotes.pdf.

- Explore the mission statement and business plan of your occupational health department to gauge how supportive they are, if they offer counselling, and if you are convinced confidentiality is maintained.
- For further details on how human and social capital can enhance learning, see:

Gopee N (2002) 'Human and social capital as facilitators of lifelong learning in nursing'. *Nurse Education Today*, 22 (7): 608–616.

RECOMMENDED FURTHER READING

9

PATIENT AND SERVICE USER INVOLVEMENT, PARTICIPATION AND PARTNERSHIP

Putting patients first is fundamental to the Government's modernisation of health and social services, and patient-focused services and patient choice are central concepts within this. The achievement of this vision is dependant upon a change in culture, together with a shift in power base to empower patients to become more actively involved both in the development of services and in the care that they personally receive. The DCM needs to keep abreast of policy developments, evaluating the implications for their practice setting and identifying ways of applying relevant ideologies to their everyday clinical practice. This chapter begins by contextualising the motivating forces for the development of choice and consumerism, together with the promotion of more patient-centred health and social care services.

Chapter objectives

On completion of this chapter you will be able to:

- identify the policy and professional drivers for the development of patient-focused services, choice and the promotion of consumerism within healthcare;
- examine the power base that underpins the practitioner-patient relationship;

- define person-centred care and identify prerequisites and barriers to the application of this concept to clinical practice;
- explore the concepts of patient involvement, participation and partnership and their application within the context of your professional practice; and
- reflect on current practice and identify strategies to enhance person-centred care within your practice setting.

Background of Patient Involvement, Participation and Partnership

Political and professional drivers, coupled with increasing public expectation, have created a demand for the provision of more patient-focused services. The advent of the initial *Patient's Charter* (DH, 1991) promoted the concepts of individualised, patient-centred care and heralded the beginning of the then Labour government's commitment to provide patients with rights regarding the healthcare services that they receive. Patient choice has more recently emerged as a central theme and it is anticipated that it will act as a catalyst for improving both the quality of service provision and patient outcomes. Research undertaken by Dixon et al. (2010), however, identified that most patients chose to be treated by their local provider, and few consulted published performance information on quality to help them choose, instead relying on past experience and the advice of their GP.

The White Paper *Equity and Excellence: Liberating the NHS* (DH, 2010a) set out the coalition Government's vision of an NHS that puts patients and the public first, where 'no decision about me, without me' is the norm. It included proposals to give patients more say over their care and treatment, together with greater opportunity to make informed choices, with the aim of securing better care and outcomes.

The Health and Social Care Act (DH, 2012a) places a duty on NHS England and the clinical commissioning groups to promote the involvement of patients and carers in decisions about their care and treatment, and to enable patient choice.

The *NHS Constitution for England* (DH, 2012d) sets out the principles and values of the NHS in England. It details the rights to which patients, public and staff are entitled, and pledges that the NHS is committed to achieve. It also sets out responsibilities for the public, patients and staff in order to ensure that the NHS operates fairly and effectively. All NHS bodies and private and third-sector providers supplying NHS services are required by law to take account of this Constitution in their decisions and actions. The pledges and rights for patients and the public are set out across seven key areas:

1 Access to health services.
2 Quality of care and environment.
3 Nationally approved treatment, drugs and programmes.
4 Respect, consent and confidentiality.

5   Informed choice.
6   Involvement in healthcare and the NHS.
7   Complaint and redress.

The constitution also sets out responsibilities for patients and the public with the intention of supporting the NHS to work effectively together with responsible resource use.

Such policy initiatives support the move from traditional paternalistic approaches of healthcare to a more empowering approach that encompasses both individual responsibility and choice. Other examples of available choice options include whether to give birth at home, in a birthing centre or in hospital, and also opportunities to self-refer to therapy services such as physiotherapy. An NHS website is available to provide patients with information about health and choices that are available to them. NHS Choices (2012) can be accessed at www.nhs.uk/Pages/HomePage.aspx and includes, amongst other features, the opportunity to compare hospitals by the treatment they provide and the facilities that they offer. Patients can also leave comments about their experiences of NHS services.

The DCM needs to be politically aware and to evaluate the impact of national and local policy on care delivery within their practice setting and has a responsibility to ensure that individualised patient-centred care, underpinned by choice, is central to the care that is provided. Mechanisms to support patient and public involvement within the NHS are highlighted in Figure 9.1 and are summarised below:

- *Health and Wellbeing Boards* bring together local commissioners of health and social care, elected representatives and representatives of Local Healthwatch to agree an integrated way to improving local health and wellbeing.
- *Healthwatch England* has a national role for people who use health and social care services to ensure that their voices are heard by the Secretary of State for Health, the CQC, NHS England, Monitor and all local authorities in England.

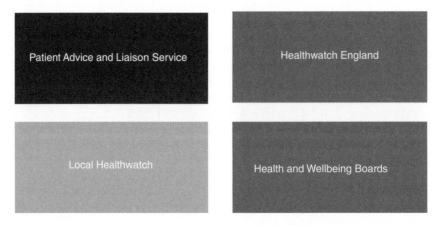

Figure 9.1   Mechanisms to support patient and public involvement

- *Local Healthwatch* are independent local organisations with a role to provide citizens and communities with a voice to influence and challenge how health and social care services are provided within their locality.
- *Patient Advice and Liaison Service (PALS)* aims to ensure that the NHS listens to patients, their relatives, carers and friends, and answers their questions and resolves their concerns as quickly as possible. PALS also provide a source of feedback to respective providers of healthcare.

We have so far explored the national agenda with regard to the modernisation of health services to support the government's vision to put patients at the heart of everything the NHS does with a focus on continuously improving those things that really matter to patients. We will now relate this concept to the role of the DCM within everyday practice.

Involvement, participation and partnership

The concepts of involvement, participation and partnership are relatively broad, and therefore are open to interpretation and are often used interchangeably (Roberts, 2002). Cahill (1996: 563) asserts that 'there is no clear consensus on what patient-participation entails' and goes on to say that as a result of this lack of clarity the concept has become 'rhetoric or even a cliché'. Cahill also argues that a hierarchical relationship exists between the three concepts of involvement, participation and partnership (Figure 9.2). Within this hierarchy Cahill states that patient involvement or collaboration is a prerequisite for patient participation, which in turn is a prerequisite for patient partnership.

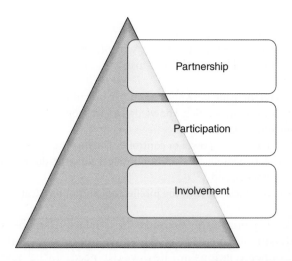

Figure 9.2   A hierarchical relationship between concepts (adapted from Cahill, 1996)

The first concept, patient involvement, is comparatively more passive in nature where, for example, the health/social care practitioner may provide information or elicit information from the patient as part of the assessment process. Participation, on the other hand, necessitates more active involvement from the patient; an example of which is where the practitioner engages the patient in an evaluation of his or her care. Working in partnership, however, is premised more upon equality within the patient– practitioner relationship, an example of which is 'contracting' with a patient through goal setting, or the development of a care, therapy or birth plan.

The degree to which equality can be achieved within the practitioner–patient relationship, however, has been questioned. Within the hierarchy of concepts, Cahill (1996), for example, considers partnership as more idealistic and not necessarily achievable in practice and concedes that there is a need, therefore, to establish the extent to which patients want to participate in their care. Conversely, Tutton (2005) identified participation as a process that occurs in the context of care giving, rather than within a hierarchy of decision-making.

Action point 9.1   Applying patient involvement, participation and partnership to the DCM role

- Draw a table with three columns, at the top of the columns insert one of the concepts of involvement, participation or partnership, one in each column.
- For each concept record a list of examples of how you apply this, or could apply this, within your role as DCM.

Within the concept analysis of patient participation completed by Cahill (1996), she identified a number of defining attributes, without which, she argues, the concept might not have surfaced. These attributes are:

- the presence of a relationship between healthcare practitioner and patient;
- a narrowing of relevant information, knowledge and/or competence gap between healthcare practitioner and patient;
- a surrendering of a degree of power or control by the healthcare practitioner;
- engagement in selective intellectual and/or physical activities during some of the phases of the healthcare process; and
- a positive benefit is associated with the intellectual and/or physical activity.

Of these defining attributes, the presence of a relationship between healthcare practitioner and patient emerged as the most important. Within the patient–healthcare practitioner relationship, however, it needs to be acknowledged that some patients are supportive of healthcare practitioners making decisions on their behalf and respect the professionalism of the healthcare practitioner to act in their best interests.

Roberts' (2002) study, for example, identified that 60 per cent (18 of 30) of patient participants stated a preference to be involved in decision-making, with 23 per cent (7) stating that they did not want to be, predominantly on the grounds of their ill health. The healthcare practitioner must acknowledge the uniqueness of each patient and recognise the necessity to treat patients as individuals, establishing the degree to which they want to participate in decisions about their healthcare.

Action point 9.2   Power and the healthcare practitioner–patient relationship

- Consider who is more powerful, the patient or the health/social care practitioner.
- Make a list of sources of power for each of these two groups.

Boxes 9.1 and 9.2 provide examples of potential sources of power for healthcare practitioners and patients, respectively. When sources of power are evaluated, the DCM needs to identify ways of shifting the balance of power more in favour of the patient.

Box 9.1   Potential sources of power: healthcare practitioners

Sources of power	Healthcare practitioner
1 Knowledge and expertise	Professional education
	Clinical experience
2 Language	Medical terminology
3 Environment	Delivering care/therapy/treatment within the environment of a healthcare institution
4 Uniform	Represents status
5 Professional autonomy	Gatekeeper to treatment/care/therapy

Box 9.2   Potential sources of power: patients

Sources of power	Patient
Knowledge and expertise	Information technology, e.g. Internet
	Impact of their illness on their everyday experiences
Environment	Care/therapy/treatment delivered within the patient's own home
Rights	Choice of care provider
	Right to complain
	Right to ask for a second opinion
	Right to refuse treatment

Power can form a significant role in the healthcare practitioner–patient relationship. Transfer of power from healthcare practitioner to patient, however, is not without challenge as it is at odds with more traditional, paternalistic approaches to care delivery where healthcare practitioners act/acted in the best interests of patients. Within contemporary practice, altering the power base more in favour of the patient will necessitate a change in culture. It needs to be recognised that power can be exerted both consciously and subconsciously, and that some healthcare practitioners will adapt more readily than others.

Decision-making needs to encompass choice, with the healthcare practitioner outlining the various options that are available to the patient. EBHC, however, can sometimes be dichotomous with 'patient choice'. A NICE guideline, for example, may indicate a particular type of treatment or therapy; conversely, the patient may express an alternative preference. Part of the initial patient assessment needs to be the identification of the individual patient's wishes regarding their preferred level of participation in their healthcare.

Brashers et al. (1999) indicated that research showed the existence of a dichotomy between the amount of healthcare information that patients consistently report that they would like, and the number of questions that they actually ask during consultations. It must, therefore, also be recognised that preferred level of participation may be affected by a number of variables and may change at different points within the patient journey.

Person-centred care

The terms 'person-centred care', 'personalised care', 'personalisation' and 'individualised care' consistently feature within government documents regarding the modernisation of both health and social care services. The Health Foundation (2013) states that person-centred care involves putting patients and their families at the heart of all decisions, where patients are regarded as equal partners in planning, developing and assessing care to make sure it is most appropriate for their needs. Figure 9.3 illustrates the HEART Choice model that has been developed from concepts identified within the literature, which includes a number of key concepts that are central to the healthcare practitioner–patient relationship in supporting the achievement of person-centred care.

Figure 9.3   Heart Choice Model: Concepts that support person-centred care

Each of the concepts within the HEART Choice model will now be explored individually.

Holism: Holism encompasses regard for the 'whole person', both physically and psychologically. Within a holistic approach, physical, social, psychological, spiritual and cultural issues are recognised as having collective impact on the wellbeing of the individual.

Empowerment: To empower is to provide power or authority to another person. This term is both widely and liberally used in everyday practice; however, often with lack of regard as to the conceptual complexities involved in truly empowering patients.

Advocacy: An advocate is someone who acts on behalf of another person. The advocate needs to understand the values, beliefs and perspectives of the person whom they are representing. Conflicting roles and responsibilities of health/social care practitioners need to be acknowledged; for example, those relating to their role of professional versus their role as an employee of the health/social care organisation. It must also be acknowledged that, within the practitioner–patient relationship, the level of advocacy required will vary from patient to patient and will be dependent upon a number of factors such as the preference of the individual patient.

Respect: To respect is to have positive regard for another person. Mutual respect and positive regard should ideally be evident on both sides of the practitioner–patient relationship.

Trust: Trust relates to the reliability of another person and having confidence in them. Within the practitioner–patient relationship, the patient must be assured that the practitioner will address their best interests.

Choice: Choice is having the opportunity to select a preference from a range of alternatives. At a more 'micro' level within the practitioner–patient relationship, the practitioner must strive to identify everyday choices that they can provide their patients with in relation to their care/therapy.

The HEART Choice model can be used to inform the achievement of true patient-centred care within everyday practice and can be applied at all levels within the organisation.

Action point 9.3   Patient-centred care, from rhetoric to reality

- Consider each of the six concepts that make up the HEART Choice model.
- For each concept, compile a list of examples of how you apply the concept within your interactions with patients.
- Within your role as DCM, as discussed in Chapter 2 for instance, you have a responsibility to monitor and supervise the care delivered by members of your team. Make a list of strategies that you can employ to facilitate the delivery of person-centred care within your practice setting.

Strategies for Promoting Person-centred Care

Everyday practice presents a wealth of opportunities for health and social care practitioners to promote person-centred working. Central to this approach, however, is the need to complete a holistic assessment that clearly identifies the values, beliefs and concerns that are important to the individual patient. Assessment skills are fundamental to the professional practice of all healthcare practitioners. Patient assessment presents a unique opportunity to provide the foundation for person-centred working. It could be argued that a skilled assessor can engage in a 'conversation with a purpose' with his/her patients to elicit personalised information, as opposed to asking them a list of predetermined questions in the order in which they appear within the assessment document. The opportunity for self-assessment can also be considered where the patient can be supported to complete their own assessment, recorded in their own words. Once a holistic assessment has been completed, the practitioner should strive to engage the patient in the planning, delivery and ongoing evaluation of their care. McCormack (2006) has developed a person-centred nursing framework comprising of four constructs:

- *Prerequisites*, which focus on the attributes of the nurse.
- *The care environment*, which focuses on the context in which care is delivered.
- *Person-centred processes*, which focus on delivering care through a range of activities.
- *Expected outcomes*, which are the results of effective person-centred nursing.

McCormack concluded that in order to deliver person-centred outcomes, account must be taken of the prerequisites and the care environment that are necessary for providing effective care through the care processes.

Action point 9.4   Person-centred assessment

- Reflect on a patient assessment that you have completed recently. How confident are you that within the assessment you identified what the patient considered to be important to them, such as their values, needs, problems, concerns and goals?
- Make a list of the strategies that you used to elicit the patient perspective, such as open questions, managing the environment to promote privacy and open body language.
- Think of ways that you could further enhance your practice in the achievement of person-centred assessment.

Practice examples that support person-centred working are outlined below; further opportunities such as case conferences, ward rounds, goal setting, ICPs and MDT meetings will be explored in Chapter 10.

A ticket to go home

She's Got a Ticket ... To Go Home (IHI, 2011) is an initiative that originates from America where patients are provided with an individual whiteboard in their room that details information regarding what they need to achieve prior to being discharged. This provides a practical tool that acts as a mechanism for three-way communication and engagement between the patient, their family/carer and healthcare practitioners. Within the United Kingdom, the essence of this approach is transferable; however, to maintain confidentiality, a person-held record may be more appropriate than an individual whiteboard.

Patient diary

The use of a patient diary presents the healthcare practitioner with an opportunity to learn from the everyday experiences of the individual patient, and to use this information in meeting their personal care/therapy needs. This approach is sometimes used within palliative care where the patient uses a diary to record symptoms, emotions and problems, for instance. The diary can be used to identify problems and needs and the impact on the individual, to monitor care and to solve problems.

The Common Assessment Framework

The development of a Common Assessment Framework (CAF) for adults was proposed in the White Paper *Our Health, Our Care, Our Say* (DH, 2006c) and was intended to build upon the experience and benefits from implementing the CPA for mental health, the SAP for older people, and person-enterd planning for people with learning disabilities as a mechanism for supporting the delivery of person-centred care.

The Single Assessment Process

The Single Assessment Process (SAP) was introduced through the *National Service Framework for Older People* (DH, 2001a), the purpose of which is to ensure that older people receive appropriate, effective and timely responses to their health and social care needs, and that professional resources are used effectively. SAP aims to:

- provide person-centred assessment and care;
- ensure that older people receive appropriate, effective and timely responses to their health and social care needs;
- prevent practitioners duplicating each other's assessments and the care they provide;
- prevent people having to repeat the same information again and again;
- ensure that information is shared (with the individual's consent) between agencies and departments;
- create a person-held record of information about the individual's needs and the care and service they receive; this will reduce the amount of time practitioners spend finding and collating information and ensure that any decisions are based on all of the information available; and
- ensure that all agencies have shared values and approaches to assessment, care planning and care provision so that people will receive a similar assessment experience wherever they are assessed.

Direct payments

Direct payments support the personalisation agenda and take the form of cash payments provided to patients in lieu of community care services they have been assessed as needing, and are intended to give patients greater choice regarding their care. The payment provided is means tested and needs to be sufficient to enable the patient to purchase services to meet their eligible needs, and must be spent on services that meet eligible needs. Patients can, for example, employ a personal assistant or commission services directly from a provider organisation (Samuel, 2012).

Personal budgets

Samuel (2012) outlines that personal budgets are an allocation of funding given to patients after an assessment which can either be taken as a direct payment and/or – while still choosing how their care needs are met and by whom – leave councils with the responsibility to commission the services. Personal budgets have become increasingly available over the past few years and personal health budgets have been piloted more recently. A personal health budget provides an amount of money to support a person's identified health and wellbeing needs, planned and agreed between the person and their local NHS team (DH, 2013b). Personal health budgets provide individuals with more choice and control over how their needs are met and CCGs are required to make personal health budgets available from 2014.

Achieving Person-centred Care – Patients with Special Needs

Within health and social care there are a number of patients who may need more specialist consideration and support in identifying and meeting their personal values, beliefs and needs. Patients may include those who, for example, are unconscious or those who experience a cognitive impairment or other mental health problem, communication deficit or learning disability. Kitwood (1997), for example, states that for people who experience advancing cognitive impairment, the aim of person-centred care is to 'maintain personhood'. Kitwood states that personhood implies 'recognition, respect and trust' and defines personhood as 'a standing or status that is bestowed upon one human being by others in the context of relationships and social being'. Strategies to support the achievement of person-centred care in more specialist circumstances can include biographical approaches and advance directives.

Biographical approaches

Biographical approaches can support the achievement of a person-centred assessment for patients who, for example, may have a cognitive impairment or learning disability. Within this approach, individual patients are afforded the opportunity to share their life experiences to provide insight into their values, needs and aspirations. A small-scale study completed by Clarke et al. (2003) identified that the use of a biographical approach can promote person-centred care through enhancing the personhood of the older person. However, Clarke et al. recognise the resource limitations of adopting this approach in everyday clinical practice and suggest that rather than being an activity in its own right, the approach can be integrated into everyday care activities, such as supporting the patient with their activities of daily living.

Advance directives

An advance directive, also known as a 'living will', enables a competent individual to outline the treatment and care that they would like to receive in the future, should they subsequently lose the capacity to decide or to communicate their preferences. The Mental Capacity Act (Legislation.gov.uk, 2005) provides a statutory framework that aims to protect vulnerable people who may be unable to make decisions on their own behalf. The Mental Capacity Act includes statutory rules that govern advance decisions to refuse treatment and outlines 'formalities' that need to be complied with, which include that the decision must be in writing and signed and witnessed and that a statement must be included which states that the advance decision stands 'even if life is at risk'.

Challenges to the Achievement of Person-centred Care

The achievement of person-centred care can pose challenges for the health/social care practitioner, some of which are directly related to individual practice, others are affected by the prevailing culture of the environment within which they work, and yet others relate to resource constraints. Challenges to the individual can include their personal values, attitudes and beliefs and the influence that these may have on their care/therapy delivery, such as in a situation where the practitioner is a non-smoker and the patient who is pregnant or has continuous obstructive pulmonary disease chooses to continue smoking.

Challenges relating to the culture of the care environment can include routine working practices, such as an expectation by the day staff that the night staff will complete a number of bed-baths before shift handover. Challenges relating to the availability of resources can include environmental factors, such as having a limited number of side rooms or showers, or relate to consumable resources such as the type of toiletries and hospital clothing available to the patient, or to care-rationing decisions that have to be made due to pressure on resources, for example, the amount of therapy time that a patient receives or whether a nurse washes a patient rather than promoting their independence and supporting them to wash themselves.

Action point 9.5   Personal, cultural and resource challenges to person-centred care

Draw a table with three columns, and label the columns 'Personal challenges', 'Cultural challenges' and 'Resource challenges'. Consider the challenges that you face as a health/social care practitioner in the provision of person-centred care to your patients and record these within the first column. In the second column make a list of challenges to the achievement of person-centred care that emanate from the culture of the practice setting where you work. In the third column record the challenges that are posed through limited availability of resources. Next to each of the challenges that you have identified, record two or three potential solutions. Solutions can be based on you as an individual working differently or may require the support of your manager and colleagues in changing the working practices within your practice setting. Now consider your role as DCM and the extent to which you can have a positive impact in promoting person-centred care during the spans of duty where you are in charge.

Webster (2004) identified a number of factors as having a negative impact on an individual's sense of self and their personhood, namely:

- Stereotyping
- Labelling
- Depersonalisation
- Stigmatisation
- Ageist attitudes and beliefs
- Changes in health status
- Lack of 'real' choice and autonomy
- Physical environment
- Rigid organisational boundaries/service access criteria
- Task orientation based on routine and tradition
- Lack of knowledge, skills and insight by care givers.

Action point 9.6   Balancing safety and patient preferences case study

Brenda is a 79-year-old widowed lady who was admitted to hospital after sustaining a fractured neck of femur. Brenda has a history of recurrent falls and has recently been diagnosed as having dementia. Following surgery to have her hip fracture pinned, Brenda experienced some initial medical problems from which she is now recovering. She has started to take a few steps with her walking frame and the supervision of one member of staff. Prior to admission, Brenda lived alone in a ground-floor council flat – her home for the past 30 years. Brenda has expressed a wish to return to her flat, once she is discharged. Members of the inter-disciplinary team, however, are concerned about Brenda's preferred discharge destination and have reservations regarding her safety and ability to cope at home. Key concerns centre on Brenda's short-term memory problems and her risk of falls.

- What factors need to be addressed as part of the decision-making relating to Brenda's pending transfer of care?
- What strategies could you use to promote Brenda's safety while also meeting her personal wishes regarding her preferred discharge destination?
- What support could you draw upon from colleagues, other agencies and services?

You may have identified some of the following within your answers:

- the need to establish whether or not, at this point in time, Brenda has the capacity to make the decision about discharge destination;
- if it is deemed that Brenda lacks capacity to make this decision at this point in time, that any subsequent actions taken are in her best interests, and that family members are consulted if this is the case, it would also need to be established whether there is someone who holds a lasting power of attorney that would allow them to act on Brenda's behalf if appropriate; or if Brenda has no family or friends to support her, a decision may need to be made regarding whether the appointment of an independent mental capacity advocate is required to represent her;
- use of advanced technology, such as community and social alarms (e.g. Telecare) which use communications and sensing technologies such as fall, flood and gas detectors;
- provision of an intensive care package that may include night sits;
- sheltered housing options; and
- allocation of a care co-ordinator.

Health and social care practitioners face numerous dilemmas during the course of their everyday professional practice. They can sometimes demonstrate paternalism in the decisions that they make, which may be due to the need to maintain safety and to reduce risks, although there is a need to balance risks against the preferences of the individual. Similarly, patient preferences and choices made may be at odds with evidence-based approaches to care, such as if four-layer bandaging may be the evidence-based treatment indicated to promote the healing of a leg ulcer; the patient, however, may refuse this treatment and request an alternative course of treatment. Similarly, a pregnant woman may request an elective caesarean section where there is no evidence to support this approach and natural delivery would be considered appropriate. Acknowledging, respecting and treating the patient as a person are fundamental to a patient-centred model of care delivery. It is important that the implications of various options are explored and that the individual is aware of any actual and potential risks associated with the various choice options that are available. In some instances, the option preferred by the patient may not be available to them either because it is not evidence-based, they do not meet the criteria for funding or it is not available on the NHS.

The health/social care practitioner–patient relationship

The health/social care practitioner–patient relationship is central to health and social care practice. Interpersonal relationships between health/social care practitioners and patients humanise care and therapy through identifying with the patients' personal experiences. The nature of this relationship needs to be explored to enable practitioners to recognise the importance of their interpersonal skills to the development of therapeutic relationships with their patients. Different types of behaviour can exert influence on the power base within the practitioner–patient relationship, namely authoritarian or democratic. Within an authoritarian approach the practitioner assumes a more powerful position and informs the patient of interventions, treatments and the outcomes of decisions made regarding their care. Within a democratic approach, the practitioner adopts a more patient-centred philosophy, identifying individual preferences and promoting choice and empowerment.

Priorities can differ between the practitioner and the patient. A patient presenting with respiratory insufficiency due to myasthenia gravis, for example, may identify social responsibilities such as providing for his family and caring for his wife and new-born baby as his main concern in the advent of an impending deterioration in condition. Healthcare practitioners may be more likely. however, to prioritise the need to maintain oxygen perfusion. This case scenario illustrates the need to identify the patient perspective to elicit values, goals and priorities to inform the provision of personalised care.

Within the literature there exists a plethora of studies that illustrate how the patient perspective can commonly contrast to that of the healthcare practitioner. A study conducted by Florin et al. (2005) found that nurses were less likely than patients to identify problems relating to nutrition, sleep, pain and emotions/spirituality. The study also identified that in relation to problems that had been identified collectively with patients, nurses underestimated the severity of the problem in nearly half of all cases (47 per cent).

A study undertaken by Duxbury and Whittington (2005) similarly identified differences between staff and patient perspectives. In this instance patients identified precursors to aggressive behaviour to be environmental conditions and poor communication, whereas nurses conversely cited patients' mental illnesses as the main reason. Magnus et al. (2004) revealed that nurses' assessments compared more favourably than patients' perceptions for the majority of care interventions provided at night with, for example, 73 per cent of nurses assessing 'night rest' positively and 95 per cent for 'information and participation' positively, compared to only 51 per cent and 49 per cent respectively by patients. Healthcare practitioners therefore need to identify strategies to elicit the patient perspective throughout the patient journey.

Identifying a patient's willingness to participate

In addition to choices regarding health and social care services, choices about health and opportunities to support wellbeing similarly need to be provided for patients. Within the public health agenda, issues of state responsibility versus individual responsibility, however, need to be addressed. Inequalities such as poverty and education are widely acknowledged as having a positive correlation to morbidity and mortality. Government policy is paying increasing attention to the prevention of ill health and maintenance of health. The Expert Patient Programme (EPP) (DH, 2001b) promulgates self-care and self-management for patients with long-term conditions. The development of patient expertise in symptom management and lifestyle choices are key approaches within this model. The DCM can support the EPP through the promotion of the role and encouraging patients to access EPP courses where appropriate. Earlier on in the chapter, treating the patient as an 'individual' and providing 'choice' were identified as central concepts to the achievement of person-centred care.

Action point 9.7   Patient choice

- Think about the choices that are offered to patients within your practice setting.
- Compile a list of choices and for each consider the actual extent of choice, together with any boundaries that may be present.
- Which aspects of care/therapy provision within your practice setting are governed by the needs of the individual, and which are governed by the needs of the institution/practice setting?
- What further choices do you think could be offered within your practice setting?

Table 9.1 highlights the availability of choices that were identified by staff who attended a multi-disciplinary person-centred care workshop. The choices are divided into those that are governed nationally, those that are available locally within individual services, together with other preferred choices that they would like to be widely available.

Many of the choices available, however, are offered within the context of boundaries, some of which relate to resource constraints. If, for example, a patient is offered a preferred time for an intervention, this in many instances is a restricted choice as other patients may similarly opt for the same time. Health and social care staff have to try to accommodate the preferences of a number of patients simultaneously while working within available resources.

Table 9.1   Healthcare choices

Choices governed nationally	Local choice availability	Other preferred choices
General practitioner	Menu	Individual room
Care provider	Time of therapy	Timing of consultations
Consent or refuse treatment	Wash or shower to meet hygiene needs	Unrestricted visiting
	Patient-held records	Individual use of a TV, DVD, telephone and laptop computer

Compliance versus non-compliance

The achievement of patient compliance with treatment, therapy and advice can be challenging for health and social care practitioners. It has been identified, for example, that as many as 50 per cent of older people may not be taking their medications as intended (Royal Pharmaceutical Society of Great Britain, 1997). Concordance related to medicine-taking is a more contemporary approach to prescribing that involves negotiation between the patient and healthcare practitioner (Marinker et al., 1997). This approach recognises the beliefs and preferences of the patient and acknowledges that to achieve compliance, patients need to know how the medication will benefit them personally. Concordance is an example of the promotion of partnership between the patient and the healthcare practitioner.

In promoting similar approaches within other areas of healthcare practice, it is important to analyse the factors that influence individual patient decisions to comply or not to comply with treatment, therapy and advice. An ethnographical study completed by Tutton and Seers (2004) identified the powerlessness of older patients and how they continually tried to identify 'what was expected of them' and tried to 'fit in' with the norms of the ward while simultaneously trying to get the care that they needed. Similarly, within a study conducted by Pearson et al. (2004), a patient respondent stated 'I told the nurse, I says "I don't take pain killers." I only took them in hospital to please them'. These two studies suggest that patients comply with convention and treatment as a strategy to achieve favour or to ensure that their needs are met. Patient compliance, therefore, should not be regarded as synonymous with patient motivation.

A further challenge that healthcare practitioners can sometimes face within their professional relationship with patients is what has been termed by Stockwell (1984) as the 'unpopular patient'. Stockwell's study explored interpersonal relationships between nurses and patients in general hospital wards and identified that the 'least' popular patients identified by nurses fell into two broad categories: those who grumbled and complained or demanded attention in other ways, and those whom the nurses considered did not need to be in hospital or on a particular ward. A study conducted by Johnson and Webb (1995) similarly identified that the 'expression of evaluations of social worth' by nurses was widespread both in terms of 'good and bad patients'. Johnson and Webb, however, identified that ascribed labels could be 're-negotiated' rather than achieving permanency as implied by Stockwell. Conway (2000) identified a degree of confusion between 'difficult' and 'difficult to nurse' and derived a 'patient rules' framework from staff's reactions to these behaviours. Conway concludes that the issue of patient behaviour is complex, and that patient 'difficulty' is a relative, as opposed to absolute, quality.

Action point 9.8   Popular and unpopular patients

- Think about a patient that you have enjoyed working with.
- Make a list of the positive attributes/influences that contributed towards the positive care practitioner–patient relationship in the example that you have identified.
- Now think about a patient that you have not enjoyed working with.
- Make a list of the attributes/influences that contributed towards the less positive care practitioner–patient relationship in the example that you have identified.

(Continued)

(Continued)

- Now compare the two lists to identify any commonalities, distinguishing factors or trends.
- For the patient that you did not enjoy working with, list the strategies that you employed to manage this situation.

It is important that all patients are treated as individuals and encouraged to be involved in their care and that the achievement of person-centred care transcends any issues regarding popularity or unpopularity. Chapter 8 explores a number of strategies for both personal and peer support to assist healthcare practitioners in the course of their professional roles.

Ways of coping

In addition to the challenges posed for practitioners in caring for less 'popular' patients, other groups of patients can also constitute a source of pressure. Morse et al. (1992), for example, proposed a model to describe nurses' responses to patients who are suffering. Within this model, engagement by the nurse is affected by their focus either on themselves or their patient, together with whether their response is reflexive or learned. Morse et al. identify a number of strategies that are used to control personal engagement with a patient who is suffering, such as pity, sympathy, consolation, compassion, commiseration and reflexive reassurance. Healthcare practitioners need to recognise the influence of their own values, attitudes and personal experiences to the quality of care that they provide.

Good practice guidelines

The following constitute good practice guidelines for patient involvement, participation and partnership in health and social care delivery:

- Establish the patient's preferred form of address and ensure that this is documented and respected by team members.
- Ensure that patient assessments are holistic and address the individual's values, beliefs, concerns and personal preferences.
- Prepare plans of care in collaboration with patients and ensure that they are reflective of the individual's values, beliefs, concerns and personal preferences.
- Involve patients in all decisions about their care and promote informed decision-making and choice.
- Use biographical approaches to support the achievement of person-centred care for patients who have a cognitive impairment or learning disability.
- Talk with and listen to patients; ask them about their experiences and evaluations of care and take positive action to address any concerns.

CHAPTER SUMMARY

This chapter began by contextualising the motivating forces for the development of choice, personalisation and consumerism, together with the promotion of more patient-focused health and social care services. The key concepts of patient involvement, participation and partnership were then explored and applied to everyday practice. The concepts person-centred care, personalised care and individualised care were analysed and opportunities identified to achieve these approaches in practice. As advocated by the Joseph Rowntree Foundation (2005), 'Involvement starts with talking but it shouldn't end there'.

The DCM needs to act as a role model to promote choice and the achievement of personalised care. To ensure that person-centred care is achieved, they need to act as a champion so that both their practice and that of fellow team members is person-centred. A wealth of opportunities exists within the practice setting to achieve this, with person-centred assessment being fundamental to success. The DCM needs to lead by example and monitor and supervise care delivery in the practice setting to ensure the achievement of patient-centred outcomes and personalised care.

The chapter has explored the key components of patient involvement, participation and partnership which impacts on the DCM's roles, and included:

- the background to patients and the public's involvement, participation and partnership in healthcare delivery;
- person-centred care including strategies to promote person-centred care, achieving person-centred care for all, including patients with special needs, and the challenges to the achievement of person-centred care; and
- the health/social care practitioner–patient relationship in the context of identifying patients' willingness to participate in safeguarding their own health and wellbeing, as well as compliance and non-compliance with treatment and advice given by health and social care practitioners.

RECOMMENDED FURTHER READING

Dixon A, Appleby J, Robertson R, Burge P, Devlin N, Magee H (2010) *Patient Choice: How Patients Choose and How Providers Respond*. London: Kings' Fund. Available from: www.kingsfund.org.uk/publications/patient-choice.

The Lancet (2012) 'Patient empowerment – who empowers whom?'. *The Lancet*, (5 May) 379 (9827) 1677. Available from: www.thelancet.com/journals/lancet/article/PIIS0140–6736%2812%2960699–0/fulltext.

The Patients Association (2012) *Partners in Care: Working Together in the South West*. Available from: www.patients-association.com/Default.aspx?tabid=96.

10

UNI-PROFESSIONAL, INTER-PROFESSIONAL AND INTER-AGENCY TEAMWORK

Maximising patient outcomes, making the best use of resources, facilitating seamless services and ensuring timely transfers of patient care are reliant upon effective team-working between primary, community, secondary and social care services.

In this chapter, models of multi-disciplinary, inter-disciplinary and trans-discipli-nary teamwork will be evaluated, and theories related to teamwork, such as Belbin's (1993) team roles, will be critiqued and applied to multi-disciplinary/multi-agency teamworking. The reader will have the opportunity to explore both their role and that of their colleagues within the teams that they belong to and to identify mecha-nisms to increase their effectiveness. Strategies that capitalise upon formal oppor-tunities for inter-disciplinary/inter-agency discussion and decision-making, such as ward rounds, goal setting meetings, MDT meetings and case conferences, will be appraised. Finally the chapter will progress to identify ways of evaluating team performance.

Chapter objectives

On completion of this chapter you will be able to:

- identify and analyse the nature of groups and teams, models and prerequisites for effective teamworking, and identify ways in which you can maximise team perfor-mance within the teams that you belong to;

- evaluate team leadership, in the context of inter-professional/inter-agency teamworking, together with the challenges to leadership and management within;
- demonstrate knowledge of the theories and practice of staff motivation and identify ways to apply them within your role in the context of uni-disciplinary and inter-professional teamworking; and
- critically analyse teamwork, the role of multi-professional communication within, and reflect upon ways to evaluate the performance of the teams that you belong to.

Theories of Teamwork

Teamwork is often premised to be a prerequisite for good practice within health and social care. Teams, however, can be very diverse in nature and range from uni-disciplinary teams such as those exclusively comprising a single professional group (e.g. nursing staff, physiotherapists, social care staff or midwives), to inter-disciplinary teams that include representation from a range of disciplines that may transcend both health and social care, together with acute and community services.

Multi-professional team approaches to healthcare are commonplace in many clinical specialities such as the care of older people, mental health, cancer and palliative care. Although such approaches are perceived to be positive, team interaction, dynamics and a shared understanding of the roles of individual disciplines can be present challenges. Each discipline has its own philosophy of care that needs to feed into the wider, shared philosophy of the inter-professional and inter-agency team.

Collaborative working is one of 15 leadership qualities identified by the NHS III (2010), the benefits of which are identified as delivery of measurable and radical health improvements in a complex and changing health and social care environment, and that effective partnership promotes the sharing of information and appropriate prioritisation of limited resources, as well as support 'joined up' provision of integrated care.

It needs to be recognised, however, that professionals can collaborate with one another without being part of a team. A healthcare professional may, for example, make a referral to a healthcare professional from another discipline who can assess the patient, provide their expert opinion and undertake therapeutic interventions. Collaboration, therefore, should be differentiated from teamwork.

Differentiating groups from teams

A group can be defined as a collective unit of people who share a common interest. A group can either be formal or informal in nature. A formal group may be configured within an organisation where there is a need to perform a specific task, for example, to develop an ICP or an integrated record. An informal group will tend to develop more naturally amongst peers; for example, a group of colleagues who socialise together.

A team, on the other hand, takes the concept of a group further by focusing on the interrelationship between members, and is premised upon the organisation of people with a shared purpose and the way in which they work together to achieve this. Consequently, a team can be defined as a group of individuals who are conversant with the organisation's mission and aims, work together to deliver the organisation's services, and feel individually and collectively accountable for the achievement of its goals. Teams can transcend organisational boundaries such as those that include both health and social care professionals.

Within healthcare, teams have been broadly classified as project teams, such as those that focus on quality improvement, and care delivery and management teams that can broadly be subdivided into three categories (Canadian Health Services Research Foundation, 2006), namely:

- Patient population, e.g. specialist old age multi-disciplinary team.
- Disease type, e.g. stroke team.
- Care delivery settings, e.g. intermediate care team.

Action point 10.1   A group or a team

Consider the various groups and teams that you are a member of as part of your clinical role, and for each one decide whether it is a group or a team. Think about the justifications for your decision(s) and base these around the definitions that were provided earlier.

Models of teamwork

A plethora of terms are used within healthcare to denote the context within which health and social care professionals work together. Leathard (2003) has identified incongruence between definitions of teamwork and cites the example of the term 'inter' that has been used to denote working between two groups, but also to a team of individuals from different backgrounds. A number of different models for the facilitation of teamwork are also in existence. Mumma and Nelson (2002), for example, differentiate between multi-disciplinary, inter-disciplinary and trans-disciplinary models of collaborative practice:

- Multi-disciplinary:

  - discipline – specific goals
  - clear boundaries between disciplines
  - effective communication is essential for success.

- Inter-disciplinary:

  - collaborate to identify patient goals
  - expanded problem-solving beyond discipline-specific boundaries/work.

- Trans-disciplinary:
  - blurring of the boundaries between disciplines
  - flexibility to minimise duplication of effort.

Action point 10.2   Team map

Figure 10.1 provides diagrammatic representation of a MDT with a central focus on the patient. Consider the various members that make up your team, and draw a diagram to illustrate this. Where does the patient sit within the team? Now consider the inter-relationship between team members, and make notes on which of the models of collaborative teamwork outlined by Mumma and Nelson (2002) best reflects your team. Consider your team in the context of its interrelationship with other teams, both within your organisation and with external organisations.

The team map that you have plotted will be beneficial for you to refer back to throughout the remainder of the chapter.

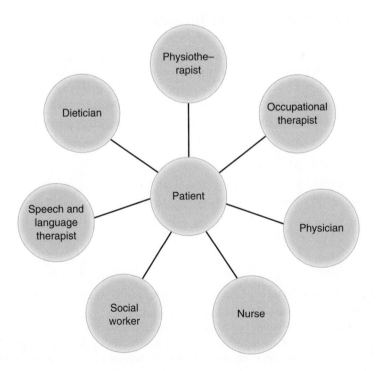

Figure 10.1   Members of the multi-professional team

Benefits of teamwork

A number of positive outcomes have been identified from working in a team that include job satisfaction, turnover, effectiveness, innovation and patient safety (Healthcare Commission, 2006). Borrill et al. (2000) identified that staff working in teams within hospital-based care reported lower levels of stress when compared to colleagues who worked alone or in less defined groupings. Moroney and Knowles (2006) similarly identified positive outcomes when they evaluated the implementation of MDT ward rounds, identifying an increase in patient involvement, a development of nurses and greater job satisfaction, and an improvement in MDT relationships, all of which improved ward culture and created a happier working environment. West (2012) differentiates between 'real' and 'pseudo' teams, and classifies the former where team members state that they have clear objectives, they work closely together to achieve those objectives, and they meet regularly to review performance and how it can be improved. West classifies 'pseudo' teams conversely as those where one or more of the three criteria are reported as not taking place. West identified fewer injuries, errors, violent assaults and cases of harassment, bullying and abuse in 'real' teams as well as reduced absenteeism when compared to 'pseudo' teams. West also reported that the data revealed that more 'real' teams in a hospital or other healthcare organisation was associated with lower patient mortality.

Characteristics of Effective Teams

The 2011 National Survey of NHS Staff (National NHS Staff Co-ordinating Centre, 2012c) identified that 94 per cent of respondents reported that they work in a team, but for many groups of staff the teams appeared to be in name only and did not display all of the characteristics of a well-structured team. A well-structured team has been identified by the Healthcare Commission (2006) as having the following characteristics:

- The team objectives are clear.
- The team members work closely to achieve team objectives.
- Regular team meetings are held to discuss effectiveness and ways for improvement of the team.
- The team does not have more than 15 members.

Action point 10.3   A well-structured team

Consider your team in relation to the four characteristics identified by the Healthcare Commission as comprising a well-structured team. Does your team possess all of these characteristics? If the answer is no, you may wish to discuss your assessment with your manager and fellow team members.

Team roles

Belbin (1993) developed a theory based on his research that individuals can contribute to teamworking in a specific number of ways. He identified nine key team roles as outlined in Table 10.1. However, he also argues that not all nine roles are necessarily essential for the successful functioning of the team. Belbin also suggested that team members can display the qualities of more than one of the identified team roles. Belbin's research focused on management teams; however, the team roles are transferable to other types of teams.

Action point 10.4   Team roles

Think about a team that you are a member of, and consider each of Belbin's team roles in turn. Make notes on which team role(s) most closely represent your contribution to this team. Consider the remaining team roles – are these covered by the roles that your colleagues adopt within this team? Are there any roles that are not covered within the team? Do colleagues appear to adopt more than one role simultaneously? Now relating your reflections to the overall functioning of the team, consider how successful the team is. How do the dynamics of the team overcome some of the 'allowable weaknesses' identified in Belbin's identified team roles?

Multi-disciplinary team roles

Each of the disciplines that collectively comprise the MDT has their own professional values and code of conduct and so on. Within nursing and midwifery, *The Code – Standards of Conduct, Performance and Ethics for Nurses and Midwives* (NMC, 2010b) outlines the requirement for the practitioner to 'work cooperatively within teams and respect the skills, expertise and contributions of your colleagues'. The NMC's (2010a) standards for competence (generic and field- or branch-specific) that nurses must acquire during their pre-registration programme identify competencies under four domains, of which the domain that refers to teamwork is entitled 'Leadership, management and teamworking', which the registrant must also demonstrate the potential to develop during their period of preceptorship and beyond.

The role of the nurse in the MDT

Within the rehabilitation literature, a number of models have been developed that address the actual and potential role of the nurse in this area of practice. Hoeman (2002), for example, discusses the care manager role of the nurse; and Long et al (2002) identified six interlinked roles for the nurse that include: assessment; co-ordination and communication; technical and physical care; therapy integration and therapy carry-on; emotional support; and involving the family.

Table 10.1   Team-role descriptions (Belbin, 1993)

Team Role	Contribution	Allowable weakness
Plant	Creative, imaginative, unorthodox. Solves difficult problems.	Ignores incidentals. Too pre-occupied to communicate effectively.
Resource Investigator	Extrovert, enthusiastic, communicative. Explores opportunities. Develops contacts.	Over-optimistic. Loses interest once initial enthusiasm has passed.
Co-ordinator	Mature, confident, a good chairperson. Clarifies goals, promotes decision-making, delegates well.	Can be seen as manipulative. Offloads personal work.
Shaper	Challenging, dynamic, thrives on pressure. The drive and courage to overcome obstacles.	Prone to provocation. Offends people's feelings.
Monitor/ Evaluator	Sober, strategic and discerning. Sees all options. Judges accurately.	Lacks drive and ability to inspire others.
Teamworker	Co-operative, mild, perceptive and diplomatic. Listens, builds, averts friction.	Indecisive in crunch situations.
Implementer	Disciplined, reliable, conservative and efficient. Turns ideas into practical actions.	Somewhat inflexible. Slow to respond to new possibilities.
Completer/ Finisher	Painstaking, conscientious, anxious. Searches out errors and omissions. Delivers on time.	Inclined to worry unduly. Reluctant to delegate.
Specialist	Single-minded, self-starting, dedicated. Provides knowledge and skills in rare supply.	Contributes on only a narrow front. Dwells on technicalities.

The 'Nursing, Midwifery and Care Staff Vision and Strategy' (DH, 2012b) acknowledges that nurses, midwives and care staff work in multidisciplinary teams and outlines the importance of collaboration at all levels and in all settings in order to underpin the delivery of excellent care. The strategy highlights the importance of leadership, and advocates that leaders and managers need to create supportive, caring cultures within their respective teams.

Team leadership

Leadership can exist outside of formal hierarchical structures, and there is therefore a need to develop leaders at all levels within the organisation to facilitate both top-down and bottom-up approaches to development. In recent years the NHS has invested significantly in leadership education and development for its staff. The achievement of effective healthcare for patients requires the input of a number of management functions and professional groups across the organisation. Some staff may work together in a collaborative function, while others may operate more as a team.

Leadership will now be explored within the context of teamwork. The leader should view fellow team members as partners and therefore having equality of status. This approach can facilitate a sharing of leadership amongst team members who are empowered to take a natural lead at times where they consider that they are in the best position to drive the team forward. The team needs to have vision and to collectively agree what it is aspiring to achieve. Effective leadership of the team is essential to ensure that it achieves its vision.

Challenges to Leadership and Management within Inter-professional Teams

Shared responsibility for outcomes is an integral feature of an inter-disciplinary team. This can present a challenge for the leader in managing accountability within shared responsibility. For some teams this may be further complicated by lack of clarity regarding team leadership. Within the inter-disciplinary team, individual members will have their lines of accountability and responsibility to their respective professional group that is often outside of the collective team.

A study conducted by Atwal and Caldwell (2006) regarding nurses' perceptions of teamwork in acute healthcare identified three barriers that hindered teamwork: (1) differing perceptions of teamwork; (2) different levels of skills acquisitions to function as a team member; and (3) the dominance of medical power that influenced interaction in teams. Gibbon et al. (2002) identified that the introduction of team co-ordinated approaches to stroke care and rehabilitation did not result in greater teamworking staff attitudes.

Experiences of teamwork

A phenomenological study conducted by Robertson and Finlay (2007) revealed occupational therapists' relationships with multi-disciplinary colleagues to be both 'valuable and satisfying' while also providing a source of 'stress and frustration'. Team membership was valued by the occupational therapists both within their unidisciplinary team and within the wider MDT. The occupational therapists, however, considered that the extent of their role was misunderstood by colleagues, this being evidenced by colleagues focusing upon certain aspects of the role, such as the provision of equipment, to the exclusivity of others. A study by Saar and Trevizan (2007) similarly identified that participants in their study were not very knowledgeable about the professional roles of their colleagues. The role of the physician, nurse and pharmacist were found to be most understood, while the role of the psychologist was identified to be least understood.

Action point 10.5   Individual team members' roles

Refer back to the members of your team that you identified in Action point 10.1 and briefly outline the role of each member together with the unique contribution that this professional group brings to the inter-disciplinary team. Discuss your interpretations with individual team members. You may also find it helpful to explore the roles through the websites and literature that are published by the various professional bodies concerned.

Challenges to leadership and management within inter-agency teams

The challenges of teamworking can be somewhat compounded within inter-agency teams; the membership, for example, comprises staff from different organisations, each of which will have targets and outcomes to achieve that can sometimes conflict with one another. Acute hospitals, for example, need to meet waiting-time targets in A&E departments and to reduce length of stay. Social care, on the other hand, is tasked with reducing reliance upon long-term institutional care and supporting independent living in the community. A focus on individual priorities rather than a whole-systems approach can be a cause of conflict between multi-agency team members. The joint appointment of a team leader across the agencies and professional disciplines, together with strong support and collective management, however, can maximise team performance.

Pooled budgets similarly present an opportunity to achieve more patient-centred services that span organisational boundaries. An example of an inter-agency team is a hospital discharge team that can include staff from social care, acute hospital care and primary care. The aim of such a team is to promote timely and seamless transfers of patient care from hospital back into the community. Benefits of this approach can include the minimising of duplication of effort, improved communication and maximising team performance. Furthermore, for teamwork to be effective, staff motivation is an important imperative, which is now explored.

Staff Motivation

The DCM needs to be knowledgeable about the concept of motivation, together with the various approaches that managers can adopt on a day-to-day basis to motivate staff in order to maximise their effectiveness.

Why should the DCM be interested in staff motivation?

A few years ago, Brown (1998) suggested that national productivity could be raised 1.5 times if what was already known about motivation was implemented. Motivation had been shown to be the single most important factor in determining business (or work or organisation) efficiency. In concluding his views on staff motivation, Brown (1998: 2) notes that 'Job satisfaction accounts for 25 per cent of the variation in productivity between organisations', and goes on to suggest 'If you make people accountable as the drivers of the business rather than bit-part players, you have a direct impact on their motivation'. A small-scale study by Valencia (2005) identified that whilst both managers and employees agreed that motivation was significant in influencing performance, there was a marked difference between the two groups regarding what constitutes successful motivation. Employees were identified as placing greater credence on 'firm' culture, congeniality and recognition, whereas managers conversely placed greater focus on monetary factors.

It is important for the DCM to recognise the importance of motivation and its relevance to their role. Chapter 2 identified 'human resource manager' as one of 12 managerial roles of the DCM; the DCM needs to identify ways to motivate colleagues and subordinates in order to maximise productivity, develop individual and team spirit and to promote recruitment and retention.

Also as noted in Chapter 2, several definitions of management and manager refer to the activities and competencies of managers, which according to Drucker (2007: 6) for example, includes motivating staff as one of the five 'basic operations' of management. Drucker also defines the manager as 'someone who directs the work of others and who does their work by getting other people to do theirs', and thereby accomplishing organisational goals. As such statements imply, managers are people to whom responsibility has been given, by virtue of the posts they are in, to ensure that the work of the organisation is carried out as specified in its strategic and operational plans. They have to decide the interventions that need to be performed, and suitable personnel to perform them, and rather than just telling employees which tasks to perform the manager needs to recognise that motivated staff will have a positive impact on productivity and quality.

Action point 10.6   Staff motivation in healthcare – an analysis

Consider the following questions and make notes in some detail:

- What motivates me to work?
- In what ways does my manager ensure that I remain motivated to do my work?
- How do I motivate my colleagues and subordinates?
- What else could managers/I do to motivate staff?

Motivation can be subdivided into two areas: *intrinsic*, which is motivation from within, and *extrinsic*, which is motivation by external rewards. Naturally one of the key reasons for working is to gain an income; other motivating factors include:

- self-identity and a vocation;
- opportunity to engage in a subject area of interest;
- gaining new knowledge and skills;
- an opportunity to help people (altruism); and
- making friends.

Your manager may use a number of ways to motivate you and your colleagues at work, many of which can also be used by the DCM; these can include:

- supporting professional development;
- being an effective communicator; sharing information and involving team members in decision-making;
- saying 'Thank you', 'Well done' at the end of a span of duty;
- setting adequately challenging tasks;
- encouraging and listening to ideas;
- identifying mutual goals through IDPRs;
- encouraging to use own initiative;
- encouraging social activities/outings;
- recognising high standards of care given, such as the absence of pressure sores and reduced re-admissions;
- allowing to introduce new ideas/methods of care (tested and untested); and
- being easily accessible, approachable and giving responsibility.

Many of the areas identified above also have relevance to the DCM role.

Theories of motivation

There are several theories of staff motivation documented in management literature. Different theories tend to apply to different circumstances and settings, and they may be combined by the user as appropriate. These theories include:

- Drucker's 'management by objectives'.
- Maslow's theory of human motivation.
- Herzberg on motivation to work.
- McGregor's theory X and theory Y.

Drucker's management by objectives

One well-recognised theory of staff motivation is Drucker's (2007) management by objectives (MBO). According to MBO, organisational goals (corporate objectives) are linked with employees' own personal needs and expectations of the job. A major point in MBO is that it directly attaches significance to individual employees' strengths and achievements at work rather than focusing on their weaknesses. MBO can be directly linked to IDPR.

Maslow's theory of human motivation

Maslow's (1987) theory of motivation is based upon the assumption that individuals are motivated to take action to fulfil particular human needs. Individuals strive to meet the more basic physiological needs first, and when this is satisfied they take action to meet their safety needs, then social needs, esteem needs, and finally their self-actualisation needs. Therefore, physical, safety and socio-economic needs have to be met first before the individual attempts to meet their higher psychological or intellectual needs and goals. However, Maslow suggested that if the self-actualisation or self-realisation needs of the individual are not satisfied, then problems of frustration, boredom and apathy might ensue.

However, meeting physiological needs does not present a problem to most individuals, and therefore they are more motivated to achieve or sustain their next level needs in the hierarchy. Several individuals knowingly jeopardise lower-level needs in the quest for higher-level needs of self-esteem and self-fulfilment, and therefore people's major needs centre around realising their full potential as individuals, via creative, worthwhile achievement. As a means of staff motivation, employing organisations and managers should endeavour to meet employees' needs as identified in Table 10.2.

Table 10.2 Application of Maslow's theory of motivation to managing an organisation

Needs level	Organisational rewards	
1 Physiological	a)	Reasonable level of pay so that employees can easily afford, housing, food, clothing etc.
	b)	Rest periods such as coffee breaks
	c)	A staff canteen
2 Safety	a)	Complying with health and safety regulations
	b)	Job security through employment contract and IDPR
	c)	Organisational policies, procedures and guidelines
3 Social	a)	Encouraging cohesive teamwork
	b)	Buddying and supportive supervision
	c)	Membership of sub-teams
4 Esteem	a)	Acceptance of the individual by the team
	b)	Recognition of a job well done
5 Self-actualisation	a)	Preceptoring and clinical supervision
	b)	Opportunities to use initiative and creativity
	c)	Staff development strategies
	d)	Opportunities for advancement and career progression

Herzberg's theory of motivation to work

Modern theories of motivation are based on preceding theories and the findings of earlier experiments. Herzberg's theory on 'motivation to work' reflects the findings of the Hawthorne experiments conducted in the earlier part of the last century. The conclusions of the Hawthorne experiments indicated that productivity increases if individuals have stability, a place where they feel they belong, work in groups, and the purpose of the work is communicated to them.

Herzberg (1974) also suggested that all attempts to motivate employees by fear, economic rewards and good working conditions achieve limited success. In his view the way to motivate employees (which he considers to be intrinsic) is that in addition to providing the economic rewards and good working conditions, employees should simultaneously be given challenging work for which they can assume responsibility and gain the satisfaction of achievement.

Herzberg identified 'motivators or growth factors' by which employees are motivated, namely: a sense of achievement, recognition, responsibility and opportunities for personal growth and advancement. In addition to motivators, employers need to address the 'dissatisfiers' at work, which are also referred to as 'hygiene' or 'maintenance' factors. These factors are:

- The level of supervision
- Interpersonal relations
- Working conditions
- Salary
- Company policies
- Administrative practices
- Job security.

McGregor's theory X and theory Y

McGregor (1987) suggests that false assumptions about human motivation lie at the root of many ineffective management strategies. He postulated that either 'theory X' or 'theory Y' about human nature and human behaviour formed the basis for every managerial decision or action. Thus managers who act in accordance with the principles of theory X tend to believe the following to be true of people and therefore their employees – that the average human being:

- has an inherent dislike of work and will avoid it if he can;
- prefers to be directed, wishes to avoid responsibility, has relatively little ambition and wants security above all; and
- must be coerced, controlled, directed and threatened with punishment to get them to put forth adequate effort towards the achievement of organisational objectives.

The assumption underpinning theory X is that most workers are interested in their work to only a limited extent, and therefore need to be coerced and threatened to ensure that they carry out their duties effectively. Theory X offers management an easy rationalisation for ineffective organisational performance. McGregor's theory Y is the polarised extreme of theory X, which reflects a more realistic assumption that recognises the importance of the individual's need for self-actualisation at work. The manager using theory Y tends to believe that for the average human being, and therefore their employees, they:

- do not inherently dislike work;
- will exercise self-direction and self-control in the service of objectives to which they are committed;
- have commitment to organisational objectives as a function of the rewards associated with their achievement;
- learn under the appropriate conditions not only to accept but also to seek responsibility;
- have capacity to exercise a relatively high degree of imagination, ingenuity and creativity in the solution of organisational problems; and
- only partially use the intellectual abilities of their individual employees.

Theory Y reflects different implications for managerial strategy than those of theory X. It is dynamic rather than static, and recognises the opportunities for personal growth and development of employees. It enables managers to view their employees as resources, with substantial potentialities, and endeavour to enable them to discover how to realise their potential through its human resources department. These assumptions are apparent in managerial policies and practices.

Inter-professional Teamworking

Inter-professional learning has been advocated as a mechanism to promote inter-professional working and over the past decade has become an integral feature of pre- and post-registration courses for health and social care professionals in the United Kingdom. The standards of proficiency for pre-registration nursing (NMC, 2010a: 5), for example, include the requirement to demonstrate knowledge of 'effective inter-professional working practices which respect and use the contributions of members of the health and social care team'. The World Health Organization (2010) advocates inter-professional education as a prerequisite in preparing a 'collaborative practice-ready' health workforce that is better prepared to respond to local health needs.

Empirical evidence to support inter-professional approaches to learning, however, is somewhat limited but emerging, and as such the approach appears to be premised upon the rationale that if the various professional groups are expected to work together in teams, then it is common sense to mirror this within educational preparation.

A multi-case study undertaken by Hollenberg et al (2009: 17) reported that when considered collectively, the group of inter-professional education programmes had an influence on the awareness, attitudes, perceptions and knowledge of individual practitioners in ways that had the 'potential to enhance inter-professional care'. Caldwell et al. (2006) conducted a study that explored pre-registration education in relation to teamwork, together with the perceptions of newly qualified practitioners regarding their confidence in working as a team member. The study identified overall positive reporting by respondents regarding their teamwork, with the exception of 'equality' where 47 per cent of respondents rated that they were either unsure or disagreed with the statement 'I have found that within my team the members work as equals'. The findings of Caldwell et al. are encouraging and would appear to support inter-professional education within pre-registration preparation; more research is needed, however, to evaluate the outcomes of such educational strategies in assessing both collective experiences and those of the respective professional disciplines.

Barr (2002) completed a systematic review of the literature regarding inter-professional education and argues that to be effective, inter-professional education must reflect the following areas:

1 *Put service users at the centre:* Involving patients and clients in designing, teaching, participating and assessing programmes.
2 *Promote collaboration:* Applying learning to collaborative practice during placements or work-based assignments, collaboration within and between professions, within and between organisations and with communities, service users and their carers.
3 *Reconcile competing objectives:* Ensure that these principles are protected as the essential qualities of inter-professional education while ensuring that they are compatible with other objectives and their implications for programme design, content and learning methods.
4 *Reinforce collaborative competence:* Reach beyond modification of attitudes and securing common knowledge bases to reinforce collaborative competencies necessary to cope with the complexity of contemporary practice.
5 *Relate collaboration in learning and practice to a coherent rationale:* For example, able to explain the beneficial outcomes of inter-professional learning.
6 *Incorporate inter-professional values:* For example, inclusion, equality, openness, humility, mutuality, generosity and reciprocity.
7 *Include common and comparative learning:* Treat comparative content as essential to inform learning from and about each other, to enhance understanding about respective roles and responsibilities and intelligent co-working.
8 *Employ a repertoire of interactive learning methods:* Avoid over-reliance on any one method.
9 *Count towards qualifications:* Inter-professional education is valued more when it is assessed towards qualifications.

10 *Assess and evaluate programmes:* It is also valued more when programmes are approved and, where feasible, evaluated.
11 *Disseminate findings:* To inform, stimulate and support wider development of inter-professional education.

Leadership, power and hierarchies

Inter-professional teamwork also requires leadership, although in healthcare it has traditionally been perceived as hierarchical in nature and defined by job title and position equating to the status of the individual within the organisation. Snelgrove and Hughes (2002) conducted interviews with medical and nursing staff in three general hospitals. Their study identified that teamwork was seen to be valuable by both professional groups; however, the 'power of medical hierarchies and the limits of nursing influence in core areas of medical work' was recognised. A study by Nugus et al. (2010) identified the exercise of both 'competitive power' and 'collaborative power' in the negotiated order of health services across all settings. The study highlights how relationships among clinicians in various occupations are mediated by the expectation that doctors assume responsibility for patient management and co-ordinating roles in healthcare teams. A qualitative case study conducted by McDonald et al. (2012) identified three themes in relation to power dynamics between health professionals: their use of power to protect their autonomy; power dynamics between private and public sector providers; and reducing their dependency on other health professionals to maintain their power. The concept 'power' relates to control, influence and authority and can be subdivided into various cognate areas as identified in Box 3.4.

The NHS Leadership Qualities Framework (NHS III, 2010) identifies 15 leadership qualities that include personal, cognitive and social qualities that are applicable to leadership roles at all levels within the health service, both existing and aspiring. The leadership qualities are arranged in three clusters: personal qualities, setting direction, and delivering the service. For each individual quality there are between three and six levels, each of which commences with a negative descriptor that describes behaviours which illustrate a lack of the individual quality. Collaborative working is one of the five qualities that feature within the 'delivering the service' cluster. The other four qualities include: leading change through people, holding to account, empowering others, and effective and strategic influencing.

You may wish to consider completing a more comprehensive self-assessment by addressing all of the qualities that are included within the Leadership Qualities Framework. Now develop a personal action plan that includes strategies for you to further develop your collaborative working. You may find it helpful to discuss this with your manager, mentor or preceptor, as appropriate.

Communication

Teams need to have effective communication to enable them to achieve their goals. Communication is central to sharing information and to the facilitation of group

Action point 10.7   Levels of working

Consider your interrelationships with key stakeholders, including patients, carers, health professionals and social care professionals together with voluntary sector organisations. For each stakeholder identified, consider which collaborative level from the following provided by the NHS III (2006) best describes your current level of working:

0. *Goes it alone*

    - Fails to involve others in bringing about integrated healthcare   Yes/No

    - Does not share information with other stakeholders   Yes/No

1   *Appreciates others' views*

    - Expresses positive expectations of internal and external   Yes/No
      stakeholders

    - Acknowledges and respects others' diverse perspectives   Yes/No

2   *Works for shared understanding*

    - Shares information with partners when appropriate   Yes/No

    - Summarises progress, taking account of differing viewpoints, so   Yes/No
      as to clarify understanding and to establish common ground

    - Surfaces conflict and supports resolution of this conflict   Yes/No

3   *Forges partnerships for the long term*

    - Works with other stakeholders where conflict impedes progress   Yes/No
      to create the conditions for successful partnership working in the
      longer term

    - Is informed on the current priorities of partners, and responds   Yes/No
      appropriately to changes in their status or circumstances

    - Ensures that the strategy for health improvement is developed in   Yes/No
      a cohesive and 'joined up' manner

Source: NHS III, 2006

problem-solving and decision-making. We communicate using a combination of verbal and non-verbal approaches. Verbal communication encompasses the words that we say, together with the way in which we say them. Non-verbal communication relates to the messages that we provide to other people through our body language, as discussed in Chapter 1. In addition to face-to-face communication, a number of other strategies are also available to support communication with members of the inter-disciplinary team, such as telephone, paper and electronic formats.

It should be borne in mind that communication encompasses much more than simply sending a message. Communication is a two-way process, the success of which is dependent upon the receiver interpreting the information in the way that the sender had intended. Messages sent electronically, for example, can be left open to interpretation by the receiver as they are unable to establish the tone in which the message has been sent.

The Situation-Background-Assessment-Recommendation (SBAR) tool (NHS III, 2008b), provides a mechanism to frame conversations and supports practitioners to clarify what information should be communicated between members of the team. The tool aims to support teamwork and foster a culture of patient safety and can be used to support communications between professionals throughout the patient journey, both within organisations and across primary, secondary, community and social care. The tool has been adapted for healthcare from military and aviation industries and consists of standardised prompt questions within four sections to ensure that staff are sharing concise and focused information.

Action point 10.8   Communication and teamwork

Identify an everyday communication situation in your area of practice; this could be, for example, telephoning a doctor to request a review of a patient, transferring the care of a patient to a district nurse or GP, or making a safeguarding referral. Think about the message that you want to deliver together with the key points that you want to get across. Now consider the four sections of SBAR and note the respective key points in each section:

1 *Situation:*

- Your name, title and workplace.
- The name of the patient and reason for the communication.
- The issue or concern.

2 *Background:*

- Relevant information about the patient, e.g. medical history, reason for admission.

3 *Assessment:*

- Your assessment of the current situation, e.g. deteriorating vital signs, medically fit for transfer of care, ready for rehabilitation etc.

(Continued)

(Continued)

4 *Recommendation:*

- What you need, e.g. doctor to assess, district nurse to visit.
- Clarify agreements, expectations and actions etc.

Once you have completed this Action point, visit the NHS web site and consider some of the suggested applications for the SBAR tool. You may want to access some of the supporting resources or seek training on the use of the tool. The tool can be accessed at: www.institute. nhs.uk/quality_and_service_improvement_tools/quality_and_service_improvement_ tools/sbar_-_situation_-_background_-_assessment_-_recommendation.html.

Poor communication is often identified as a key contributing factor in the investigation of complaints about health services. The Parliamentary and Health Service Ombudsman report (2012b), for example, reported that poor communication with patients and their families is repeatedly at the core of what goes wrong. The report also highlighted that in 2011/12, 50 per cent more complaints were received from people who felt that the NHS had not acknowledged mistakes in care.

Strategies to support multi-professional communication

Team meetings are essential to ensure effective communication between team members. The team may engage in various meetings together, each of which should fulfil a different function. These can include meetings to discuss patient progress and to set patient goals, together with meetings to maximise the effectiveness of the team, for instance, where team goals are set and outcomes are monitored.

Getting the most out of group/team meetings

Meetings need to be managed effectively to ensure that they are productive and meet the needs of the team and its members. As the DCM, in addition to being a team member, you may also find yourself in the position of leading a group/team meeting; this could be for a handover report to colleagues, or for discussing your patients as part of a MDT meeting. To maximise the outcomes of these meetings, there are a number of principles that should be adhered to:

- Always start and finish the meeting on time.
- Review progress achieved since the last meeting.
- Encourage all members to participate.
- Keep focused on the nature of the business.

- Summarise key points.
- Agree the outcomes to be achieved by the next meeting.
- Confirm date and time of next meeting.

In addition to face-to-face communication, the MDT needs to ensure effective record-keeping, both as a formal record of the care provided, together with providing a mechanism to share information. Traditional record-keeping systems maintained by each discipline are not conducive to teamwork and can lead to duplication of effort. Therapists, for example, may maintain their discipline-specific records and additionally record a brief summary of interventions and treatments in the patient's notes. Integrated record-keeping systems can be more conducive to teamwork, as they contain a comprehensive account of the interventions of each member of the MDT. The SAP, as outlined in Chapter 9, provides an example of an integrated record that can be multi-professional and multi-agency, and can also be used as a patient-held record.

The National Programme for Information Technology (NPfIT) in the NHS was launched in 2002 with the aim of reforming the way that the NHS in England used information, and to improve services and the quality of patient care. A report by the National Audit Office in 2011, however, highlighted that although some care records systems were in place, progress against DH plans had fallen far below expectations and care records systems had not been delivered across the NHS, or with the required functionality that would enable it to achieve the original aspirations of the Programme. In 2012, the DH published a new information strategy that sets out a 10-year framework which aims to transform information for health and social care through harnessing information and new technologies to achieve higher quality care and improve outcomes for patients and service users (DH, 2012i). The strategy is underpinned by the Health and Social Care Act 2012, and includes public health, healthcare and social care in adult and children's services in England. The new strategy builds upon information systems already in place and looks at linking systems together rather than designing or reinventing large-scale information systems.

Ineffective teamwork

Whilst the various merits of teamwork are espoused and this model of working is widely promoted, it must be recognised that not all teams are effective. The report of the public inquiry into children's heart surgery at the British Royal Infirmary between 1984 and 1995 (Kennedy, 2001), for example, cited failings in communication together with a lack of leadership and teamwork as a contributing factor for the failings. A clear lack of clinical leadership was identified as being responsible for the poor teamwork that was in existence. This report made a number of recommendations that included the need for managers, doctors and nurses to work together and to have clear lines of accountability.

As identified in Chapter 4, conflict can provide a source of challenge for groups and teams. To facilitate effective teamwork, individual team members need to have clarity regarding their personal role as well as the roles of their fellow team members. The language used by team members can provide insight into team cohesiveness: language such as 'we' and 'us, for example, suggests ownership and a unified approach.

Action point 10.9   Effective teams and ineffective teams

First, consider a successful team that you have been a member of. Make notes on what the characteristics were that made the team a success. What skills and attributes did the leader of the team demonstrate?

Second, consider a less effective team that you have been a member of. Why was this team less effective? How did the skills and attributes of the leader differ to those of the more effective leader in the successful team that you identified?

Evaluating team performance

Throughout the chapter, reference has been made to the numerous challenges associated with teamwork. Within healthcare there is a need to maximise the use of resources and to ensure best outcomes for patients.

Measures that can be used to measure the effectiveness of teamwork can include:

- *Patient outcomes:* e.g. functional independence, independent living, quality of life.
- *Service efficiency:* e.g. length of stay, service costs.
- *Patient satisfaction:* e.g. communication, seamless transfer of care.

In order to evaluate the effectiveness of a team it is helpful to have clarity of purpose that can be used as a benchmark against which to assess team performance. First, it is helpful to establish if the team has:

- a mission statement that articulates shared purpose and values;
- shared goals; and
- agreed SMART objectives.

'SMART' is an acronym for Specific, Measurable, Achievable, Realistic and Timed. It is worth exploring how recently the mission statement, goals and objectives have been reviewed to ensure clarity and focus for the team. Mechanisms to appraise team performance should also be agreed.

Action point 10.10   The successful team

Think about your team: how effective do you consider it to be? What has the team achieved during the past 12 months? What strategies, both formal and informal are used to provide both the whole team and individual members with feedback? You may find it beneficial to ask members of your team the same questions and to explore with your manager and as a team how you can further enhance teamworking and maximise outcomes.

Celebrating and sharing success

When the team evaluates its performance against the goals that it had set, it is important to make it a priority to both celebrate and share its achievements. There are a number of ways that this can be achieved: for example, organising a team celebration or night out; informing managers of the accomplishments; submitting an abstract to present a paper at a conference; writing an article for publication in a professional journal and submitting an application for an award.

Guidelines for coherent and effective inter-professional teamwork

The following constitute good practice guidelines for coherent and effective inter-professional teamwork:

- Ensure that the patient is the focus of your teamwork and is involved in the decision-making process.
- As a team, develop and agree your mission statement and goals.
- Set SMART objectives.
- Ensure that your team and its objectives support the wider organisation.
- Agree how you will communicate with team members and the wider organisation.
- Monitor team performance and evaluate outcomes.
- Celebrate and share team success.

Teamwork is premised as an important mechanism for healthcare management and delivery. Whether uni-disciplinary, inter-disciplinary or inter-agency, the team needs to have clarity of purpose, together with clear objectives to enable it to be effective. Individual teams also need to operate within the overarching objectives of the wider organisation. Effective teamwork is dependant upon good working relationships and effective communication between team members. The DCM has an important role in co-ordinating uni-disciplinary, inter-disciplinary

(Continued)

CHAPTER SUMMARY

(Continued)

and inter-agency care, and the needs of the patient should be central to the focus of such teamwork.

This chapter has focused on uni-professional, inter-professional and inter-agency teamwork in healthcare and therefore focused on:

- theories of teamwork, which entailed differentiation between groups and teams, identifying models and benefits of teamwork, the characteristics of effective teams and MDT roles, including the role of the nurse in the MDT;
- team leadership, including experiences of teamwork, challenges to leadership and management within inter-professional teams and within inter-agency teams;
- staff motivation, which started by exploring why the DCM should have knowledge and understanding of staff motivation, what motivation is, theories of motivation such as management by objectives, Maslow's theory of human motivation based on human needs, Herzberg's theory comprising motivators and hygiene factors and McGregor's theory X and theory Y with regard to how employees are perceived by managers; and
- inter-professional education, which included exploring power and hierarchies within and between healthcare professions, multi-professional communication and strategies to ensure that they are effective, getting the most out of inter-professional team meetings, ineffective teamwork, evaluation of team performance and guidelines for coherent and effective inter-professional teamwork.

RECOMMENDED FURTHER READING

West M A (2012) *Effective Teamwork: Practical Lessons from Organisational Research* (3rd edn). Chichester: Wiley.

11

MANAGING LEARNING IN HEALTH AND SOCIAL CARE

Various organisations proudly and strategically display Investors in People (IIP) shields and use the logo on their organisations' headed paper to indicate that both employees and employers value continuing professional learning to ensure that employees perform their duties in the light of the most up-to-date evidence base. Formally, continuing learning is referred to as 'continuing professional development' (CPD) and 'lifelong learning', which are essential activities for professional revalidation and which also enrich the learning ethos in health and social care settings, leading to improved care for patients and service users. Such environments encourage and invest in formal modes of learning, and also support informal learning activities. 'Informal learning' generally refers to various non-structured learning and teaching activities that care organisations quiescently support.

The DCM's role is crucial in demonstrating educational leadership in enhancing the learning ethos in their care setting. This chapter analyses the way in which a learning ethos can prevail throughout care settings, and thereby ensure that employees as well as patients and service users benefit from up-to-date knowledge, competence and expertise. It examines ways in which continuing learning is managed for care professionals in care settings, including accessing funding for structured CPD courses, as well as learning for care profession students, preceptorship and management coaching.

Chapter objectives

On completion of this chapter you will be able to:

- identify the ways in which registrants progress from being a preceptee through to functioning competently as a DCM, and beyond;

(Continued)

(Continued)

- demonstrate knowledge of what makes care settings learning environments, and how the DCM can manage and sustain a learning ethos in these settings;
- demonstrate substantial insight into how the DCM can influence an organisational culture that values and supports learning;
- suggest how to use and maximise opportunities for the acquisition of knowledge and professional competence in the development and education of care practitioners; and
- recognise developmental processes that incorporate CPD, lifelong learning, professional regulation and funding for CPD.

Progressing from Registrant to Duty Care Manager

Health and social care settings that are effective learning environments are those that enable the professional and personal development of care practitioners. It involves supporting learning for everyone, including care professionals who are on structured post-qualifying courses and those who are not, and includes mentoring, preceptorship and clinical supervision, as well as educating patients and service users. It also includes identifying and developing learning opportunities for all care profession students and learners. Mentoring in healthcare, which is also known by various other titles such as 'practice supervision' and 'clinical education', tends to refer to facilitation of learning for pre-registration students while on placement in care settings. Preceptoring refers to facilitation of learning for new registrants. Learning beyond preceptoring includes learning relevant expanded role skills, then later attending specialist or advanced practice courses, and/or management coaching. Peer support and peer-learning for qualified staff were discussed under 'Clinical supervision' and 'Peer review' in Chapter 8.

Preceptor and preceptee

On first qualifying and registering with the appropriate professional regulatory body, the registrant undergoes a period of preceptorship, which involves supervised practice for a specified but flexible length of time. Starting a first job as a qualified professional can be both exciting and daunting.

Action point 11.1 Hopes and fears of finalist care profession students

Consider the hopes and fears of emerging health and social care professionals at the point of registration, and jot down these hopes and fears, together with some of the possible reasons for them as well as potential solutions.

Various hopes and fears are experienced by new registrants when they seek their first employment as a registrant on gaining their professional qualification. Some of the hopes and fears of aspiring care practitioners are identified in Table 11.1.

Table 11.1   Hopes and fears of aspiring registrants

Hopes	Fears
Acceptance by the care team and support from them	Isolation (lack of support) due to staff shortages
Orientation to the practice setting and associated areas, and systems	Not fitting into the MDT
Space (time) for gaining experience and confidence	Personal expectations not being met
Support for further professional education	Not being valued
An identified preceptorship period, and clinical supervision	Making mistakes
To learn how to practise safely and effectively	Personality clashes
A payband 5 development programme	Aggressive patients/staff
To further develop patient or service user care skills	Anxiety due to lack of confidence in own competence, and fear of litigation
Equal opportunities for all team members	Insufficient professional development time
To be valued as an important member of the care team	Dealing with complaints – due to lack of experience

As can be expected, new registrants' hopes vary from individual to individual. Some of the ways in which fears can be prevented from materialising are as follows. For fear of isolation (lack of support) due to staff shortages, or fear of making mistakes for instance, the registrant needs to invest full effort into their day-to-day care interventions, look for role models and observe experienced colleagues. They can also support their activities through further reading and attending appropriate structured learning events.

Access to structured preceptorship can play a crucial role. For personality clashes, they would need to learn experientially how to resolve these by using systematic problem-solving approaches. It may help to discuss the problem with the preceptor, and also attend assertiveness training. For overcoming inexperience and lack of self-confidence in dealing with complaints, the registrant needs to become fully conversant with appropriate policies and procedures, which include documentation, and accessing relevant departments in the organisation.

Several authorities, including the NMC (2006), indicate that the support and guidance of an experienced professional colleague can be invaluable for a newly registered care professional, for a registrant who has returned to practice following a break of five years or more, or for a registrant changing their area of practice, and for qualified nurses from other European Economic Area States and overseas. The provision of such support and guidance is referred to as 'preceptorship', and has been recommended for some time as a form of formal support that incorporates learning time which is protected during the first year of qualified practice, depending on the preceptee's ability and experience.

The DCM may have to take a preceptor role for one of the above-mentioned categories of novices, or be responsible for allocating another appropriately knowledgeable and skilled team member for this role.

The preceptor's role has different meanings in different professions, and even in nursing in different countries. In England and Wales, preceptorship refers to a specified but negotiable period of structured support and facilitation of learning for registrants who are new to the specialism, to consolidate existing skills and theoretical knowledge, and to develop new skills that are required for the specialism. The DH (2010e: 6) defines a preceptor as 'a registered practitioner who has been given a formal responsibility to support a newly registered practitioner through preceptorship'.

Preceptoring aims to reduce the phenomenon of 'reality shock' (Kramer, 1974; Bain, 1996), which can occur on transition from being a mentored pre-registration student to an accountable practitioner and is characterised by an initial period of disorientation. Therefore, preceptorship prepares newly qualified care professionals for responsible and accountable professional practice and protects the public from the inexperienced. It also initiates socialisation of the newly qualified care professional into the team and its routines, and can lead to higher morale and better retention and recruitment of staff.

The NMC notes that preceptors will not, however, be accountable for the actions or omissions of preceptees, as they are registered professionals and therefore accountable for their practice in their own right. Preceptorship is not a mandatory requirement (although this has been recommended), and the NMC has no power to enforce the system but emphatically states that structured preceptorship reflects sound professional practice, and advises that local policies should be developed or amended for this purpose. The NMC's (2006) recommendations for preceptors are that they should:

- facilitate the transition from student to a registrant who is confident in his/her practice, sensitive to the needs of patients, an effective team member and up-to-date with their practice and knowledge;
- provide feedback to new registrants on good performance;
- provide honest, constructive and objective feedback on performance that needs improving, and provide support to remedy this; and
- facilitate new registrants to gain new knowledge and skills.

Preceptorship constitutes an intensive but short-term teaching and supervisory role. A preceptor is therefore a person, generally a staff nurse (in the nursing profession), who teaches, counsels, inspires, serves as a role model and supports the professional growth and development of an individual (the novice) for a fixed period of time with the specific purpose of enabling skill development and socialising the novice into the new role.

The NMC (2006) also indicates that healthcare professionals who take on the role of preceptor should be first-level registrants who have had at least 12 months (or equivalent) experience in the same area of practice as the registrant requiring support. Registrants may be in full or part-time employment, but they must appreciate the additional demands it places upon them, and have appropriate preparation for the role. The preceptor and the preceptee should agree the nature of their working relationship and define intended outcomes, which at times comprise an adaptation of the induction programme for new employees and can be documented as a learning contract. Midwives also have the support of a named supervisor of midwives allocated upon starting to practise midwifery.

Furthermore, Sharples and Elcock (2011: 7) identify some of the benefits of preceptorship as: enhanced recruitment; improved retention of staff; increased confidence and competence of new registrants; professional socialisation into the work environment; and taking personal responsibility for keeping up to date. They also examine a range of methods of learning that can add impetus to their pre-registration mentoring process as including reflective practice, identifying the preceptee's learning style and so forth.

Preceptors can be called upon if the registrant needs help with a procedure that they are unfamiliar with, or with a situation not encountered before, or if guidance is needed with certain aspect of practice. However, there can be barriers to effective functioning of the preceptorship role, which can include poor staffing levels, lack of time to precept and lack of baseline criteria to measure progress against.

More constructively though, based partly on extensive research entitled 'Flying Start' in Scotland, the DH (2010e) presents a framework for implementation of preceptorship for all care professions. The framework comprises 'elements of preceptorship' from the perspectives of (1) the newly registered practitioner, (2) the preceptor and (3) the employer. From the preceptor's perspective, it indicates that the preceptor:

- has responsibility to develop others professionally to achieve potential;
- acts as a conduit to formalise and demonstrate CPD;
- has responsibility to discuss individual practice and provide feedback;
- has responsibility to share individual knowledge and experience;
- has insight and empathy with the newly registered practitioner during the transition phase;
- acts as an exemplary role model;
- receives preparation for the role; and
- enables the embracement of the principles of the NHS constitution.

The NHS Constitution (DH, 2012d) mentioned in the last bullet point presented above was discussed in Chapter 1. The DH (2010e) document also identifies the attributes of an effective preceptor, the indicative content and design of preceptorship programmes, and outcome measures, as well as standards for preceptorship, such as:

- Systems are in place to identify all staff requiring preceptorship.
- Systems are in place to monitor and track newly registered practitioners from their appointment through to completion of the preceptorship period.

- Preceptors are identified from the workforce within care areas and demonstrate the attributes outlined (in this framework).
- Organisations demonstrate that preceptors are appropriately prepared and supported to undertake the role, and that the effectiveness of the preceptor is monitored through appraisal.
- An evaluative framework is in place that demonstrates benefits and value for money.

Flying Start England (NHS Flying Start England, 2013) is a national preceptorship development programme for newly qualified nurses, midwives and AHPs in England that has been designed to support the transition from student to newly qualified care professional by supporting their learning in everyday practice through a range of learning activities.

These up-to-date, well-informed critiques and guidelines for preceptorship are useful components of the DCM's repertoire of knowledge for their role as care managers. As for the preparation of preceptors, structured preceptorship programmes can be provided locally by employing organisations. There are no formal qualifications associated with being a preceptor, but preparation as a mentor or practice teacher should provide a working basis for anyone undertaking the role. Funding for preceptorship preparation programmes have been available through the recommendations of the Darzi Report (DH, 2008a), but may not recur as the United Kingdom experiences serious financial constraints that are also impacting on funding for the NHS overall. Some British universities offer a single-module preceptorship preparation course. Accessing funding for continuing professional education will be examined later in this chapter.

Management Coaching for the Duty Care Manager

The careers of care professionals often progress to management positions such as DCMs which can take the guise of various job titles such as ward manager, team leader, ward sister and so on. Taken from the viewpoint that care practitioners' functions can be grouped under key areas such as the six core dimensions (or components) stipulated in the *NHS KSF* (DH, 2004a), the four components identified by Scottish Government (2008) as clinical, management, education and research, or the six components of the DCM's roles identified at the beginning of Chapter 1 of this book, these are the areas or components that can be learnt by newly qualified health and social care professionals under the preceptorship provision, as just discussed.

The care professional develops their practice or clinical skills over the duration of their careers as they develop from being competent to proficient, and eventually experts (see Figure 11.1). Teaching skills can be learnt through both pre-registration and mentoring courses, and the teaching role of the registrant is clearly identified by the NMC (2008) and other professional bodies. Research skills can be acquired

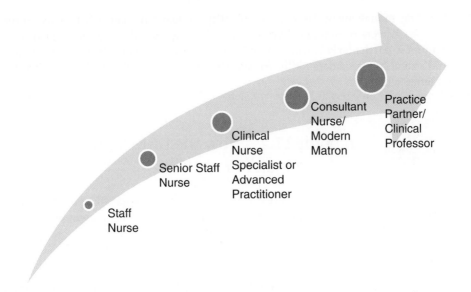

Figure 11.1 The potential career progression of the new registrant

through attending specific courses, journal clubs, completing assignments and conducting research under the guidance of a research supervisor.

The management component of the role of care professionals is also identified in the *NHS KSF* (DH, 2004a). As one of the DH's (2004a) policies, the *NHS KSF* has relevance for the DCM's role in that it is a framework of job definitions for healthcare employees and identifies posts into pay bands. It is designed to:

- identify the knowledge and skills that individuals need to apply in their post;
- help to guide the development of individuals;
- provide a framework on which to base review and development for all staff; and
- provide the basis of pay progression in the service.

Thereby, one of the key principles on which the *NHS KSF* is based is that of identifying a competence framework that should be able to support the ongoing development of the NHS itself. The *NHS KSF is* therefore also used in development reviews, with managers working with individual members of staff to plan their training and development and review their work; that is, for conducting IDPRs. Training and development for care professionals include development of their leadership and/or management skills. Leadership development programmes were examined in Chapter 3, and the next section of this chapter explores development of management and leadership skills through coaching.

Attending management courses is one way to learn management skills. Some insight into aspects of management will have been gained through pre-registration programmes, particularly during the final practice placement. However, to a substantial extent, management skills are acquired through work-based experiences in the practice setting.

Action point 11.2   How the DCM learns management skills

Consider from your own experiences how DCMs learn management skills that are inherent components of their jobs. Consider care professionals on payband 5 or 6 who you know, and reflect on how they acquired their management skills.

In addition to work-based experiential learning, DCMs as first-level managers often learn management skills from their own line manager or more senior managers, either through direct advice or reflective conversations. WBL theories, which are discussed shortly, significantly underpin this. Management coaching is another systematic means of acquiring management skills.

As a term that is generally used in sports and general physical fitness, as well as in management training, 'coaching' tends to refer to one-to-one and team guidance in developing or improving skills and performance. Driscoll and Cooper (2005) suggest that coaching is a holistic term for the support of continuing personal and professional development. This function includes enabling the coachee to reflect on and to draw their own conclusions about the best way to develop and enhance their skills. This applies to the DCM as a developing manager, as they are both empowered and accountable for their management functions. This form of learning can comprise regular one-to-one meetings between the DCM and the coach, supported by structured study days.

Various management skills were identified in Table 2.1 as day-to-day management activities of the DCM. It is important, of course, for the coach to be competent in both coaching and management skills. Garvey et al. (2009: 66) note that coaching is prevalent in various arenas, such as in sports coaching, life coaching and executive coaching, and they even identify evidence-based coaching as a concept that can be empirically investigated. They also acknowledge the 'GROW' model of coaching, which is an acronym for **G**oal, **R**eality, **O**ptions and **W**ill and seen as the four key elements of a coaching session:

- *Goal:* of the session, or outcome to be achieved.
- *Reality:* seeing clearly the current situation objectively.
- *Options:* exploring the range of options or possible ways of achieving the outcome.
- *Will:* the motivation of the coachee to achieve the outcome.

'W' is often taken to stand for a number of other elements such as 'Wrap-up', or for What, Where, Why, When and How. However, there is a risk that using such a framework can reduce coaching to a technical tick-box exercise. Whilst acknowledging the use of a self-selected model of coaching, Garvey et al. (2009) argue that using a framework is contrary to the humanistic tradition of coaching and mentoring whereby aspects of coaching depends to a good extent of empathising with the coachee (see Recommended Further Reading at the end of the chapter for more on executive coaching).

Furthermore, Byrne (2007), among others, advocates 'leadership coaching' for care professionals at all levels, although current initiatives have generally only been available for senior nurses (e.g. lead nurses and modern matrons). She identifies the benefits of such individually tailored programmes as feelings of empowerment, increased motivation and so on, and subsequent positive effects on patient and service user care.

An alternative to management coaching can be management mentoring for trainee managers. The Chartered Institute of Personnel and Development (2011) provides extensive details through various publications on coaching, albeit predominantly executive coaching. They indicate that coaching and mentoring are development techniques based on the use of one-to-one discussions to enhance an individual's skills, knowledge or work performance, and that in practice these terms tend to be used interchangeably. Fields (1994) suggest that if a mentoring relationship is used instead of a coach, then the management mentor should be a more senior and experienced manager, but not in a line management relationship with the mentee. They could be from a different part of the organisation, or even external to the organisation.

Here a clear distinction is being made between a management coach and a management mentor. The definition of a mentor would in this case be different from the NMC (2008) definition which specifically refers to facilitation of learning and assessment of competence. Instead, as Byrne and Keefe (2002) suggest, the mentor is a person who helps a more junior person develop professionally through a combination of advising, skill development, creation of opportunities and personal growth in an intense manner over an extended period of time. Fields (1994) suggests that typically the management mentor should be chosen by the trainee manager, with the knowledge that the mentor has certain specific qualities or attributes that are desirable. It is also preferable for the mentor to have undertaken educational preparation for the role.

Furthermore, Driscoll and Cooper (2005) differentiate between management coaching and clinical supervision, and note that while the latter is still viewed with suspicion by supervisees, and is at times difficult to implement due to lack of time, the former is already available to some senior managers in care organisations, whereupon individually tailored personal and professional development meetings intended to improve organisational performance are held. Gould et al. (2001) report on a study exploring nurse managers' perceptions of factors that help or hinder their performance, in which the latter reported poor preparation to undertake key aspects of their roles. Educational preparation for management roles can be accessed in various ways (e.g. through in-service courses) and open learning programmes (e.g. the Master of Business Administration courses offered by some higher education institutes).

However, Garvey et al. (2009), who have investigated management coaching for several years, acknowledge that there is a drive to link the outcome of coaching to some organisational purpose (e.g. the purpose of the *NHS KSF*).

Supervising Learning

Supervision of care profession students and learners is an important role of the DCM. The various learners and care profession students whose learning needs to be facilitated in the care setting can include CSWs on national vocational qualification courses, and nursing, medical and AHP students. 'Mentoring' refers to enabling pre-registration student nurses to develop clinical skills. The NMC (2008) has identified competencies for mentors, and the outcomes that mentors have to achieve through the educational preparation for mentorship. The mentoring role usually incorporates the assessment of learners' competence (e.g. DH, 2001c; NMC, 2008), and recording them in appropriate documents. Gopee (2011) identifies various approaches and models of mentoring, including one-to-one mentoring with a named mentor being allocated to a student or team mentoring, reflective mentoring, classical mentoring and so on.

Occasionally, a student might be offered the opportunity to select a mentor in the placement, although usually they are allocated their mentor. The role has developed a step further to the role of 'sign-off mentor', whose function is to assess final placement students on the NMC's standards of proficiency to ensure that the student is 'fit for practice' on qualifying.

A similar arrangement can apply to preceptorship, which refers to supervising learning for newly qualified care professionals as discussed earlier in this chapter. There are common elements and differences between mentoring and preceptoring, but the principles of facilitation of learning for qualified staff (i.e. preceptoring) are similar to those of mentoring, and it is generally expected that the preceptor already holds a mentor qualification (NMC, 2008).

Action point 11.3   Allocating mentors and preceptors

How are mentors and preceptors allocated to learners in your workplace? Explore, and decide whether you have any views on how they could be allocated more effectively.

The NMC (2006, 2008) indicates that both roles require identifying a named person, but one who is supported by team members. Furthermore, an independent report into the future of nurse education published in November 2012 recommended that healthcare employers must ensure mentors have dedicated time for their mentorship role, and that mentors must be selected for their knowledge, skills and motivation and be well supported (Willis Commission, 2012).

Enhancing the care setting as a learning environment

It is the responsibility of the DCM to supervise and monitor the practice of all individuals in the work setting so that competent, safe and effective care is delivered at all times. Individual employees also have the responsibility to ensure that they acknowledge any limitations in their knowledge and skills, and are amenable to development of identified new knowledge and skills. To achieve this, an enquiring open-minded trusting ethos in the workplace is essential. This section explores this aspect of care settings, and includes professionalism and CPD, the care setting as a learning environment, work-based or practice-based learning, care settings as learning organisations and organisational culture.

Professionalism and CPD

It is every health and social care practitioner's responsibility to engage in CPD, a concept which is a subset of lifelong learning (DH, 2001d; Gopee, 2001). This is to ensure that their care delivery is informed by current knowledge and evidence. As noted in Chapter 8, this is achieved through formal and non-formal processes; that is, through attending structured courses or more informal training and education. Non-formal learning refers to structured teaching and learning strategies that do not involve attending structured courses. It therefore includes short courses held in the care organisation's post-graduate or in-service training department, for instance. Each trust has staff development strategies in their annual business plans. They work in tandem with IDPRs and personal development plans as indicated in the *NHS KSF* (DH, 2004a).

Furthermore, substantial learning of knowledge and competence occurs while engaging in direct patient or service user care, and hence the concept of WBL. It is logical to deduce, therefore, that the patient-care setting and general work ethos should reflect an environment where learning is fostered and supported. Teaching and learning (i.e. facilitating the acquisition of knowledge and competence in practice settings) is also a feature of professionalism, as indicated in the NMC (2010b) *The Code – Standards of Conduct, Performance and Ethics for Nurses and Midwives*, for instance. However, such learning can also be referred to as 'incidental learning', which can be seen positively as 'opportunistic' learning or with reservation as unstructured and partial learning.

CPD and lifelong learning

To avoid waiting for opportunities to learn, the care professional can endeavour to be more proactive, anticipate problematic situations and encounter them as natural challenges. This tends to implicate ongoing learning. Various policy documents including *The PREP Handbook* (NMC, 2011a), *Working Together – Learning Together* (DH, 2001d), *Continuing Professional Development* (GMC, 2012b) recognise the importance of CPD and lifelong learning for all throughout our professional careers. Clinical supervision, as discussed in Chapter 8, is one formal medium through which individuals can identify their professional development needs; IDPR is another. More informal means of support and identifying professional development needs include peer-assessment, peer-reviews, action learning sets, and even social networking, as discussed in Chapter 8.

Furthermore, as noted in Chapter 7, Handy (1984) suggests that people should be treated as assets, not costs, and that the workplace has a vital role to play in fostering continuing learning. Thus, as lifelong learning is becoming increasingly appreciated as an essential ingredient for ensuring high quality patient care, it would seem that employers and employees need to be sensitive to, and nurture, all structures that can facilitate this. Apart from the organisational mechanisms that are in situ to facilitate CPD for care professionals, informal learning tends to go unrecognised or is underused, as also noted in Chapter 8.

Learning opportunities for care professionals

Numerous avenues of learning have been developed during the last two decades. Professional development courses run at universities and short courses in healthcare trusts' own in-service/post-graduate training departments constitute the majority of professional development provision. Others include:

- structured teaching by practice facilitators, medical staff, and clinical nurse specialists, for instance;
- conferences organised locally by care organisations;
- conferences organised by professional forums;
- e-learning or blended learning opportunities;
- professional development learning and assessment provision in professional journals; and
- inter-professional learning.

In the current ethos of efficiency, effectiveness and close monitoring of funding for care provision and delivery, teaching and learning can easily be relegated to being an occasional fringe activity. Therefore DCMs should ensure that opportunities for the acquisition of knowledge and competencies are maximised. Such opportunities could include of use of e-learning and blended learning that can be accessed from care settings. Additionally, DCMs can apply for scholarship from various sources to support their learning (e.g. from the Florence Nightingale Foundation: www.florence-nightingale-foundation.org.uk/).

The care setting as a learning environment

Nursing and AHPs are practice-based professions, and a substantial part of learning that the 'novice' professionals undertake occurs in the care setting.

Action point 11.4   The care setting as a learning environment

Reflect on your experiences of the various care settings where you have worked. Consider the question: 'What makes a care and treatment setting a learning environment?' Think of the settings where you or learners have had a positive learning experience and contrast them with those where learning is less well supported.

The NMC (2008: 53) identifies a learning environment as one 'where practice is valued and developed, that provides appropriate professional and inter-professional learning opportunities and support for learning to maximise achievement for individuals.' It refers to a range of care settings, including hospital wards, health centres and schools, which self-evidently constitute important learning environments.

Dunn and Hansford (1997) note that a clinical learning environment comprises an interactive network of forces that influence student learning outcomes in practice settings. These descriptions implicitly recognise the psycho-social factors that are essential for practice settings to be learning environments, and therefore Gopee (2011: 122) deduces that a practice setting which constitutes a learning environment comprises 'a psycho-social ethos and culture, with related supportive resources, that fosters mutual learning amongst all care professionals, learners and clientele, and where care and treatment are founded on evidence-based practice.' Stuart (2007) suggests that there are four categories of factors that make a care setting a learning environment, namely:

1   The people, such as the team leader, team members, student and mentors.
2   Learning opportunities and experiences provided through care activities.
3   Staff commitment to teaching (supervision) and learning (CPD).
4   Material resources.

Both above authors expressly avoid too much focus on learning environments as places where students merely achieve their course objectives, which policy definitions such as that of the NMC (2008) tends to do.

Earlier studies on clinical learning environments explored how effectively and adequately learning occurs in practice settings. It formed the focus of research studies by various authors, some of the earliest being by Fretwell (1980) and Orton (1981). The recommendations from these studies have been implemented fairly widely. From her study of practice settings as learning environments, Fretwell (1980) concluded that the key components of the 'ideal learning environment' are anti-hierarchy, teamwork, negotiation, communication and availability of trained nurses; and the practice setting sister's leadership in teaching is crucial in maintaining a learning ethos on the area, as also noted more recently by Webb and Shakespeare (2008).

Orton's (1981) study concluded with the identification of the characteristics of wards that are 'high student-oriented' and those that were 'low student-orientated'. In the former, all individuals in the practice setting including students and patients were manifestly valued, and staff showed willingness to teach. In the latter, however, there was a lack of open-mindedness, lack of respect for individuals, and the atmosphere was not relaxed which made students anxious about asking questions. The responses in these earlier studies could be categorised as key factors that promote learning in the care setting and those that hinder, a number of which are identified in Box 11.1.

Box 11.1   Factors that promote learning and those that hinder learning in care settings

Factors that promote learning

- Mentors and preceptors repertoire of knowledge and skills
- Adequate time to teach
- Explanation of procedures
- Practical demonstration of skills
- Students feel they can take their time to practise the skills
- A learning ethos
- Teaching on a one-to-one basis
- Adequate staffing levels
- Adequate planning and preparation
- Reinforcing learning resources and information
- Approachable staff

Factors that hinder learning

- Interruptions
- Busy ward area
- Lack of time
- Staff, patient and learners' attitudes
- Availability of relevant medical equipment, e.g. hoists
- Not enough information communicated
- Learner–staff ratio too high
- Inadequate staffing levels
- Student not interested
- Disorganised programme of teaching
- Poor leadership

Rotem and Hart's (1995) findings are also consistent with the above research findings in that some practice settings and institutions are found to be more conducive to learning than others. Later studies focused on exploring the extent to which particular practice settings were suitable for students' practice placements, and therefore on educational auditing (also known as the 'clinical learning environment profile'). For example, Orton et al. (1993) identified various components or criteria under orientation to the placement, theory and practice, supernumerary status, staff attitudes and behaviour, the mentor and progressive assessment.

The DH (2001c) *Placements in Focus* guidance identified such criteria under four key headings: providing practice placements, practice learning environment, student support, and assessment of practice. Under practice learning environment, the criteria include, for instance, care provision being founded on relevant research-based and evidence-based findings where available, and students gaining experience as part of a multi-professional team.

Various more recent studies still endeavour to identify more suitable contemporary criteria for education audits. Newton et al. (2010), for instance, tested a 'clinical learning environment inventory' comprising 42 criteria under five sections: personalisation, student involvement, task orientation, innovation, and satisfaction and individualisation. They conclude their test by suggesting modification to the inventory, indicating that even 30 years after Fretwell's research the best educational audit tool has not yet been established.

Action point 11.5   The 'learning environment profile' of your care setting

Consider the learning ethos in your care setting, and complete a SWOT analysis of the setting as a learning environment using the proforma presented below.

Alternatively, or additionally, locate your practice setting's copy of the 'learning environment profile' (or education audit) document to complete this Action point.

STRENGTHS	WEAKNESSES
• • •	• • •
THREATS	OPPORTUNITIES
• • •	• • •

Other than in hospital wards, based on the first-hand experience of community nurses, Gopee et al. (2004) identified other specific requirements for enhancing primary care settings as effective clinical learning environments. These requirements include mentor–mentee matching in accordance with the seniority of the care professional and the student's particular learning needs, ensuring that particular student practice outcomes are achievable within particular primary care settings, together with access to clinical supervision for all qualified staff.

Education audits of care settings also invite care professionals to identify formal and informal learning opportunities in their own settings. These opportunities include teaching during care delivery (or care interventions), that is, WBL, talks by medical device representatives, lectures or seminars presented by doctors, and opportunistic learning such as when a patient with a new condition is admitted. Such learning opportunities need to be recognised and nurtured by the DCM to ensure that the learning ethos endures.

For some decades, the responsibility for ensuring that clinical learning environments are suitable as practice placement areas has been that of the particular higher education institution offering the pre- and post-registration courses, but from 2006 this has been the responsibility of care organisations themselves (NMC, 2008), usually through practice education facilitators.

The factors that are important for the creation of a positive learning environment include friendly staff, a positive attitude and allocated time for teaching. Good communication is of course paramount, as is the learner feeling that they are part of the team. Staff demonstrating up-to-date knowledge and use of latest research findings in their specialism generally portray a positive impression. The availability and accessibility of research literature in the work environment may be kept in the learning resources section or in a resource room, which also contributes to a learning culture.

Furthermore, you might have noted that staff showing genuine interest in students' individual learning needs, and their stage of knowledge and competence development, also creates positive impressions. The enthusiasm of all those who teach in care settings, and practice educators' input, generate impetus for learning and constructive criticism in an appropriate environment which is usually appreciated by students. A culture in which care staff are open to new ideas and share new learning from courses also present healthy perspectives, as is good staff morale.

From the DCM's perspective, learning in the care setting needs to be approached from a management perspective, including allocation of mentors, preceptors and clinical supervisors, and evaluation, analysis, introducing changes and so on.

Action point 11.6   Analysis of a care setting as a learning environment

Following on from Action point 11.5, this exercise involves identifying actions that can be taken in respect of reviewing the effectiveness of your practice setting as a learning environment and identifying objectives and strategies for ensuring that they are effective. Consequently, consider your thoughts on the actions that you can take as a DCM to enhance your care setting as a learning environment.

More recent studies on care settings as learning environments focus on specific aspects of learning in practice settings. Lewin (2007) reports on a study evaluating five key components of effective learning environments, comprising the grade of staff students worked with most, how often practical procedures were demonstrated to them, and undertaken with them, how much of the time they were personally supervised and how often they worked with mentors who assessed them. This study, which is a replication of another study that was undertaken 25 years earlier, revealed a 20 per cent improvement in the five component areas.

Andrews et al. (2006) explored students' experiences during clinical placements, and concluded that commitment, collective vision, co-ordination and effective communication are crucially important requirements for successful practice placement experiences. Another perspective is provided by Henderson et al. (2006), who found that the psycho-social support available to students during clinical placements plays a very significant role. To investigate the factors that enhance the learning experiences of student nurses whilst they are on practice placement, Warne et al. (2010) conducted a survey of 1,903 students undertaking general nurse training in nine European countries using the validated 'Clinical Learning Environment, Supervision and Nurse Teacher (CLES + T)' education audit tool. They found that:

- respondents were generally satisfied with their clinical placements;
- there was clear support for mentorship – 57 per cent of respondents had a successful mentorship experience whilst 18 per cent experienced unsuccessful supervision;
- most satisfied students were supported by individualised mentorship relationships; and
- learning requires time and a supportive supervisory relationship.

The components identified specifically for ascertaining the extent to which care settings are learning environments comprise frameworks or models of clinical learning environments. Various such frameworks extracted from research and in policy documents are available. Lewin's (2007) five-component framework of learning environments is one, Orton et al.'s (1993) is another, those identified by the DH (2001c) is yet another, as are those in the trust–university education audit (or learning environment profile) documents.

As noted in Chapters 1 and 5, in their role as inspectors of quality of patients' or service users' care and treatment, the CQC has a pivotal say in deciding whether a care setting is suitable for student placement. Williams (2011) reports in the *Health Services Journal* for example, that in July 2011, the NMC withdrew 100 students from practice placements at a British hospital as the CQC explored allegations of abuse and neglect at the healthcare trust.

Work-based learning and reflective learning

It has long been recognised that care practitioners develop their competence through learning-by-doing in work settings, which includes learning care skills that might be assessed and signed by the mentor, and also accredited. Thus the concept and role of WBL (or practice-based learning) has been evolving and increasingly recognised in care professions. Such learning is recognised in module details of care profession courses, and therefore also commands a specific number of academic credit points.

Some years ago, Guile and Young (1996) amongst others have suggested that WBL as a concept is innovative in that it places firm emphasis on the importance of the workplace as a site of learning, and Flanagan et al. (2000) suggested that WBL is a team-based, structured and learner-managed approach to maximising opportunities for learning and professional development in the workplace.

Some of the issues related to WBL include (Guile and Young, 1996) the limitations of the concept competence, which can reflect behaviourist assumptions and reductionist descriptions of work performance (i.e. as simply tasks) and therefore overlook theoretical knowledge, and also comparability and equivalence between academic and work-based learning.

Furthermore, 'work-based learning' is a rather vague term in that it has been variously interpreted as learning that takes place in the workplace, learning that is based on the workplace, and learning for the workplace. 'Workplace' sometimes refers to a specific place of work, and at other times it signifies workplaces in general. There is very little research on the benefits of any of these three forms. Nonetheless, WBL is supported by professional regulatory bodies such as the NMC (2008), and by the DH's *NHS KSF* (2004a) framework as it enhances the likelihood of 'fitness for practise' on qualifying, and supports lifelong learning.

The care setting as a learning organisation

It was argued in Chapter 8 that social capital thrives in settings that reflect the features of a learning organisation. The work environment in which health and social care professionals deliver care seems to have considerable effect on their learning.

The learning organisation (or the learning company) as a concept goes beyond the notion of the care environment in that it signifies support for learning from higher-level structures such as the management team of an acute NHS trust. A learning organisation therefore implies that a learning attitude prevails in the management structure and organisational strategies.

Impinging on how much the care area as an organisation functions as a learning organisation is 'organisational culture', which in turn has an effect on staff morale and on how conflict is resolved. Watkins and Marsick (1992: 118) noted that a learning organisation is characterised by 'total employee involvement in a process of collaboratively initiated, collaboratively conducted, collectively accountable change of direction towards shared values and principles.' Bahn (2001: 115) discusses this in the context of social learning theory, and notes that the social environment has considerable impact on the 'collaborative approach to learning through the use of peers and expert practitioners as role models'. This is also related to the concept of 'informal organisation', which refers to non-formal structures that constitute a powerful force in shaping culture in organisations.

The notion of the care setting being a learning organisation has not been as widely researched and documented as the 'clinical learning environment'. However, as is obvious from the foregoing discussion on learning in care settings and the concepts discussed in Chapter 8, learning needs to be a fundamental underlying component of all activities in care settings. It must not be a superficial add-on activity, but rather an intrinsic facet that ultimately ensures more informed patient or service user care. It should be a feature of organisational culture in healthcare organisations. Staff development strategies should already be built into the organisational business plans, and are also evident in various DH policies and guidelines (e.g. DH, 1998, 2000d, 2001d). It is therefore well ingrained into the psycho-social ethos and organisational culture of care organisations.

The learning culture in practice settings

According to the dictionary (Brown, 2002), 'culture' refers to the distinctive cus-toms, achievements, products and outlook of a group, their way of life. Organisa-tional culture is defined by Buchanan and Huczynski (2010: 623) as 'the collection of relatively uniform and enduring values, beliefs, customs, traditions, and practices that are shared by an organisation's members, learned by new recruits, and transmit-ted from one generation of employees to the next.' This definition clearly suggests recognising local attitudes that are ingrained and enduring, but focuses on the achievement of both the organisation's and its employees' goals for the organisation.

Mullins (2010) notes that culture is created and sustained through particular pat-terns of communication, values and beliefs that determine particular patterns of behaviour, and unconsciously held basic assumptions that determine group mem-bers' perceptions and feelings about modes of interactions within the organisation, along with the dynamics of the informal organisation. Four types of organisational culture are identified by Handy (1993), ranging from power culture, role, task or person cultures:

- *Power culture:* a setting in which power is vested generally in one individual, or in a small group of individuals, who control all activities of the organisation.
- *Role culture:* an organisational culture in which each employee's role and functions are clearly demarcated, and wherein work is allocated on the basis of their ability to do the task.
- *Task culture:* a product-oriented culture, wherein the whole focus is on getting the job done, which involves appointing individuals with the right skills and allowing them to be productive in the job.
- *Person culture:* an organisation that heeds the basic needs of each individual employee.

The DCM needs to be sensitive to the prevailing culture in their workplace, as it reflects the values and beliefs of individuals in the team, as well as the team as a whole.

Action point 11.7   Organisational culture

Which of the four types of organisational culture prevail in your care setting? How far does the identified culture(s) support a lasting ethos for learning in your workplace?

Kane-Urrabazo (2006) notes that regardless of the four types of culture, there are also three critical components of organisational culture: (1) trustworthiness and trust, (2) empowerment and delegation, (3) consistency and mentorship, all of which influence employees' job satisfaction, and consequently organisational effectiveness. She suggests that managers should install support systems and mechanisms that enable employees' growth and development.

It is important, however, to distinguish between organisational culture and organisational climate, two concepts that are at times used interchangeably. 'Culture' is something that endures over very long periods of time, while 'climate' in this context refers to more transient and changeable attitude and behaviour. Increasingly this includes effective inter-professional learning.

Managing Continuing Learning

Having examined ways in which care settings can be effective learning environments and learning organisations, and then the mechanisms for developing and educating the workforce on a lifelong spectrum, this section explores how policy-directed learning can be achieved and how this interfaces with professional regulation.

Managing funding for learning

It is up to the registrant to ensure they are up to date and competent in their care activities. However, it is one of the roles of the DCM to ascertain the skill needs of the care setting, in consultation with the organisation's management, and also to match the skill needs with the CPD interests of individual employees. The issues discussed in the preceding sections relate to the point that care dynamics can affect learning in care settings, and indicate that learning and teaching in care settings need to be managed and resourced.

The *NHS KSF* (DH, 2004a) clearly identifies the functions of groups of members of staff, and the professional development requirements and aspirations of each employee through IDPR. These can be documented in personal development plans, which are usually based on IDPRs.

Formal education programmes for care professionals have until recently generally been funded by local SHAs through monies identified in yearly budgets specifically for this purpose, for each NHS trust. This funding has been designated for initial professional educational preparation as well as for post-registration professional development. HEE has taken over this role from April 2013 through the newly established LETBs (DH, 2012j).

The DH (2012j) indicates that all providers of NHS services must be a member of a LETB (p.3 of executive summary), and as a governing body of HEE, LETB is instituted to determine local education and training strategy for healthcare trusts' employees, in primary, secondary and community care, as well as lead planning and education commissioning, thereby ensuring security of supply of competent health and care workforce locally. Each LETB works through a number of identified Local Education and Training Councils (LETC) (see Figure 11.2 for the interface between HEE, LETB and LETC).

LETBs also have to heed ongoing statutory requirements of the health and social care profession regulators to ensure that national professional standards are met, and include working in collaboration with other key bodies including professional bodies and royal colleges to contribute to the regulators' quality assurance frameworks.

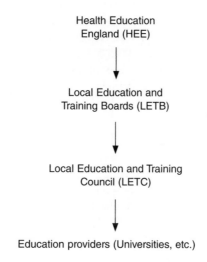

Health Education
England (HEE)

Local Education and
Training Boards (LETB)

Local Education and Training
Council (LETC)

Education providers (Universities, etc.)

Figure 11.2   HEE, LETB and LETC

HEE itself has been instituted a Special Health Authority in its own right, with a chief executive, a board and so on, and its role is to provide leadership and oversee (DH, 2012j: 14) the strategic planning, as well as education and training for the local health and social care workforce. Whilst LETBs work with service providers (e.g. NHS Trusts), CCGs and education providers (e.g. universities), they are accountable to HEE for their decision-making and activities, together with their quality assurance mechanisms. HEE works in collaboration with the various organisations identified in Chapter 1, as illustrated in Figure 11.3.

The Investors in People award

A learning culture in the care setting that is supported by an appropriately devised operational strategy directly impacts on the extent of formal and informal learning and also on achievement of the Investors in People (IIP) award. The IIP framework (Investors in People, 2012) comprises three core principles and ten indicators against which organisations (or smaller units or departments) are assessed for the IIP award. The three core principles are:

- *Plan:* Develop strategies to improve performance.
- *Do:* Take action to improve performance.
- *Review:* Evaluate and improve performance.

These indicators include people-management strategy, recognition and reward, and performance measurement. It involves the capability of leaders and managers being more closely measured. The IIP assessor looks to see how plans for professional education and CPD figure in the organisation's strategic plans, and how the impact of learning and development upon performance is measured and evaluated.

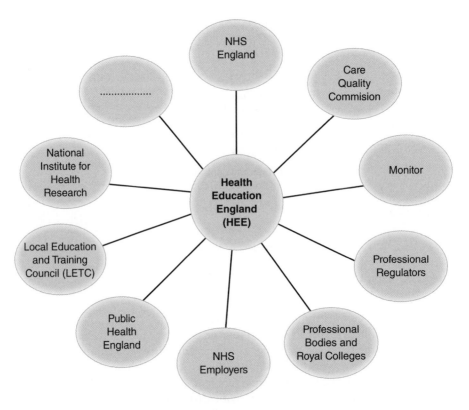

Figure 11.3   Organisations with whom HEE collaborates

Mandatory Learning and Regulating Care Professionals

Another dimension of managing learning is 'mandatory learning'. This notion, as a mechanism for CPD, is well known in nursing and midwifery circles in the form of post-registration education and practice (known as PREP) (NMC, 2011a), which has been in force for a number of years. Mandatory learning entails the registrant self-declaring to the NMC that they have updated their knowledge and competence, and are then allowed to remain on the register and to practise in that capacity. Further-more, registrants are expected to be lifelong learners (e.g. DH, 2001d). Doctors are expected to undertake similar activities (e.g. GMC, 2012a), as are AHPs (e.g. HCPC, 2011) and others (e.g. DH, 2004b *NHS Improvement Plan*).

The requirement for continuing education, revalidation and professional regula-tion of care registrants has been evolving over time. The NMC was established in 2002, replacing the UK Central Council for Nursing, Midwifery and Health Visiting, to self-regulate the nursing and midwifery professions. The other nine regulators of health and social care professions in the United Kingdom who are overseen by the PSA include the Health and Care Professions Council, General Chiropractic Council, General Dental Council, General Medical Council, Pharmaceutical Society of Northern Ireland and so forth.

In 2012, regulation of social care professionals transferred from the General Social Care Council to the HCPC (the new name for the Health Professions Council), which in turn is answerable to the PSA, whose aim is to promote consistency across the 13 regulators. The DCM needs to be aware of this as the new proposed rules will directly impact on their day-to-day roles.

However, there have been strong recommendations for more central regulation of healthcare professions. The central regulation of healthcare professions was initiated through the government white paper *Trust, Assurance and Safety – The Regulation of Health Professionals in the 21st Century* (DH, 2007), which comprises a major development that outlines how healthcare professions will be regulated imminently. It set out a programme of reform that is based on consultation of two reviews of professional regulation, one by the Chief Medical Officer published in July 2006 entitled *Good Doctors, Safer Patients* (DH, 2006d) and another by the DH known as the Foster Report entitled *The Regulation of the Non-Medical Healthcare Professions* (DH, 2006e), as well as other contemporary reports of incompetence on the part of some healthcare practitioners. It is complemented by the government's response to the Shipman Inquiry and similar reports.

However, care regulators such as the NMC, HCPC and GMC in conjunction with health unions such as UNISON have resisted central regulation (Kendall-Raynor, 2006). This was because of a fear that professional regulation led by government departments might not be as insightful regarding the 'whys and hows' of care interventions and might impose inappropriate penalties on suspected poor performance, for instance, than professional regulators might do. Professional development imposed by central regulators could be undertaken less wholeheartedly than if they were imposed by professional self-regulators.

The DH (2007) White Paper in essence, however, proposes that the responsibility for ensuring that nurses are up to date should be transferred from the NMC to healthcare employers, thus replacing PREP by another system linked to the *NHS KSF*, and will be known as 're-validation'.

Guidelines for managing learning in the care setting

The criteria contained within the 'learning environment profile' (educational audit) document, as well as those required for achieving the IIP award, together with other various policy documents constitute guidelines for good practice for sustaining a learning ethos in care settings. These criteria, however, usually identify structured mechanisms for learning, and also need to recognise informal and peer-learning where they occur.

This chapter has focused on the DCM's role in ensuring that continuing learning occurs in their work setting. This entailed examining:

- the route the newly qualified registrant, takes in progressing from being a care practitioner to becoming a DCM, which includes being a preceptee to learning to become a manager, which in turn includes supervising learning;
- how to create, maintain and develop a learning ethos in care settings, which includes the registrant's professionalism and CPD, and developing learning opportunities for care practitioners and learners, the care setting as a learning environment, work-based or practice-based learning and reflective learning, workplaces as learning organisations, and a culture for learning in care settings; and
- how to achieve the IIP award, mandatory continuing learning and professional regulation by various agencies, and managing learning in workplaces, as well as guidelines for sustaining the learning ethos in care settings.

- For detailed guidance on the implementation of preceptorship in the United Kingdom, see the following publications:

Department of Health (2010) *Preceptorship Framework for Newly Registered Nurses, Midwives and Allied Health Professionals*. Available from: www.dh.gov.uk/prod_consum_dh/groups/dh_digitalassets/@dh/@en/@abous/documents/digitalasset/dh_114116.pdf.

Scottish Government (2010) *Flying Start NHS*. Available from: www.flyingstart.scot.nhs.uk/index.htm.

NHS Flying Start England (2013) *Welcome to Flying Start England*. Available from: www.flyingstartengland.nhs.uk/

- For detailed exploration of management coaching, see:

Garvey R, Stokes P, Megginson D (2009) *Coaching and Mentoring – Theory and Practice*. London: Sage.

- For guides, leaflets and other publications and learning materials on coaching, see:

Chartered Institute of Personnel and Development (2011) *Coaching and Mentoring – Resource Summary*. Available from: www.cipd.co.uk/hr-resources/factsheets/coaching-mentoring.aspx.

- For more on executive coaching, see:

'Coaching for Business Leaders' – Available from:www.linkageinc.com/offerings/training/Pages/Coaching_for Optimum_Performance_and_Results.aspx.

- For further information on the roles of LETB, see:

Department of Health (2012) *Summary of Local Education and Training Board Authorization Process*. Available from: www.dh.gov.uk/health/2012/10/local-education-training/.

GLOSSARY

Budget	A budget is a statement of revenues and costs in financial terms that are anticipated and identified in advance of a period of time for spending on specific activities that reflect the agreed policies and strategies for meeting the objectives of the organisation.
Care	Used as a generic term that represents health and/or social care.
Care intervention	Clinical practice, direct patient or service user care and treatment activities.
Care professional	A qualified health or social care member of staff whose name appears in the relevant care regulatory body's professional register.
Care organisation	Health and social care organisation where patient or service user care is delivered, e.g. NHS Trusts, nursing home, primary health care centre etc.
Care setting/ practice setting	Terms used interchangeably referring to locations where healthcare practitioners/professionals regularly work, and deliver patient/service user care, i.e. perform care interventions; include wards, clinics, GP surgeries, patient's own home etc.
Clinical support worker	Healthcare staff who are not registered with a professional regulatory body. Also known as healthcare assistant or healthcare support worker.
Duty care manager	A health or social care professional who has management and leadership responsibility for a group of patients and a team of staff who deliver care in a practice setting or in the patient or service user's home. The responsibility may be for the duration of a span of duty, or may be more long-term in nature, and entails fulfilling the role and responsibilities of the appointed manager and identified figurehead in the practice setting.

Efficiency	The achievement of expected objectives at minimum financial costs, in the minimum amount of time, but to the required standard.
Effectiveness	The achievement of expected patient outcomes.
Healthcare organisation	A care organisation where healthcare is delivered, e.g. Acute NHS trusts, Foundation trust, Teaching NHS trust, GP practice, nursing home, primary health care centre etc.
Healthcare practitioner/Care practitioner/ Health or social care practitioner	All qualified health and social care staff who are directly involved in patient or service user care delivery.
Healthcare professional/Care professional/ Health or social care professional	An individual healthcare professional registered with their appropriate regulatory body, e.g. nurse, physiotherapist etc.
Manpower equivalents (MPE)	The total number of staff hours expressed as a percentage of full-time positions.
Patients or service users	A generic term referring to 'users' of health and social care in the widest sense and therefore also represents patients, service users and clients.
Practice setting/ care setting	Used interchangeably, referring to locations where care practitioners deliver patients and service users care, i.e. perform care interventions, which include wards, clinics, GP surgeries, the patient's own home etc.
Randomised controlled trials (RCT)	Also referred to as randomized clinical trials or randomized controlled clinical trials, a RCT is a specific type of scientific experiment (research), that is often used to test the efficacy of particular types of interventions (e.g. medication, therapy) within a patient population, when the effect on one group who receives the intervention is compared to an identical group who receives an alternative treatment.
Qualitative studies	Qualitative research as a method used mainly in social sciences to obtain an in-depth understanding of a social concept or issue, often using smaller but focused samples, and research methods such as individual interviews, case studies etc. to draw general conclusions.

Quantitative studies	Quantitative research whereby a systematic empirical investigation of social phenomena is conducted incorporating statistical and mathematical measurement, and the findings are expressed in numerical forms such as statistics or percentages, often to show co-relation between components of the study, and the results are discussed in the context of generalisation to some larger population.
Registrant	Used interchangeably with 'healthcare professional', registrant refers to qualified nurses, doctors, allied health professionals and health scientists, etc. who are registered with their respective professional regulatory bodies.
Skill mix	The numbers and ratio, capability and experience of qualified and unqualified staff, which in the case of nursing are required for the delivery of safe and effective care.
Span of duty	The duration of time that the practitioner is on duty on any particular day, e.g. the duration of their shift.
Strategic planning	The organisation planning for the forthcoming 3, 5 or 10 years; different from operational planning, which in turn refers to planning for one financial year.

REFERENCES

Adair J (2005) *Effective Leadership Development*. London: Chartered Institute of Personnel and Development.

Alexander C (1997) 'Influencing decision making'. *Nursing Standard*, 11 (38): 39–44.

Almio-Metcalf B (1996) 'Leaders or managers'. *Nursing Management*, 3 (1): 22–24.

Andrews G J, Brodie D A, Andrews J P, Hillan E, Thomas B G, Wong J and Rixon L (2006) 'Professional roles and communications in clinical placements: a qualitative study of nursing students' perceptions and some models for practice'. *International Journal of Nursing Studies*, 43 (7): 861–874.

Andrews-Evans M (2012) 'Senior nurses' views about factors that lead to service failures'. *Nursing Management*, 10 (18): 26–31.

Anonymous (1998) 'Leadership – great expectations ... the role of the team leader'. *Nursing Times*, 94 (30): 66–67.

Armstrong M (2012) *A Handbook of Human Resource Management Practice* (12th edn). London: Kogan Page.

Ashridge Psychometrics (2012) *Myers-Briggs Type Indicator*. Available from: www.ashridge.org.uk/Website/Content.nsf/wELNPSY/Psychometric+Instruments+-+Myers-Briggs+Type+Indicator+(MBTI)?opendocument (accessed 20 December 2012).

Atwal A and Caldwell K (2006) 'Nurses' perceptions of multidisciplinary team work in acute health-care'. *International Journal of Nursing Practice*, 12 (6): 359–365.

Bahn D (2001) 'Social learning theory: its application in the context of nurse education'. *Nurse Education Today*, 21 (2): 110–117.

Bain L (1996) 'Preceptorship: a review of literature'. *Journal of Advanced Nursing*, 24 (1): 104–107.

Ballard J (1994) 'District nurses – who's looking after them?'. *Occupational Health Review*, 52 (Nov/Dec): 10–19.

Baron S, Field J and Schuller T (eds) (2000) *Social Capital: Critical Perspectives*. Oxford: Oxford University Press.

Barr H (2002) *Interprofessional Education Today, Yesterday and Tomorrow: A Review*. London: LTSN HS&P.

Bass B M (1990) *Bass and Stogdills Handbook of Leadership: Theory, Research and Managerial Applications* (3rd edn). New York: Free Press.

Bass B M and Riggio R E (2006) *Transformational Leadership*. London: Lawrence Erlbaum.

BBC News (2013) *Nurse Leaders Issue Warning over Staff Numbers* (12 May). Available from: www.bbc.co.uk/news/health-22481151 (accessed 13 May 2013).

Beckhard R and Harris R T (1987) *Organisational Transitions: Managing Complex Change* (2nd edn). Boston, MA: Addison-Wesley.

Belbin RM (1993) *Team Roles at Work*. Available from: www.belbin.com/rte.asp?id=8 (accessed 29 January 2013).

Benner P (2001) *From Novice to Expert: Excellence and Power in Clinical Nursing Practice*. Menlo Park, CA: Addison-Wesley.

Binnie A (1998) 'How to grow more leaders'. *Nursing Times*, 94 (28): 24–26.

Blake R R and McCanse A A (1991) *Leadership Dilemmas – Grid Solutions*. Houston, TX: Gulf Publishing. Available from: www.iwise2.com/blake-mouton-mccanse-leadership-grid (accessed 20 December 2012).

Boaden R, Harvey G, Moxham C and Proudlove M (2008) *Quality Improvement: Theory and Practice in Healthcare*. Coventry: NHS Institute for Innovation and Improvement.

Bond M and Holland S (2010) *Skills in Clinical Supervision for Nurses: A Practical Guide for Supervisees, Clinical Supervisors and Managers* (2nd edn). Buckingham: Open University Press.

Borrill C S, West M A, Shapiro D and Rees A (2000) 'Team working and effectiveness in health care'. *British Journal of Health Care Management*, 6 (8): 534–535.

Botting L (2011) 'Transformational change in action'. *Nursing Management*, 17 (9): 14–19.

Boud D, Keogh R and Walker D (eds) (1985) *Reflection: Turning Experience into Learning*. London: Kogan Page. (Reprinted 2002.)

Brashers D E, Haas S M and Neidig J L (1999) 'The Patient Self-Advocacy Scale: measuring patient involvement in health care decision-making interactions'. *Health Communication*, 11 (2): 97–121.

Brookes J (2011) 'Engaging staff in the change process'. *Nursing Management*, 18 (5): 16–19.

Brooks N and Moriarty A (2009) 'Implementation of a peer-support system in the clinical setting'. *Nursing Standard*, 23 (27) 35–39.

Brown L (editor-in-chief) (2002) *Shorter Oxford English Dictionary* (5th edn). Oxford: Oxford University Press.

Brown P (1998) 'Endangered species'. *The Times*, 29 October, p. 2.

Buchanan D A and Huczynski A A (2010) *Organisational Behaviour* (7th edn). London: Prentice Hall/Financial Times.

Burns D (2009) 'Clinical leadership for general practice nurses, 2: facilitating factors'. *Practice Nursing*, 20 (10) 519–523.

BusinessDictionary.com (2012) *Total Quality Management (TQM)*. Available from: www. businessdictionary.com/definition/total-quality-management-TQM.html (accessed 24 December 2012).

Byrne G (2007) 'Unlocking potential – coaching as a means to enhance leadership and role performance in nursing'. *Journal of Clinical Nursing*, 16 (11): 1987–1988.

Byrne M W and Keefe M R (2002) 'Building research competence in nursing through mentoring'. *Journal of Nursing Scholarship*, 34 (4): 391–396.

Cahill J (1996) 'Patient participation: a concept analysis'. *Journal of Advanced Nursing*, 24 (3): 561–571.

Cairns J (1998) 'Clinical supervision and the practice nurse'. *Journal of Community Nursing*, 12 (9): 20–24.

Caldwell K, Atwall A, Copp G, Brett-Richards M and Coleman K (2006) 'Preparing for practice: how well are practitioners prepared for teamwork'. *British Journal of Nursing*, 15 (22): 1250–1254.

Calpin-Davies F (2000) 'Nurse manager, change thyself'. *Nursing Management*, 6 (9): 16–20.

Canadian Health Services Research Foundation (2006) *Teamwork in Healthcare: Promoting Effective Teamwork in Healthcare in Canada*. Ontario: CHSRF.

Care Quality Commission (2011a) *Annual Report and Accounts 2010/11*. Available from: www.cqc.org.uk/sites/default/files/media/documents/20110713_care_quality_commission_annual_report__accounts_2010–11_tagged_1.pdf (accessed 16 March 2012).

Care Quality Commission (2011b) 2010 *NHS Staff Survey*. Available from: www.cqc.org.uk/public/news/2010-nhs-staff-survey (accessed 3 April 2012).

Care Quality Commission (2012) *The State of Health Care and Adult Social Care in England*. Available from: www.cqc.org.uk/sites/default/files/media/documents/cqc__soc_201112_final_tag.pdf (accessed July 2013).

Care Quality Commission (2013) *Safeguarding People*. Available from: www.cqc.org.uk/public/what-are-standards/safeguarding-people (accessed 27 May 2013).

Carper B A (1978) 'Fundamental patterns of knowing in nursing'. *Advances in Nursing Science*, 1 (1): 13–23.

Carver N, Ashmore R and Clibbens N (2006) 'Group clinical supervision in pre-registration nurse training: the views of mental health nursing students'. *Nurse Education Today*, 27 (7): 768–776.

Castle A (2007) 'Lean thinking on the wards'. *Nursing Standard*, 22 (8): 16–18.

Charns M P and Tewksbury L S (1993) *Collaborative Management in Health Care: Implementing the Integrating Organisation*. San Francisco, CA: Jossey-Bass.

Chartered Institute of Personnel and Development (2011) *Coaching and Mentoring – Resource Summary*. Available from: www.cipd.co.uk/hr-resources/factsheets/coaching-mentoring.aspx (accessed 7 April 2012).

Chief Nursing Officer Bulletin (2012) *Consultation on Ensuring Fair and Transparent Pricing for NHS Services*. Available from: http://cno.dh.gov.uk/2012/10/08/pricing-consultation/ (accessed 29 December 2012).

Clarke A, Hanson E J and Ross H (2003) 'Seeing the person behind the patient: enhancing the care of older people using a biographical approach'. *Journal of Clinical Nursing*, 12 (5): 697–706.

Clegg A (2000) 'Leadership: improving the quality of patient care'. *Nursing Standard*, 14 (30): 43–45.

Clinical Governance Support Team (2013) *About CG – What Is Clinical Governance?* Available from: http://collections.europarchive.org/tna/20081112112652/http://www.cgsupport.nhs.uk/About_CG/default.asp. (accessed 3 April 2013).

College of Social Work (2012) *PCF levels and domains information*. Available from: www.collegeofsocialwork.org/uploadedFiles/TheCollege/Media_centre/PCF%20levels%20and%20domains.pdf (accessed 12 March 2012).

Conway P (2000) *The Unpopular Patient Revisited: Characteristics or Traits of Patients which May Result in Their Being Considered as 'Difficult' by Nurses*. Available from: www.leeds.ac.uk/educol/documents/00001415.htm (accessed 6 January 2013).

Cook M J (2001) 'The attributes of effective clinical nurse leaders. *Nursing Standard*, 18 (35): 33–36.

Covey S (1992) *Principle-Centred Leadership*. New York: Simon and Schuster.

Cunningham G and Kitson A (2000) 'An evaluation of the RCN Clinical Leadership Development Programme'. *Nursing Standard*, (part 1) 15 (12): 34–37 and (part 2) 15 (13): 34–40.

Curtis E and Nicholl H (2004) 'Delegation: a key function of nursing'. *Nursing Management*, 11 (4): 26–31.

Davies H and Mannion R (2013) 'Will prescriptions for cultural change improve the NHS?'. *British Medical Journal*. Available from: http://eprints.bham.ac.uk/1267/5/Will_prescriptions_for_cultural_change_improve_the_NHS.pdf (accessed 19 May 2013).

Davis, L., Taylor, H. and Reyes, H. (2013) 'Lifelong learning in nursing: a Delphi study'. *Nurse Education Today*. In press.

Dearlove D (1997) 'No substitute for bright ideas'. *The Times*, 3 July, p. 5.

Department for Education (2013) *What is the Difference between Safeguarding and Child Protection?* Available from: www.education.gov.uk/popularquestions/a0064461/safeguarding-and-child-protection (accessed 1 June 2013).

Department of Health (1991) *The Patient's Charter*. London: The Stationery Office.

Department of Health (1993) *Clinical Audit: Meeting and Improving Standards*. London: The Stationery Office.

Department of Health (1998) *A First Class Service: Quality in the NHS*. London: HMSO.

Department of Health (1999a) *Health Service Circular 1999/198*. Available from: http://webarchive.nationalarchives.gov.uk/+/www.dh.gov.uk/en/Publicationsandstatistics/Lettersandcirculars/Healthservicecirculars/DH_4004385 (accessed 3 July 2013).

Department of Health (1999b) *Making a Difference*. London: The Stationery Office.

Department of Health (2000a) *An Organisation with Memory – Report of an Expert Group on Learning from Adverse Events in the NHS Chaired by the Chief Medical Officer*. Available from: www.dh.gov.uk/en/Publicationsandstatistics/Publications/PublicationsPolicyAndGuidance/DH_4065083 (accessed 4 January 2013).

Department of Health (2000b) *The NHS Plan: A Plan for Investment, a Plan for Reform*. London: The Stationery Office.

Department of Health (2000c) *A Health Service for All the Talents: Developing NHS Workforce*. London: The Stationery Office.

Department of Health (2000d) *Improving Working Lives Standard*. London: The Stationery Office.

Department of Health (2000e) *No Secrets: Guidance on Developing and Implementing Multi-agency Policies and Procedures to Protect Vulnerable Adults from Abuse*. Available from: www.dh.gov.uk/prod_consum_dh/groups/dh_digitalassets/@dh/@en/documents/digitalasset/dh_4012677.pdf (accessed 27 May 13).

Department of Health (2001a) *National Service Framework for Older People*. London: The Stationery Office.

Department of Health (2001b) *Expert Patient Programme*. London: The Stationery Office.

Department of Health (2001c) *Placements in Focus – Guidance for Education in Practice for Health Care Professions*. Available from: www.dh.gov.uk/en/Publicationsandstatistics/Publications/PublicationsPolicyAndGuidance/DH_4009511 (accessed 29 December 2011).

Department of Health (2001d) *Working Together – Learning Together. A Framework for Lifelong Learning for the NHS*. London: The Stationery Office.

Department of Health (2002) *Securing Our Future Health: Taking a Long-Term View (The Wanless Report)*. Available from: http://webarchive.nationalarchives.gov.uk/+/www.dh.gov.uk/en/Publicationsandstatistics/Publications/PublicationsPolicyAndGuidance/DH_4009293 (accessed 3 January 2013).

Department of Health (2004a) *NHS Knowledge and Skills Framework*. Available from: www.dh.gov.uk/en/Publicationsandstatistics/Publications/PublicationsPolicyAndGuidance/DH_4090843 (accessed 15 July 2007).

Department of Health (2004b) *The NHS Improvement Plan: Putting People at the Heart of Public Services*. London: The Stationery Office.

Department of Health (2004c) *Agenda for Change*. London: The Stationery Office.

Department of Health (2006a) *Standards for Better Health*. Available from: www.dh.gov.uk/prod_consum_dh/groups/dh_digitalassets/@dh/@en/documents/digitalasset/dh_4086666.pdf (accessed 29 January 2013).

Department of Health (2006b) *The Chief Medical Officer on the State of Public Health Annual Report 2005*. London: The Stationery Office.

Department of Health (2006c) *Our Health, Our Care, Our Say: A New Direction for Community Services*. London: The Stationery Office.

Department of Health (2006d) *Good Doctors, Safer Patients: Proposals to Strengthen the System to Assure and Improve the Performance of Doctors and to Protect the Safety of Patients*. London: The Stationery Office.

Department of Health (2006e) *The Regulation of the Non-medical Healthcare Professions: A Review by the Department of Health*. London: The Stationery Office.

Department of Health (2007) *Trust, Assurance and Safety – The Regulation of Health Professionals in the 21st Century White Paper*. Available from: www.dh.gov.uk/en/

Publicationsandstatistics/Publications/PublicationsPolicyAndGuidance/DH_065946 (accessed 29 January 2013).

Department of Health (2008a) *High Quality Care For All – NHS Next Stage Review Final Report.* Available from: www.dh.gov.uk/en/Publicationsandstatistics/Publications/PublicationsPolicyAndGuidance/DH_085825 (accessed 30 December 2012).

Department of Health (2008b) *Delivering Care Closer to Home: Meeting the Challenge.* Available from: www.dh.gov.uk/prod_consum_dh/groups/dh_digitalassets/@dh/@en/documents/digitalasset/dh_086051.pdf (accessed 15 December 2012).

Department of Health (2009) *Listening, Responding, Improving: A Guide to Better Customer Care.* Available from: www.dh.gov.uk/en/Publicationsandstatistics/Publications/PublicationsPolicyAndGuidance/DH_095408 (accessed 3 July 2013).

Department of Health (2010a) *Equity and Excellence: Liberating the NHS.* Available from: www.dh.gov.uk/en/Publicationsandstatistics/Publications/PublicationsPolicyAndGuidance/DH_117353 (accessed 3 January 2013).

Department of Health (2010b) *Midwifery 2020: Delivering Expectations.* Available from: www.dh.gov.uk/prod_consum_dh/groups/dh_digitalassets/@dh/@en/@ps/documents/digitalasset/dh_119470.pdf (accessed 15 December 2012).

Department of Health (2010c) *Liberating the NHS: Legislative Framework and Next Steps.* Available from: www.dh.gov.uk/en/Publicationsandstatistics/Publications/PublicationsPolicyAndGuidance/DH_122661 (accessed 30 December 2012).

Department of Health (2010d) *NHS Outcomes Framework.* Available from: www.dh.gov.uk/en/Publicationsandstatistics/Publications/PublicationsPolicyAndGuidance/DH_122944 (accessed 2 January 2013).

Department of Health (2010e) *Preceptorship Framework for Newly Registered Nurses, Midwives and Allied Health Professionals.* Available from: www.dh.gov.uk/prod_consum_dh/groups/dh_digitalassets/@dh/@en/@abous/documents/digitalasset/dh_114116.pdf (accessed 29 December 2011).

Department of Health (2011a) *Quality, Innovation, Productivity and Prevention (QIPP).* Available from: www.dh.gov.uk/en/Healthcare/Qualityandproductivity/QIPP/index.htm (accessed 29 April 2012).

Department of Health (2011b) *Health and Social Care Bill 2011.* Available from: www.dh.gov.uk/en/Publicationsandstatistics/Legislation/Actsandbills/HealthandSocialCareBill2011/index.htm (accessed 31 December 2012).

Department of Health (2011c) *Healthy Lives, Healthy People: Update and the Way Forward.* Available from: www.dh.gov.uk/en/Publicationsandstatistics/Publications/PublicationsPolicyAndGuidance/DH_128120. (accessed 31 December 2012).

Department of Health (2011d) *Clinical Governance Guidance.* Available from: www.dh.gov.uk/health/2011/09/clinical-governance/ (accessed 26 December 2012).

Department of Health (2011e) *National Search for New Ideas to Improve the Lives of People with Dementia.* Available from: http://mediacentre.dh.gov.uk/2011/08/15/improve-the-lives-of-people-with-dementia/ (accessed 25 December 2012).

Department of Health (2011f) *Implementing Innovation.* Available from: http://ahp.dh.gov.uk/2011/03/24/implementing-innovation/ (accessed 4 January 2013).

Department of Health (2011g) *Statement of Government Policy on Adult Safeguarding.* Available from: www.dh.gov.uk/government/uploads/system/uploads/attachment_data/file/147310/dh_126770.pdf.pdf (accessed 1 June 2013).

Department of Health (2012a) *Health and Social Care Act 2012.* Available from: www.legislation.gov.uk/ukpga/2012/7/enacted (accessed 12 September 2012).

Department of Health (2012b) *Compassion in Practice – Nursing, Midwifery and Care Staff Our Vision and Strategy*. Available from: www.commissioningboard.nhs.uk/files/2012/12/compassion-in-practice.pdf (accessed 10 December 2012).

Department of Health (2012c) *Energise for Excellence*. Available from: http://webarchive.nationalarchives.gov.uk/+/www.dh.gov.uk/en/Aboutus/Chiefprofessionalofficers/Chiefnursingofficer/Energiseforexcellence/index.htm (accessed 30 December 2012).

Department of Health (2012d) *The NHS Constitution for England*. Available from: www.dh.gov.uk/en/Publicationsandstatistics/Publications/PublicationsPolicyAndGuidance/DH_132961 (accessed 29 December 2012).

Department of Health (2012e) *Public Health England*. Available from: www.dh.gov.uk/health/tag/public-health-england/ (accessed 3 January 2013).

Department of Health (2012f) *NHS Foundation Trusts: Review of Three Months to 30 June 2012*. Available from: http://mdbulletin.dh.gov.uk/2012/11/27/nhs-foundation-trusts-review/ (accessed 15 December 2012).

Department of Health (2012g) *Simple Guide to Payment by Results*. Available from: www.dh.gov.uk/health/2012/11/pbrguide/ (accessed 29 December 2012).

Department of Health (2012h) *Quality in the New Health System*. Available from: http://mdbulletin.dh.gov.uk/2012/09/21/nqb-quality-in-the-new-health-system/ (accessed 29 January 2013).

Department of Health (2012i) *The Power of Information: Putting All of Us in Control of the Health and Care Information We Need*. Available from: http://informationstrategy.dh.gov.uk/executive-summary/ (accessed 20th January 2013).

Department of Health (2012j) *Local Education and Training Board Authorization: Summary Document*. Available from: www.gov.uk/government/uploads/system/uploads/attachment_data/file/127015/270912-local-ed-training-board-authorisation-summary.pdf.pdf. (accessed 1 April 2013).

Department of Health (2013a) *The Mid-Staffordshire NHS Foundation Trust Public Enquiry – Chaired by Robert Francis – Final Report*. Available from: www.midstaffspublicinquiry.com/report. (accessed 16 April 2013).

Department of Health (2013b) *Personal Health Budgets*. Available from: www.personalhealthbudgets.england.nhs.uk/About/healthCareProfessionals/ (accessed 23 June 2013).

Dickson R (1996) 'Dissemination and implementation: the wider picture'. *Nurse Researcher*, 4 (1): 5–14.

Dixon A, Appleby J, Robertson R, Burge P, Devlin N and Magee H (2010) *Patient Choice: How Patients Choose and How Providers Respond*. London: Kings Fund. Available from: www.kingsfund.org.uk/publications/patient-choice (accessed 12 January 2013).

Donabedian A (1988) 'The quality of care. How can it be assessed?'. *American Journal of Public Health*, 260 (12): 1743.

Drennan V (2007) *Nurse, Midwife and Health Visitor Entrepreneurship in the UK*. Paper presented at The 2007 International Nursing Research Conference, Dundee.

Driscoll J and Cooper R (2005) 'Coaching for clinicians', *Nursing Management*, 12 (1): 18–23.

Drucker P F (2007) *The Practice of Management* (The Classic Drucker Collection edition). Oxford: Butterworth-Heinemann.

Duffin C (2012) 'Study finds 42% nurse burnout in England'. *Nursing Management*, 19 (2): 5.

Dunn S V and Hansford B (1997) 'Undergraduate nursing students' perceptions of their clinical learning environment'. *Journal of Advanced Nursing*, 25 (6): 1299–1306.

Duxbury J and Whittington R (2005) 'Causes and management of patient aggression and violence: staff and patient perspectives'. *Journal of Advanced Nursing*, 50 (5): 469–478.

Ellis J (1995) 'Using benchmarking to improve practice'. *Nursing Standard*, 9 (35): 25–28.

Ellis R B, Gates B and Kenworthy N (2003) *Interpersonal Communication in Nursing* (2nd edn). Edinburgh: Churchill Livingstone.

England Centre for Practice Development (2013) *What is Practice Development?* Available from: www.canterbury.ac.uk/health/EnglandCentreforPracticeDevelopment/ Whatispracticedevelopment/Whatispracticedevelopment.aspx (accessed 29 January 2013).

Evans L (2002) 'An exploration of district nurses' perception of occupational stress'. *British Journal of Nursing*, 11 (8): 576–585.

Faugier J and Woolnough H (2003) 'Lessons from LEO'. *Nursing Management*, 10 (2): 22–25.

Fayol H (2012) *Five Functions of Management*. Available from: www.provenmodels.com/3/ five-functions-of-management/henri-fayol/ (accessed 28 January 2012).

Field J (1999) 'Participation under the magnifying glass'. *Adults Learning* (November 1999), 11 (3): 10–13.

Fields H (1994) 'Coaching and mentoring'. *Nursing Standard*, 8 (30): 105–111.

Filley A C (1975) *Interpersonal Conflict Resolution*. Glenview, IL: Scott & Foresman. Available from: www.amazon.co.uk/Interpersonal-Conflict-Resolution-Alan-Filley/dp/0673075893 (accessed 29 April 2012).

Flanagan J, Baldwin S and Clarke D (2000) 'Work-based learning as a means of developing and assessing nursing competence'. *Journal of Clinical Nursing*, 9 (3): 360–368.

Florin J, Ehrenberg A and Ehnfors M (2005) 'Patients' and nurses' perceptions of nursing problems in an acute setting'. *Journal of Advanced Nursing*, 51 (2): 140–149.

Ford S (2009) 'Creating a "new culture of leadership"'. *Nursing Times*. Available from: www.nursingtimes.net/nursing-times-this-weeks-issue/creating-a-new-culture-of-leadership/1969886.article (accessed 9 April 2012).

Francis F (2013) *The Mid Staffordshire NHS Foundation Trust Public Inquiry*. London: The Stationery Office. Available from: www.midstaffspublicinquiry.com/sites/default/files/ report/Executive%20summary.pdf (accessed 19 May 2013).

Fretwell, J E (1980) 'An inquiry into the ward learning environment'. *Nursing Times*, 26 June, 69–75.

Galloway J (2011) 'Dignity, values, attitudes and patient-centred care' in Hindle A and Coates A (ed.) *Nursing Care of Older People*. Oxford: Oxford University Press.

Garbett R and McCormack B (2002) 'A concept analysis of practice development'. *NTResearch*, 7 (2): 87–100.

Garbett R, Hardy S, Manley K, Titchen A and McCormack B (2007) 'Developing a qualitative approach to 360-degree feedback to aid understanding and development of clinical expertise'. *Journal of Nursing Management*, 15 (3): 342–347.

Garvey R, Stokes P, Megginson D (2009) *Coaching and Mentoring – Theory and Practice*. London, Sage.

General Medical Council (2010) *Standards for Curricula and Assessment Systems*. Available from: www.gmc-uk.org/Standards_for_curricula_and_assessment_systems_0410.pdf_48904896. pdf (accessed 15 January 2013).

General Medical Council (2012a) *Doctors under Investigation – Performance Assessments*. Available from: www.gmc-uk.org/concerns/doctors_under_investigation/performance_ assessments.asp (accessed 29 January 2013).

General Medical Council (2012b) *New Guidance on Continuing Professional Development*. Available from: www.gmc-uk.org/publications/13684.asp (accessed 29 January 2013).

Ghaye A (2011) *Teaching and Learning through Reflective Practice: A Practical Guide for Positive Action* (2nd edn). London, Routledge.

Gibbon B, Watkins C, Barber D, Waters K, Davies S, Lightbody L and Leathley M (2002) 'Can staff attitudes to team working in stroke care be improved?'. *Journal of Advanced Nursing*, 40 (1): 105–111.

Gilmore A (2001) 'Clinical supervision in nursing and health visiting – a review of the UK literature' in Cutcliffe J, Butterworth T and Proctor B (eds) *Fundamental Themes in Clinical Supervision*. London: Routledge.

Goldsmith M, Stewart L and Ferguson L (2006) 'Peer learning partnership: innovative strategy to enhance skill acquisition in nursing students'. *Nurse Education Today*, 26 (2): 123–130.

Goleman D (2000) 'Leadership that gets results'. *Harvard Business Review*, (March–April) 78 (2): 78–90.

Gopee N (2000) 'Self-assessment and the concept of the lifelong learning nurse'. *British Journal of Nursing*, 9 (11): 724–729.

Gopee N (2001) 'Lifelong learning in nursing – perceptions and realities'. *Nurse Education Today*, 21 (8): 607–615.

Gopee N. (2002) 'Human and social capital as facilitators of lifelong learning in nursing'. *Nurse Education Today*, 22 (7): 608–616.

Gopee N (2011) *Mentoring and Supervision in Healthcare* (2nd edn). London: Sage.

Gopee N, Tyrrell A, Raven S, Thomas K and Hari T (2004) 'Effective clinical learning in primary care settings'. *Nursing Standard*, 18 (37): 33–37.

Gould D, Kelly D and Gouldstone L (2001) 'Preparing nurse managers to mentor students'. *Nursing Standard*, 16 (11): 39–42.

Govier I and Nash S (2009) 'Examining transformational approaches to effective leadership in healthcare settings'. *Nursing Times*, 105 (18) 24–27.

Gov.uk (2013) *The Government's Response to the Francis Report*. Available from: www.gov.uk/government/speeches/the-government-s-response-to-the-francis-report. (accessed 16 April 2013).

Gratton L (2000) *Living Strategy: Putting People at the Heart of Corporate Purpose*. London: Financial Times/Prentice Hall.

Gray J A M (2001) *Evidence-based Healthcare. How to Make Policy and Management Decisions* (2nd edn). Edinburgh: Churchill Livingstone.

Greenleaf, R K (2003). *The Servant-Leader Within: A Transformative Path*. New York: Paulist Press.

Guile D and Young M (1996) 'Further professional development and further education teachers: setting a new agenda for work-based learning' in Woodward I (ed.) *Continuing Professional Development: Issues in Design and Delivery*. London: Cassell.

Gullick J, Shepherd B and Ronald T (2004) 'The effect of an organisational model on the standard of care'. *Nursing Times*, 100 (10): 36–39.

Hamm R M (1988) 'Clinical intuition and clinical analysis: expertise and the cognitive continuum' in Dowie J and Elstein A (eds) *Professional Judgement: A Reader in Clinical Decision Making*. Milton Keynes: Open University Press.

Handy C (1984) *The Future of Work: A Guide to a Changing Society*. Oxford: Blackwell.

Handy C (1993) *Understanding Organizations* (4th edn). Harmondsworth: Penguin.

Hawkins P and Shohet R (2012) *Supervision in the Helping Professions* (4th edn). Maidenhead: Open University Press.

Hawksley B (2007) 'Work-related stress, work/life balance and personal life coaching'. *British Journal of Community Nursing*, 12 (1) 34–36.

Health and Care Professions Council (2011) *Your Guide to Our Standards for Continuing Professional Development*. Available from: www.hpc-uk.org/publications/index.asp?id=1 01#publicationSearchResults (accessed 1 April 2013).

Health and Care Professions Council (2012a) *Standards of Conduct, Performance and Ethics*. Available from: www.hpc-uk.org/assets/documents/10003B6EStandardsofconduct,performanceandethics.pdf (accessed 3 January 2013).

Health and Care Professions Council (2012b) *Other Health Regulators*. Available from: www.hpc-uk.org/aboutregistration/regulators/ (accessed 29 December 2011).

Health and Safety Executive (2008) *Safe Use of Work Equipment. Provision and Use of Work Equipment Regulations 1998. Approved Code of Practice and Guidance*. Available from: www.hse.gov.uk/pubns/books/l22.htm (accessed 1 January 2013).

Health Foundation (2013) *Person Centred Care*. Available from: www.health.org.uk/areas-of-work/topics/person-centred-care/ (accessed 12 January 2013).

Healthcare Commission [transferred to CQC] (2005) *Acute Hospital Portfolio: Ward Staffing, Commission for Healthcare, Audit and Inspection*. Available from: http://archive.cqc.org.uk/_db/_documents/04018124.pdf (accessed 1 January 2013).

Healthcare Commission (2006) *National Survey of NHS Staff 2005*. Available from: http://archive.cqc.org.uk/_db/_documents/National_survey_of_NHS_staff_2005_-_Summary_of_key_findings.pdf (accessed 7 February 2013).

Hellriegel D, Jackson S E and Slocum J W (2007) *Management: A Competency-based Approach* (11th edn). Mason, OH: Thomson South-Western.

Henderson A, Twentyman M, Heel A and Lloyd B (2006) 'Students' perception of the psychosocial clinical learning environment: an evaluation of placement models'. *Nurse Education Today*, 26 (7): 564–571.

Heron J (1989) *Six Category Intervention Analysis. Human Potential Research Project* (2nd edn). Guildford: University of Surrey.

Herzberg F (1974) *Work and the Nature of Man*. London: Staples Press.

HM Government (2013) *Working Together to Safeguard Children: A Guide to Inter-agency Working to Safeguard and Promote the Welfare of Children*. Available from: http://media.education.gov.uk/assets/files/pdf/w/working%20together.pdf (accessed 27 May 2013).

Hoeman S P (ed.) *Rehabilitation Nursing: Process, Application and Outcomes*. St Louis, MO: Mosby.

Hollenberg E, Reeves S, Beduz M A, Jeffs L, Kwan D, Lowe M, Merkley J, Sinclair L, Tassone M and Oandasan L (2009) '"Mainstreaming" interprofessional education within hospital settings: findings from a multiple case study'. *Journal of Research in Inter-professional Practice and Education*. Available from: www.jripe.org/index.php/journal/article/view/3/16 (accessed 24 January 2013).

Hollingsworth M J (1999) 'Purpose and values'. *The British Journal of Administrative Management*, January/February: 22–23.

Hollis V (1991) 'Self-directed learning as a post-basic educational continuum'. *British Journal of Occupational Therapy*, 54 (2): 45–48.

Home Office (2010) *The Equality Act 2010*. Available from: www.homeoffice.gov.uk/equalities/equality-act/ (accessed 27 March 2012).

Howatson-Jones I L (2004) 'The servant leader'. *Nursing Management*, 11 (3): 20–24.

Hurst K (2006) 'Nursing by numbers'. *Nursing Standard*, 21 (7): 22–25.

Hyrkas K, Appelqvist-Schmidlechner K and Kivimaki K (2005) 'First-line managers' views of the long-term effects of clinical supervision: how does clinical supervision support and develop leadership in health care?'. *Journal of Nursing Management*, 13 (3): 209–220.

Institute for Healthcare Improvement (2011) *She's Got A Ticket ... To Go Home*. Available from: www.ihi.org/knowledge/Pages/ImprovementStories/ShesGotaTicketToGoHome.aspx (accessed 6 January 2013).

Institute for Healthcare Improvement (2012) *Evidence-based Care Bundles*. Available from: www.ihi.org/explore/bundles/Pages/default.aspx (accessed 30 December 2012).

Investors in People (2012) *How it Works – Plan, Do, Review*. Available from: www.investorsinpeople.co.uk/Facts/Framework/Pages/PlanDoReview.aspx (accessed 15 January 2013).

Jarvis P and Gibson S (1997) *The Teacher Practitioner and Mentor* (2nd edn). Cheltenham: Stanley Thornes.

Joanna Briggs Institute (2011) *Transformational Leadership – Systematic Review*. Available from: www.joannabriggs.edu.au/events/pastEvents/2011/docs/Day2/Hickinbotham/session3/C_Holly.pdf (accessed 19 December 2012).

Joanna Briggs Institute (2012) *Welcome to the Joanna Briggs Institute*. Available from: www.joannabriggs.edu.au/ (accessed 26 December 2012).

Johnson M and Webb C (1995) 'Rediscovering unpopular patients: the concept of social judgement'. *Journal of Advanced Nursing*, 21 (3): 466–475.

Jones A (2006) 'Clinical supervision: what do we know and what do we need to know? A review and commentary. *Journal of Nursing Management*, 14 (8): 577–585.

Joseph Rowntree Foundation (2005) *Involving older People: What Standards Should We Expect*. York: Joseph Rowntree Foundation.

Kane-Urrabazo C (2006) 'Management's role in shaping organization culture'. *Journal of Nursing Management*, 14 (3): 188–194.

Kendall-Raynor P (2006) 'Foster regulation proposals rejected by unions and NMC'. *Nursing Standard*, 21 (10): 5.

Kennedy I (2001) *Learning from Bristol: The Report of the Public Inquiry into Children's Heart Surgery at the Bristol Royal Infirmary 1984–1995*. London: The Stationery Office.

Kerridge J (2012) 'Leading change'. *Nursing Times*, 108 (4): 12–15; 108 (5): 23–25; and 108 (6): 23–25.

Kitwood T M (1997) *Dementia Reconsidered: The Person Comes First*. Buckingham: Open University Press.

Kotter J (2009) 'What leaders really do' in Billsberry J (ed.) *Discovering Leadership*. Basingstoke: Palgrave Macmillan.

Kouzes J M and Posner B Z (2012) *The Leadership Challenge* (5th edn). San Francisco, CA: Jossey-Bass.

Kramer M (1974) *Reality Shock: Why Nurses Leave Nursing*. St Louis, MO: Mosby.

Lancet, The (2012) 'Patient empowerment – who empowers whom?'. *The Lancet*, (5 May) 379 (9827): 1677. Available from: www.thelancet.com/journals/lancet/article/PIIS0140–6736%2812%2960699–0/fulltext (accessed 3 July 2013).

Leathard A (2003) *Interprofessional Collaboration in Health and Social Care*. Hove: Brunner-Routledge.

Legislation.gov.uk (2005) *Mental Capacity Act 2005*. Available from: www.legislation.gov.uk/ukpga/2005/9/contents (accessed 3 January 2013).

Leners D W, Wilson V W, Connor P and Fenton J (2006) 'Mentorship: increasing retention probabilities'. *Journal of Nursing Management*, 14 (8): 652–654.

Lewin D (2007) 'Clinical learning environments for student nurses: key indices from two studies compared over a 25 year period'. *Nurse Education in Practice*, 7 (4): 238–246.

Lewin K (1951) *Field Theory in Social Science*. London: Harper Row.

Liefer D (2005) 'My practice: government policy changes allowed an entrepreneurial nurse to pave the way for nurse-led general practices'. *Nursing Standard*, 19 (22): 58.

Lipley N (2004) 'Two-year funding to train more leaders'. *Nursing Management*, 11 (6): 4.

Lipman-Blumen J (2000) *Connective Leadership: Managing in a Changing World*. Oxford: Oxford University Press.

Long A F, Kneafsey R, Ryan J and Berry J (2002), The role of the nurse within the multi-professional rehabilitation team. *Journal of Advanced Nursing*, 37: 70–78.

Maben J, Morrow E, Ball J, Robert G, Griffiths P (2012) *High Quality Care Metrics for Nursing*. London: National Nursing Research Unit, King's College London.

Magnus O, Johansson P and Fridlund B (2004) 'Nursing care at night: an evaluation using the Night Nursing Care Instrument'. *Journal of Advanced Nursing*, 47 (1): 25–32.

Malby B and Manning S (1998) 'Promoting change through peer review'. *Nursing Management*, 5 (2): 24–25.

Manley K (1997) 'A conceptual framework for advanced practice: an action research project operationalizing and advanced practitioner/consultant nurse role'. *Journal of Clinical Nursing*, 6 (3): 179–190.

Manley K, McCormack B and Wilson V (2008) *International Practice Development in Nursing and Healthcare*. Oxford: Blackwell.

Map of Medicine (2012) *How People are Using Care Maps*. Available from: www. mapofmedicine.com (accessed 22 December 2012).

Marie Curie Palliative Care Institute (2012) *Liverpool Care Pathway for the Dying Patient*. Available from: www.liv.ac.uk/mcpcil/liverpool-care-pathway (accessed 22 December 2012).

Marinker M, Blenkinsopp A, Bond C, Britten N and Feely M (1997) *From Compliance to Concordance: Achieving Shared Goals in Medicine Taking*. London: Royal Pharmaceutical Society of Great Britain.

Marquis B L and Huston C J (2012) *Leadership Roles and Management Functions in Nursing* (7th edn). Philadelphia, PA: Lippincott Williams and Wilkins.

Marriner Tomey A (2004) *Guide to Nursing Management and Leadership* (7th edn). St Louis, MO: Mosby.

Maslin-Prothero S (1997) 'A perspective on lifelong learning and its implications for nurses'. *Nurse Education Today*, 17 (6): 431–436.

Maslow A H (1987) *Motivation and Personality* (3rd edn). London: Harper and Row.

Maxwell R (1984) 'Quality assessment in health'. *British Medical Journal*, 288 (6428): 1470–1472.

McAllister M and Osborne Y (1997) 'Peer review – a strategy to enhance co-operative student learning'. *Nurse Educator*, 22 (1): 40–44.

McCaughan D (2002) 'What decisions do nurses make?' in Thompson C and Dowding D (eds) *Clinical Decision Making and Judgement in Nursing*. Edinburgh: Churchill Livingstone.

McColgan K and Rice C (2012) 'An online training resource for clinical supervision'. *Nursing Standard*, 26 (24): 35–39.

McCormack B (2006) 'Development of a framework for person-centred nursing'. *Journal of Advanced Nursing*. 56 (5): 472–479.

McCormack B, Dewar B, Wright J, Garbett R, Harvey G and Ballantine K (2006) *A Realist Synthesis of Evidence Relating to Practice Development*. Available from: http://jrn. sagepub.com/content/15/2/189.refs (accessed 29 January 2013).

McDonald J, Jayasuriya R, Harris M F (2012) 'The influence of power dynamics and trust on multidisciplinary collaboration: a qualitative case study of type 2 diabetes mellitus'. *BMC Health Services Research*, March 13 (12): 63.

McGill I and Beatty L (2001) *Action Learning – A Guide for Professional, Management & Educational Development* (2nd edn). London: Kogan Page.

McGregor D (1987) *The Human Side of Enterprise*. Harmondsworth: Penguin.

McNichol E and Smith S (2001) 'Measure your leadership skills'. *Nursing Standard*, 15 (22): 77.

Meadows S, Levenson R and Baeza J (2000) *The Last Straw – Explaining the NHS Nursing Shortage*. London: King's Fund Centre.

Menzies I E (1960) 'A case study in the functioning of social systems as a defence against anxiety: a report of a study of nursing services of a general hospital'. *The Tavistock Institute of Human Relations*, 13 (2): 95–121.

Middleton S and Roberts A (eds) (2000) *Integrated Care Pathways: A Practical Approach to Implementation*. Oxford: Butterworth Heinemann.

Mintzberg H (1990) *The Nature of Managerial Work*. London: Prentice Hall.

Monitor (2012) *What We Do*. Available from: www.monitor-nhsft.gov.uk/about-monitor/what-we-do-0 (accessed 10 April 2012).

Mooney H (2008) 'Health fair at Hindu temple puts a focus on diabetes'. *Nursing Times*, 104 (40): 7.

Moore J (2007) 'Managing change in your practice'. *Podiatry Management*, 26 (2): 53–56.

Morgan C (2005) 'Growing your own – a model for encouraging and nurturing aspiring leaders'. *Nursing Management*, 11 (9): 27–30.

Moroney N and Knowles C (2006) 'Innovation and teamwork: introducing multi-disciplinary team ward rounds'. *Nursing Management*, 13 (1): 28–31.

Morse J, Bottorff J, Anderson G, O'Brien B and Solberg S (1992) 'Beyond empathy: expanding expressions of caring'. *Journal of Advanced Nursing*, 17 (7): 809–821.

Mortlock S (2011) 'A framework to develop leadership potential'. *Nursing Management*, 18 (7): 29–32.

Morton Medical Limited (2004) *Unistik 2 Single Use Needle Safe Capillary Blood Sampling Device*. Available from: www.mortonmedicalshop.co.uk/Unistik_2_Capillary_Blood_Sampling_Device.htm (accessed 19th February 2012).

Mouton J S, Blake R R (1984) *Synergogy*. San Francisco, CA: Jossey-Bass.

Mullins L J (2010) *Management and Organisational Behaviour* (9th edn). London: Financial Times/Prentice Hall.

Mumma C M and Nelson A (2002) 'Theory and practice models for rehabilitation nursing' in Hoeman S P (ed.) *Rehabilitation Nursing: Process, Application and Outcomes*. St Louis, MO: Mosby.

Murphy L (2005) 'Transformational leadership: a cascading chain reaction'. *Journal of Nursing Management*, 13 (2): 128–136.

National Audit Office (2011) *The National Programme for IT in the NHS: An Update on the Delivery of Detailed Care Records Systems*. London: The Stationery Office. Available from: www.nao.org.uk/publications/1012/npfit.as (accessed 20 January 2013).

National Audit Office (2012) *Healthcare across the UK: A Comparison of the NHS in England, Scotland, Wales and Northern Ireland*. Available from: www.official-documents.gov.uk/document/hc1213/hc01/0192/0192.pdf (accessed 5 November 2012).

National Health Service Litigation Authority (2012a) *Fact Sheet One: Background Information*. Available from: www.nhsla.com/CurrentActivity/Pages/FOIFactSheets.aspx (accessed 23 December 2012).

National Health Service Litigation Authority (2012b) *Fact Sheet Three: Claims Information (England-wide)*. Available from: www.nhsla.com/CurrentActivity/Pages/FOIFactSheets.aspx (accessed 23 December 2012).

National Institute for Health and Clinical Excellence (2012) *Quality Standard for Patient Experience in Adult NHS Services*. Available from: http://publications.nice.org.uk/quality-standard-for-patient-experience-in-adult-nhs-services-qs15 (accessed 27 December 2012).

National NHS Staff Survey Co-ordination Centre (2012a) *NHS Staff Survey 2011 Results*. Available from: http://nhsstaffsurveys.com/cms/ (accessed 5 April 2012).

National NHS Staff Survey Co-ordination Centre (2012b) *Guidance Manual for the NHS Staff Survey 2011*. Available from: http://nhsstaffsurveys.com/cms/uploads/ST11_GuidanceNotes.pdf (accessed 26 February 2012).

National NHS Staff Survey Co-ordination Centre (2012c) *Briefing Note: Issues Highlighted by the 2011 NHS Staff Survey in England*. Available from: http://nhsstaffsurveys.com/cms/uploads/NHS%20staff%20survey%202011_nationalbriefing_final.pdf (accessed 21 January 2013).

National Nursing Research Unit (2013) *Cultural Barometer Project Summary*. London: King's College. Available from: www.kcl.ac.uk/nursing/research/nnru/research-programme/Organisa tions,environmentandwaysofworking/Cultural-Care-Barometer.aspx (accessed 29 June 2013).

Newton J M, Jolly B C, Ockerby C M and Cross W M (2010) 'clinical learning environment inventory: factor analysis'. *Journal of Advanced Nursing*, 66 (6): 1371–1381.

NHS Change Model website (2013) *NHS Change Model – Everything We Know about Delivering Change in the NHS, All in One Place*. Available from www.changemodel.nhs.uk/pg/dashboard (accessed 19 August 2013).

NHS Choices (2012) *Your Health, Your Choices*. Available from: www.nhs.uk/ /Pages/HomePage.aspx (accessed 30 March 2013).

NHS Employers (2006a) *Stop Bullying: It's in Your Hands*. London: NHS Employers. Available from: www.nhsemployers.org/SiteCollectionDocuments/Stop_bullying_its_in_your_hands_guidance_SC_010406.pdf (accessed 28 January 2013).

NHS Employers (2006b) *NHS Employers Guidance – Bullying and Harassment*. Available from: www.nhsemployers.org/Aboutus/Publications/Documents/Bullying%20and%20harassment.pdf (accessed 28 January 2013).

NHS Executive (1996) *Clinical Guidelines*. Leeds: NHSE.

NHS Flying Start England (2013) *Welcome to Flying Start England*. Available from: www.flyingstartengland.nhs.uk/ (accessed 31 March 2013).

NHS Institute for Innovation and Improvement (2006) *Releasing Time to Care: Productive Ward*. Coventry: Institute for Innovation and Improvement.

NHS Institute for Innovation and Improvement (2008a) *Quality and Service Improvement Tools – Plan, Do, Study, Act (PDSA)*. Available from: www.institute.nhs.uk/quality_and_service_improvement_tools/quality_and_service_improvement_tools/plan_do_study_act.html (accessed 29 January 2013).

NHS Institute for Innovation and Improvement (2008b) *Situation-Background-Assessment-Recommendation*. Available from: www.institute.nhs.uk/quality_and_service_improvement_tools/quality_and_service_improvement_tools/sbar_-_situation_-_background_-_assessment_-_recommendation.html (accessed 20 January 2013).

NHS Institute for Innovation and Improvement (2010) *Evaluation of the Leadership Qualities Framework 360 Review Process*. Available from: www.institute.nhs.uk/research_and_evaluation_reports/reports/evaluation_of_the_leadership_qualities_framework_360_review_process.html (accessed 6 February 2013).

NHS Institute for Innovation and Improvement (2011) *Leadership is for Everyone: Take the Leadership Challenge with the New Self Assessment Tool*. Available from: www.institute.nhs.uk/index.php?option=com_content&task=view&id=4330&Itemid=3834 (accessed 29 January 2013).

NHS Management Executive (1993) *A Vision for the Future*. London: Department of Health.

Nugus P, Greenfield D, Travaglia J, Westbrook J and Braithwaite J (2010) 'How and where clinicians exercise power: interprofessional relations in health care'. *Social Science & Medicine*, 71 (5): 898–909.

Nursing & Midwifery Council (2001) *Standards for Specialist Education and Practice*. Available from: www.nmc-uk.org/Documents/Standards/nmcStandardsForSpecialistEducationand Practice.pdf (accessed 31 December 2012).

Nursing & Midwifery Council (2006) *Preceptorship Guidelines* – NMC Circular 21/2006). Available from: www.nmc-uk.org/Documents/Circulars/2006circulars/NMC%20circular%20 21_2006.pdf (accessed 29 January 2013).

Nursing & Midwifery Council (2008) *A Standard to Support Learning and Assessment in Practice*. London: NMC.

Nursing & Midwifery Council (2010a) *Standards for Pre-Registration Nursing Education*. Available from: http://standards.nmc-uk.org/PublishedDocuments/Standards%20for%20 preregistration%20nursing%20education%2016082010.pdf (accessed 26 March 2012).

Nursing & Midwifery Council (2010b) *The Code – Standards of Conduct, Performance and Ethics for Nurses and Midwives*. Available from: www.nmc-uk.org/ (accessed 26 March 2012).

Nursing & Midwifery Council (2010c) *Midwives Rules and Standards*. Available from: www.nmc-uk.org/Documents/Standards/nmcMidwivesRulesandStandards.pdf (accessed 5 April 2012).

Nursing & Midwifery Council (2011a) *The PREP Handbook*. Available from: www.nmc-uk.org/Educators/Standards-for-education/The-Prep-handbook/ (accessed 29 December 2012).

Nursing & Midwifery Council (2011b) *Social Networking Sites*. Available from: www.nmc-uk.org/Nurses-and-midwives/Advice-by-topic/A/Advice/Social-networking-sites (accessed 27 March 2012).

Nursing & Midwifery Council (2012a) *Delegation*. Available from: www.nmc-uk.org/Nurses-and-midwives/Regulation-in-practice/Regulation-in-Practice-Topics/Delegation/ (accessed 20 December 2012).

Nursing & Midwifery Council (2012b) *Conduct and Competence Committee – Substantive Hearing, 12–15 March 2012*. Available from: www.nmc-uk.org/Documents/FTPOutcomes/2012/ March/Reasons%20COCHRANE%20CCCSH%2020120315.pdf (accessed 28 December 2012).

Nursing Standard News (2009) 'Enterprising nurses win extra funding'. *Nursing Standard*, 24 (12): 2.

Odiorne S (1979) *MBO II: A System of Managerial Leadership for the 80s*. Belmont, CA: Fearon Pitman.

Office for National Statistics (2011) *National Population Projections 2010-based Statistical Bulletin*. Available from: www.ons.gov.uk/ons/dcp171778_235886.pdf (accessed 20 November 2012).

Orton H (1981) 'Ward learning climate and student nurse response'. *Nursing Times*, (4 June): 65–68.

Orton H D, Prowse J and Millen C (1993) *Charting the Way to Excellence (Ward Learning Climate Project)*. Sheffield: Sheffield Hallam University.

Palfreyman S, Tod A and Doyle J (2003) 'Comparing evidence-based practice of nurses and physiotherapists'. *British Journal of Nursing*, 12 (4): 246–253.

Parish C (2006) '"Being nice is not enough" for good leadership on the wards'. *Nursing Standard*, 20 (41): 6.

Parliamentary and Health Service Ombudsman (2012a) *Ombudsman's Principles*. Available from: www.ombudsman.org.uk/improving-public-service/ombudsmansprinciples/ombudsmans-introduction-to-the-principles (accessed 27 December 2012).

Parliamentary and Health Service Ombudsman (2012b) *Listening and Learning: The Ombudsman's Review of Complaint Handling by the NHS in England 2011–12*. London: The Stationery Office. Available from: www.ombudsman.org.uk/__data/assets/pdf_ file/0018/18126/FINAL_Listening_and_Learning_NHS_report_2011–12optimised.pdf (accessed 20 January 2013).

Patients Association (2012) *Partners in Care: Working Together in the South West.* Available from: www.patients-association.com/Default.aspx?tabid=96 (accessed 20 July 2013).

Pearson P, Procter S, Wilcockson J and Allgar V (2004) 'The process of hospital discharge for medical patients: a model'. *Journal of Advanced Nursing,* 46 (5): 496–505.

Pedler M, Burgoyne J and Boydell T (2007) *A Manager's Guide to Self-Development* (5th edn). London: McGraw-Hill Education.

Petersen A and Bunton R (eds) (1997) *Foucault, Health and Medicine.* New York: Routledge.

Proctor B (2001) 'Training for the supervision alliance attitude, skills and intention' in Cutcliffe J, Butterworth T and Proctor B (eds) *Fundamental Themes in Clinical* Supervision. London: Routledge.

Putnam R (1993) 'The prosperous community: social capital and public life'. *American Prospect,* 13 (Spring): 35–42.

Rafferty A M, Clarke S P, Coles J, Ball J, James P, McKee M and Aiken L H (2007) 'Outcomes of variation in hospital nurse staffing in English hospitals: cross-sectional analysis of survey data and discharge records'. *International Journal of Nursing Studies,* 44 (2): 175–182.

Randle J, Stevenson K and Grayling I (2007) 'Reducing workplace bullying in healthcare organizations'. *Nursing Standard,* 21 (22): 49–56.

Resuscitation Council (2010) *Resuscitation Guidelines.* Available from: www.resus.org.uk/pages/GL2010.pdf (accessed 19 February 2012).

Roberts K (2002) 'Exploring participation: older people on discharge from hospital'. *Journal of Advanced Nursing,* 40 (4): 413–420.

Robertson C and Finlay L (2007) 'Making a difference, teamwork and coping: the meaning of practice in acute physical settings'. *British Journal of Occupational Therapy,* 70 (2): 73–80.

Rogers C and Freiberg H J (1994) *Freedom to Learn* (3rd edn). Upper Saddle River, NJ: Pearson Education.

Rogers E and Shoemaker F (1971) *Communication of Innovations: A Cross-Cultural Report* (2nd edn). New York: The Free Press.

Rolfe G (1999) 'The pleasure of the bottomless: postmodernism, chaos and paradigm shift'. *Nurse Education Today,* 19 (8): 668–672.

Rotem A and Hart G (1995) 'The clinical learning environment: nurses' perceptions of professional development in clinical settings'. *Nurse Education Today,* 15 (1): 3–10.

Royal J (2012) 'Evaluating human, social and cultural capital in nurse education'. *Nurse Education Today,* 32 (5): e19–e22.

Royal College of Nursing (1996) *Clinical Effectiveness. A Royal College of Nursing Guide.* London: RCN.

Royal College of Nursing (2005a) *Transforming Clinical Leaders to become Agents of Positive Change – Executive Summary.* Available from: www.rcn.org.uk/__data/assets/pdf_file/0009/78651/002524.pdf (accessed 9 April 2012).

Royal College of Nursing (2005b) *Maxi Nurses: Nurses Working in Advanced and Extended Roles Promoting and Developing Patient-centred Healthcare.* London: RCN.

Royal College of Nursing (2005c) *Bullying and Harassment at Work.* London: RCN.

Royal College of Nursing (2006) *Setting Appropriate Ward Nurse Staffing Levels in NHS Acute Trusts.* Available from: www.rcn.org.uk/__data/assets/pdf_file/0007/287710/setting_appropriate_ward_nurse_staffing_levels_in_nhs_acut.pdf. (accessed 30 March 2013).

Royal College of Nursing (2007) *Nurse Entrepreneurs: Turning Initiative into Independence.* Available from: www.rcn.org.uk/__data/assets/pdf_file/0018/115632/003215.pdf (accessed 3 April 2012).

Royal College of Nursing (2010) *RCN Policy Position: Evidence-Based Nurse Staffing Levels*. Available from: www.rcn.org.uk/__data/assets/pdf_file/0007/353239/003870.pdf (accessed 28 January 2013).

Royal College of Nursing (2011) *Accountability and Delegation: What you Need to Know*. Available from: www.rcn.org.uk/__data/assets/pdf_file/0003/381720/003942.pdf (accessed 27 January 2013).

Royal College of Nursing (2012a) *RCN Clinical Leadership Programme*. Available from: www.rcn.org.uk/development/practice/leadership (accessed 20 December 2012).

Royal College of Nursing (2012b) *Stress at Work*. Available from: www.rcn.org.uk/support/services/counselling/stress_at_work (accessed 28 December 2012).

Royal Pharmaceutical Society of Great Britain (1997) *From Compliance to Concordance—Achieving Partnership in Medicine Taking*. London: RPSGB.

Saar S R and Trevizan M A (2007) 'Professional roles of a health team: a view of its components'. *Latin American Journal of Nursing*, 15 (1): 106–112.

Samuel M (2012) 'Expert guide to direct payments, personal budgets and individual budgets', *Community Care*. Available from: www.communitycare.co.uk/articles/25/07/2012/102669/direct-payments-personal-budgets-and-individual-budgets.htm (accessed 12 January 2013).

Schon D (1995) *The Reflective Practitioner – How Professionals Think in Action*. Aldershot: Arena.

Scott T, Mannion R, Davies H and Marshall M (2003) 'The quantitative measurement of organizational culture in health care: a review of the available instruments', *Health Services Research*, 38: 923–945. Available from: www.ncbi.nlm.nih.gov/pmc/articles/PMC1360923/ (accessed 29 June 2013).

Scottish Government (2008) *Supporting the Development of Advanced Nursing Practice – A Toolkit Approach*. Available from: www.advancedpractice.scot.nhs.uk/definitions/achieving-consensus.aspx (accessed 29 December 2011).

Scottish Government (2010) *Flying Start NHS*. Available from: www.flyingstart.scot.nhs.uk/index.htm.

Scullion P (2002) 'Effective dissemination strategies'. *Nurse Researcher: Qualitative Approaches*, 10 (1): 65–67.

Shanley M J and Stevenson C (2006) 'Clinical supervision revisited'. *Journal of Nursing Management*, 14 (8): 586–592.

Sharples K, Elcock K (2011) *Preceptorship for Newly Registered Nurses*. Exeter: Learning Matters.

Shoup R (2000) *Take Control of Your Life*. London: McGraw-Hill.

Sizmur S and Redding D (2009) *Core Domains for Measuring Inpatient's Experiences of Their Care*. Available from: www.pickereurope.org/assets/content/pdf/Survey_data_analyses/Discussion_Paper_1_core_domains_inpatient_experience_Dec_09_final.pdf (accessed 27 December 2012).

Sloan G and Watson H (2002) 'Clinical supervision models for nursing: structure, research and limitations'. *Nursing Standard*, 17 (4): 41–46.

Smith R (1992) 'Audit and Research'. *British Medical Journal*, 305 (6859): 905–906.

Snelgrove S and Hughes D (2002) 'Perceptions of teamwork in acute medical wards' in Allen D and Hughes D (eds) *Nursing and the Division of Labour in Healthcare*. Basingstoke: Palgrave Macmillan.

Social Care Institute for Excellence (2011) *Protecting Adults at Risk: London Multi-agency Policy and Procedures to Safeguard Adults from Abuse*. Available from www.scie.org.uk/publications/reports/report39.pdf (accessed 27 May 2013).

Social Care Institute for Excellence (2013) *Adult Safeguarding*. Available from www.scie.org.uk/adults/safeguarding/ (accessed 1 June 2013).

Stewart R (1993) *The Reality of Organisations*. London: Macmillan.

Stewart R (1999) *The Reality of Management* (3rd edn). Oxford: Butterworth-Heinemann.

Stockwell F (1984) *The Unpopular Patient*. Beckenham: Croome Helm.

Stuart C C (2007) *Assessment, Supervision and Support in Clinical Practice* (2nd edn). Edinburgh: Churchill Livingstone.

Sullivan E J and Decker P J (2013) *Effective Leadership and Management in Nursing* (8th edn). London: Prentice Hall International.

Taylor R (2012) 'Social capital and the nursing student experience'. *Nurse Education Today*, 32 (3): 250–254.

Team Technology (2012) *Myers Briggs Personality Types*. Available from: www.teamtechnology.co.uk/myers-briggs/myers-briggs.htm (accessed 28 January 2012).

Thiroux J and Krasemann K (2011) *Ethics, Theory and Practice* (11th edn). Upper Saddle River, NJ: Pearson and Prentice Hall.

Thompson C (1999) 'A conceptual treadmill: the need for "middle ground" in clinical decision-making theory in nursing'. *Journal of Advanced Nursing*, 30 (5): 1222–1229.

Thompson C (2002) 'The value of research in clinical decision-making'. *Nursing Times*, 98 (42): 30–34.

Titchen A (2003) 'The practice development diamond' in RCN (ed.) *Annual International Nursing Research Conference Report*. London, RCN.

Tutton E M M (2005) 'Patient participation on a ward for frail older people'. *Journal of Advanced Nursing*, 50 (2): 43–152.

Tutton E and Seers K (2004) 'Comfort on a ward for older people'. *Journal of Advanced Nursing*, 46 (4): 380–389.

UNISON (2012) *Care in the Balance*. Available from: www.nursingtimes.net/Journals/2012/04/23/x/s/q/20727.pdf (accessed 30 December 2012).

Valencia C (2005) *Motivation and Productivity in the Workplace*. London: Westminster College. Available from: www.westminstercollege.edu/myriad/index.cfm?parent=2514&detail=4475&content=4798 (accessed 24 January 2013).

Vincent C A (2000) 'Reducing error in medicine'. Presentation at BMJ Conference, London. Cited in Department of Health (2000) *An Organisation with a Memory: Report of an Expert Group on Learning from Adverse Events in the NHS Chaired by the Chief Medical Officer*. London: The Stationery Office.

Wales S (2003) 'Integrated care pathways: what are they and how can they be used?'. *Clinical Governance Bulletin*, 4 (2): 2–4.

Warne T, Johansson U, Papastavrou E, Tichelaar E, Tomietto M, Van den Bossche K, Moreno M F V and Saarikoski M (2010) 'An exploration of the clinical learning experience of nursing students in nine European countries'. *Nurse Education Today*, 30 (8): 809–815.

Waterman H (2011) 'Principles of "servant leadership" and how they can enhance practice'. *Nursing Management*, 17 (9): 24–26.

Watkins K and Marsick V (1992) 'Building the learning organisation: a new role for human resource developers'. *Studies in Continuing Education*, 14 (2): 115–129.

Webb C and Shakespeare P (2008) 'Judgement about mentoring relationships in nurse education'. *Nurse Education Today*, 28 (5): 563–571.

Webster J (2004) 'Person-centred assessment with older people'. *Nursing Older People*, 16 (3): 22–27.

Welsh M (2006) 'Engaging with peer-assessment in post-registration nurse education'. *Nurse Education in Practice*, 7 (2): 75–81.

West E, Barron D N, Dowsett J and Newton J N (1999) 'Hierarchies and cliques in the social networks of healthcare professionals: implications for the design of dissemination strategies'. *Social Science and Medicine*, 48 (56): 633–646.

West M A (2012) *Effective Teamwork: Practical Lessons from Organisational Research* (3rd edn). Chichester: Wiley.

Wheeler H (2012) *Law, Ethics and Professional Issues for Nursing: A Reflective and Portfolio-Building Approach*. Abingdon: Routledge, Taylor & Francis.

Williams D (2011) 'Student nurses withdrawn from hospital amid CQC concerns'. *Health Service Journal*, (29 July). Available from: www.hsj.co.uk/news/acute-care/student-nurses-withdrawn-from-hospital-amid-cqc-concerns/5033230.article (accessed 15 January 2013).

Willis Commission (2012) *Quality with Compassion: The Future of Nursing Education – Report of the Willis Commission*. Available from: www.williscommission.org.uk/recommendations (accessed 21 November 2012).

World Health Organization (2010) *Framework for Action on Interprofessional Education and Collaborative Practice*. Available from: http://whqlibdoc.who.int/hq/2010/WHO_HRH_HPN_10.3_eng.pdf (accessed 24 January 2013).

Wright S (1996) 'Unlock the leadership potential'. *Nursing Management*, 3 (2): 8–10.

Yoder-Wise P S (2010) *Leading and Managing in Nursing* (5th edn). St Louis, MO: Mosby.

Yuen Loke A J T and Chow F L W (2007) 'Learning partnership – the experience of peer tutoring among nursing students: a qualitative study'. *International Journal of Nursing Studies*, 44 (2): 237–244.

Yukl G A (2002) *Leadership in Organizations*. Upper Saddle River, NJ: Prentice Hall.

INDEX